D0019708

"The church is growing around the world! B[...] stronger than ever and is thriving in unexpec[...] p[...]. [...] this behind-the-scenes exploration of the global church, Brian Stiller describes and gives examples of what's driving this remarkable expansion of Christianity. Be encouraged. Christian faith is alive and well around the world."

Ed Stetzer, executive director of the Billy Graham Center for Evangelism, Wheaton College

"*From Jerusalem to Timbuktu* is a must-read for anyone trying to understand Christianity in today's world. Brian Stiller provides a practical explanation for the amazing growth of evangelical Christianity by identifying and unpacking five drivers of growth. His practical experience combined with exceptional research creates a powerful and informative read. After taking this 'world tour' on the growth of Christianity, you will be left asking . . . what will God do next?"

William M. Wilson, president, Oral Roberts University

"While many authors have written ably on the shift of Christianity to the Global South, Stiller offers a captivating personal story of remarkable connections with church leaders from all parts of the globe. His expansive vision for the Spirit, the Bible, indigenous Christianity, the public square, and a holistic gospel articulates a clear and hopeful direction for the future of Christianity."

Todd M. Johnson, associate professor of global Christianity, Gordon-Conwell Theological Seminary

"This book filled me with hope for the gospel. The gospel is about a personal relationship with God, and the church continues to be adapted into personal and cultural forms that make it the most relevant for everyday life. Dr. Stiller teaches us great lessons of the gospel's growth throughout history, but also leads us to the Lord of that history."

Joel C. Hunter, former senior pastor, Northland Church, Florida

"Combining years of global relationships, extensive research, millions of miles traveled, and a wide knowledge of Christian history, Brian Stiller has produced a must-read masterpiece! I know of no other book that so encapsulates mission history, current trends, and real-life anecdotes of faithful followers of Jesus Christ. The stories of the church around the world will encourage every Christian that we are part of the forward move of God. The walk through Christian history will educate and help the reader to know how our faith has traveled through the ages. And the overall message of the book will stimulate every reader to faithfulness right where we live."

Paul Borthwick, mission specialist, author of *A Mind for Missions* and *How to Be a World-Class Christian*

"It is important for us to be firmly planted in the context where God has called us to live and serve. But for our own health, we sometimes need to take a few steps back and look at the big picture of what is happening with God's people in the rest of the world. This book serves this purpose admirably. As we read, we are sometimes thrilled, sometimes sobered, and always we find lessons to help us in our life and witness. But this is not only a historical survey. Undergirding what is said are deeply sensitive reflections on the theological issues facing the church today as illustrated by the events reported. Brian Stiller's wide experience as a global ambassador for Evangelicals and his considerable learning are combined to give an inspiring and instructive book."

Ajith Fernando, teaching director, Youth for Christ, Sri Lanka

"If you've ever watched the news and thought the Western world is becoming increasingly pagan, you need to read this book. In *From Jerusalem to Timbuktu*, Brian Stiller methodically shares how—despite encroaching secularism and increasing global violence and religious turmoil—the church is indeed spreading, and in the most remarkable ways! Bridging the gap between 'us' and 'them,' this is a must-read primer for budding missiologists and all believers with a heart for the nations."

Rob Hoskins, president, OneHope

"*From Jerusalem to Timbuktu* offers an expansive introduction to the momentous fact that the majority of Christians now live in the Global South. Stiller helps us understand the multifaceted implications of this reality and presents a vigorous invitation to embrace the future of Christianity. Important."

Ronald J. Sider, distinguished professor of theology, holistic ministry, and public policy, Palmer Seminary at Eastern University

"This book tells the exciting story of why Christianity continues to grow at a phenomenal rate in the twenty-first century—this despite setbacks, persecutions, and the dying of the light in lands where biblical faith was once vibrant and strong. Brian Stiller is a world Christian statesman and he tells this story with passion, insight, and in the power of the Spirit. Highly recommended!"

Timothy George, founding dean of Beeson Divinity School, Samford University, general editor, the Reformation Commentary on Scripture

FROM
JERUSALEM
TO
TIMBUKTU

A WORLD TOUR OF THE
SPREAD OF CHRISTIANITY

BRIAN C. STILLER

IVP Books

An imprint of InterVarsity Press
Downers Grove, Illinois

InterVarsity Press
P.O. Box 1400, Downers Grove, IL 60515-1426
ivpress.com
email@ivpress.com

*InterVarsity Press® is the book-publishing division of InterVarsity Christian Fellowship/USA®,
a movement of students and faculty active on campus at hundreds of universities, colleges, and schools
of nursing in the United States of America, and a member movement of the International Fellowship
of Evangelical Students. For information about local and regional activities, visit intervarsity.org.*

*All Scripture quotations, unless otherwise indicated, are taken from The Holy Bible, New International
Version®, NIV®. Copyright © 1973, 1978, 1984, 2011 by Biblica, Inc.™ Used by permission of Zondervan.
All rights reserved worldwide. www.zondervan.com. The "NIV" and "New International Version"
are trademarks registered in the United States Patent and Trademark Office by Biblica, Inc.™*

*While any stories in this book are true, some names and identifying information may have been
changed to protect the privacy of individuals.*

Published in association with the literary agency of Mark Sweeney & Associates.

Cover design: David Fassett
Interior design: Daniel van Loon
Images: ancient map: © Abraham Cresques / Getty Images
    map grid: © tyndyra / iStockphoto
    tree: © shaunl / iStockphoto

ISBN 978-0-8308-4527-9 (print)
ISBN 978-0-8308-8761-3 (digital)

Printed in the United States of America ∞

*InterVarsity Press is committed to ecological stewardship and to the conservation of natural resources
in all our operations. This book was printed using sustainably sourced paper.*

Library of Congress Cataloging-in-Publication Data

A catalog record for this book is available from the Library of Congress.

P 25 24 23 22 21 20 19 18 17 16 15 14 13 12 11 10 9 8 7 6 5 4 3 2 1

Y 37 36 35 34 33 32 31 30 29 28 27 26 25 24 23 22 21 20 19 18

I dedicate this book to

DR. DONALD S. REIMER.

His uncommon global vision,

his passion for making known the gospel,

his engagement with leadership in sponsored initiatives,

and his modeling of philanthropy to new generations

has marked out new pathways of effective witness.

CONTENTS

PREFACE

It all started in Jerusalem, the home place of Christian witness. It then moved out into Asia and Europe, and in time elsewhere, but Europe continued for centuries to be the center of gravity. But then, in the twentieth century, the witness of Jesus broke out in new ways. It spread down through Africa, and a renewed form of faith infused Latin America and took hold in Asia. That center of gravity that once hovered over Jerusalem shifted westward, then south, with it now being around Timbuktu.

Today in every corner of the world, to over two billion people, Jesus has gone global.

Each book has a story. This one began years ago as I traveled, working with colleagues internationally, speaking at churches and staff conferences in various parts of the world. But it particularly took hold of me when in 2011, after stepping down as a university and seminary president, I was invited to immerse my life in the Christian community as global ambassador for the World Evangelical Alliance.

Be it in my home country of Canada or in visiting abroad, I was asked to speak on what I was seeing globally. In study and research, reflection, conversation, and observation, I saw particular forces (or as I note, *drivers*) at work, growing and reshaping the church. I tested these with missiologists, seeking to fairly and accurately identify what is at work today in our global Christian community.

Many factors impinge on and free up the gospel witness. Much has been written, as is indicated in the bibliography. My interest was to get to the heart of the drivers creating such remarkable growth. As Patrick Johnstone has noted about this period, "Evangelical Christianity grew at a rate faster than any other world religion or global religious movement."[1] In 1960, Evangelicals numbered just under 90 million, and by 2010 that had reached close to 600 million. I wanted to find out who and what they were. I also wanted to see what, within my lifetime, has engaged and continues to engage the reshaping of the church to which I belonged.

My life has been lived in the convictions and practices of an Evangelical community. Raised in the home of a Pentecostal church leader, after university—and for more than fifty years—I served in various Evangelical ministries, all the while building friendships and partnerships with Roman Catholics, Orthodox, and mainline Protestants. However, I know best *this* Christian communion. In general my writing concerns itself with the Evangelical world, although occasionally statistics will encompass the entire Christian community.

A number of labels are used to describe this Christian world of "Evangelicals." I include Pentecostals, as their history and theology is family in the Evangelical community. In some cases, to give emphasis, I use terms such as *Evangelical/Pentecostal*, or *Evangelicals and Pentecostals*, as in some countries Pentecostals make up more than half of Evangelicals.

The shifting force of faith, in a world most often described in materialistic and commercial terms, is a factor that no longer can be denied, be it by a country leader, academic, or social observer. Each year, as more and more people in the Global South embrace Christian faith, the center of density of Christian populations pushes farther south, leaving the real (and emblematic) city of Timbuktu toward places never before imagined.

PART I
FROM JERUSALEM
TO TIMBUKTU

ONE

FAITH IS ON THE RISE

I BREATHED IN HOT, DRY AIR, walking toward the conference center to the rhythm of a drum and twanging notes from guitars. Two hundred young people were on their feet in worship, in a setting outside Erbil, Iraq, just miles from towns controlled by the genocidal forces of ISIS. Iraqi young people arrived, public in faith, bold in witness, determined to live for Christ regardless of what other forces attempted to dictate.

With their entire lives ahead of them, why would they choose to clearly identify with Christian faith and immerse themselves in its life and witness? Surely, when faced by religious hostilities and Islamic militants threatening their existence, they would temper their enthusiasm or at least camouflage their identity. This is a picture of the kind of resilient and progressive faith that is playing itself out in communities, countries, and regions around the globe today. Why and how is this happening? This question led to the writing of this book. I simply had to find out for myself.

Weeks earlier, I had driven north from Cairo toward Alexandria, through mile after mile of desert, much of it fenced, marking it as military property. Our driver pulled across the expressway to a sandy road, bumping along for a few kilometers. Taking a sharp turn in the desert, we arrived at the Wadi Conference Center, a 150-acre facility with its own 250-room hotel, soccer field, and sports facilities. The center was host to a conference on missions, attended by more than four hundred Egyptians, whose average age was in the mid-thirties. It was an outreach of the Kasr El Dobara Evangelical Church, which meets just off the (in)famous Tahrir Square in downtown Cairo. The church became well known during the Arab Spring of 2011. As students were gunned down, Pastor Sameh Tawfik, trained as a medical doctor, turned the church into a field hospital.

At the conference, I wondered who could imagine that hundreds, mostly young people, would attend a conference on Christian missions in a country overwhelmed by the Arab Spring, and unglued by political wars, religious domination, and social revolution. Rather than hide, defend, or simply maintain its existence, this church in downtown Cairo models risk-taking faith, not only within its national borders, but also through its missional activities into Iraq and throughout the Middle East. If you want to know what is going on among Christians, this is a good place to start. Here in the face of opposition, persecution, and killings, in places where one doesn't expect vital and active faith, there are bold, exceptional, and unafraid people, "youth-full" with energy—an exuberant faith that is lived not just for themselves but oriented toward making it known to others.

◀━━━━━▶

As the refugee crises tore holes in borders, defied governmental policies, disrupted border patrols, and drove frazzled bureaucrats to frenzy, we arrived in Lesbos, the Greek island between the mainland and Turkey.[1] The twin-engine plane banked to the left as we skirted the beach and lined up for the island runway. Suddenly something bright and orange caught my eye. It was a congregation of lifejackets: thousands on thousands, littering the shoreline.

The beach closest to Turkey's mainland is eleven kilometers away across the open water. Up to ten thousand people a day risked their lives to cross the strait. One family crawled out of a fragile boat holding fifty people. Having bribed and paid their way across Syria, they hid in bushes on Turkey's western seashore. Smugglers found them and for a thousand euros (minimum) each, the smugglers provided a rubber dinghy powered by a small twenty-five-horsepower outboard motor and life jackets (some were children's plastic water wings). This family was among the fortunate: they crossed the strait in ninety minutes, as the sea was calm that day, winds modest and temperature 10 degrees Celsius. On other days refugees were caught in storms, confused by direction, lost, struggling for hours to make it to land. According to the Missing Migrant Project, some 3,692 drowned that year.[2]

And who was there to greet them, with dry clothes, a hot drink, food, and medical help? I saw primarily Christians from Greece and elsewhere. Most migrating refugees were Muslims, but those who call themselves by Jesus' name, with nothing but an open heart of welcome and well stocked with provisions, made sure they were greeted and helped along their way. Responses to disaster, I've come to learn, are usually served by people of faith, out of something that is part of their spiritual makeup and intuition. When Jesus said, "Love your neighbor as yourself," he wasn't suggesting this as a good idea: love is a spiritual force causing us to help instinctively as his followers.[3]

Go back now to 1990, when there were four or five known Christians in Mongolia. After the Soviet Union lost its grip, windows of faith opened. Freed from Soviet domination, it was a country searching for identity. Mungunkhet, a fifteen-year-old, was walking downtown one evening when he saw the *Jesus* film being shown on a big screen on the street. He stopped and watched. "At that moment," he says, "I wanted to get into the story." His parents had divorced; his father murdered the man who had taken his mother and he was now in jail. In six months, Mungunkhet joined a church in his town begun by other teenagers who had come to faith after seeing the movie. In time he became its pastor.

Today, as head of a television company, Mungunkhet remarks, "In 1200 a Mongolian army of 100,000 conquered much of the world—through sword and fear. Today with 45,000 Christians, in his power and love, we can reach our world, for love is more powerful than fear."

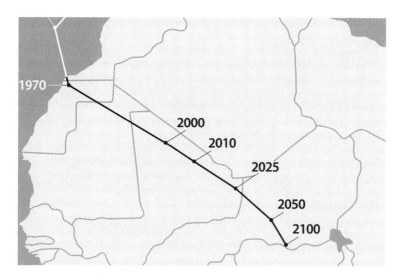

Figure 1. The movement of the center of world Christianity

Two thousand years ago the Christian church began on the day of Pentecost in the city of Jerusalem. Since then the demographic "center" of Christian populations has made its way across Europe.[4] With the surprising growth of the Christian community globally in the past fifty years, the demographic weight of Christianity in Africa and Asia has pulled this global center south and west. Demographers now place the center of population density of Christians in Africa (see figure 1).

The metaphorical center of world Christianity has literally moved from Jerusalem to Timbuktu in the nation of Mali. This is not merely some clever title—it is a remarkable sign that points out what we otherwise might miss. Long a city name used as a metaphor for a far-away and unreachable place, today Timbuktu signifies this massive shift, as the location of the center represents a mighty upsurge in Christian faith around the shrinking globe.

What is the extent of that growth? The answer might come as something of a surprise, particularly to those in the West. Even those least inclined to dismiss religion from ideological modernist presumptions—the Lutheran sociologist Peter Berger, for example—during the 1960s fell into the trap of assuming that the trends in former state-church Western European nations (such as France and Sweden) were part and parcel of modernization. In 1968, Berger projected that by "the twenty-first century, religious believers are likely to be found only in small sects, huddled together to resist a worldwide secular culture"[5] typified by the fragmentation of life and the division of labor. Thirty years later, however, these projections seemed far less plausible. As Peter Berger now notes, "The assumption that we live in a secularized world is false. The world today . . . is as furiously religious as it ever was, and in some places more so than ever. This means that a whole body of literature by historians and social scientists loosely labeled 'secularization theory' is essentially mistaken."[6]

The journey from Jerusalem to Timbuktu, with its relocation of the Christian center out of its centuries-long European habitat, alerts us that much is going on. As we will see, this growth and relocation is not driven merely by external forces, but also by reexpressions of faith in five major ways. It is those reasons, or *drivers,* that we will explore in this book. Some expand the witness of the gospel, resulting in remarkable growth of churches and the Christian population. Others do more in reshaping the vision and heart of the gospel, its self-understanding and ways of seeing its surrounding world.

SECULAR ASSUMPTIONS

An analogy (of sorts) takes me back more than a few years, to my university days.

The small graduate class in Montreal met in our professor's home; it was the late 1960s. As he outlined why faith as a working framework for life was reaching its end, I heard background music coming from the kitchen—so I asked if we could listen. It was Judy Collins singing "Amazing Grace," the longest-playing number-one song on the music charts, ever. The incongruity was striking. While the academy allowed that faith might have a sort of personal value, or even have a "cohering" or binding effect for people in need, the idea that it might become an overarching story, a *meta* narrative or a basis for an ethics of civic life, was dismissed out of hand. Religion in the postmodern age was merely a matter of aesthetics.

Science, it was assumed, would displace faith as a way to understand humanity, history would discredit religion's explanations, democracy would give citizens power to overturn religion, and global industrialization would fix human dilemmas of poverty and sickness. In summary, secularism worked from the premise that "religion's regress spelled humanity's progress."[7] Secularism would drive out its predecessors from the "dark ages" of religious belief.

What is the basis for this conjecture? The "hard secularization" thesis claims that, as societies become increasingly scientific, both interest and need for religious faith will be replaced by self-confidence, leaving little need for a God (at least insofar as to how one actually lives).[8] After all, if we can put an astronaut on the moon, what need is there to rely on a Creator Being? If we can multitransplant organs, what need have we of a Healer Being? If we can bring about psychological healing, what need is there of a Therapist Being? If social engineering can elevate the poor, what need is there of a Supplier Being? "No need," at all, seemed to be the received wisdom of the West.

Despite such declarations, faith in the Majority World is on the rise. Even as public policy and the dominant elites in the West act as though faith is on the losing side, Western public interventions abroad are constantly confronted with surging faith. This is true not only in secluded worlds of congregations, mosques, or temples, but in the wider spheres of human activity—politics, business, sports, media, arts, and science.

Even for that small group of university students in Montreal in 1969, our *experience* was different from what we heard in the academic bubble. Even as secularists posited their predictions—in the late 1960s and early 1970s—a grassroots Christian faith was turning the secular assumption on its head among (of all people) countercultural hippies.[9] It was a movement of escapism. Ironically, as it turned out, the religious response of long-haired Christian humanitarians was much more closely aligned with what was really happening in the world.[10]

A SURPRISING SURGE

Even as that secularist current moved its way through our world, another stream was gathering strength. There is an unstoppable tide rising in most regions outside the West.[11]

Africa. The 1910 World Missionary Conference in Edinburgh predicted that by the end of the century, Africa would be Islamic. It hasn't happened. Within my lifetime, the Christianization of much of Africa would have amazed even David Livingston. In 1900 Africa was home to 8.7 million Christians. Today there are 542 million, with estimates that by 2050 this will rise to 1.2 billion. While Africa makes up 14.9 percent of the global population, it holds 21.9 percent of the world's Christians.[12] In 1970, 38.7 percent of Africa was Christian (mostly in sub-Saharan Africa); by 2020 that will rise to 49.3 percent.[13]

This continent is sharply divided. A dominant Islamic presence in the north—Egypt, Somalia, Libya, Algeria, Tunisia, Sudan, and Morocco—has been joined by the gradual but determined Islamic move below the Sahara. But sub-Saharan Africa now is mostly Christian. The historic presence of mission work has built a core of Christian churches, and the many educational and medical initiatives have created a bulwark of witness, beyond which a vast indigenization of the faith has taken place.

Asia. When the Kuomintang government fell to Mao Tse-tung and his forces in 1949, there were under a million Christians in China. Through the Cultural Revolution, Christians were not only "reeducated," but many were also killed. Today the exploding population of Chinese Christians is estimated to number 100 million or more. "If the growth continues at the rate of 7 percent, Christians could be 32.5 percent of the Chinese population by 2040 and 66.7 percent by 2050."[14]

Best known in Asia (and symbolic of church growth in the Majority World) is the Yoido Full Gospel Church in Seoul, South Korea. Located near the government's national assembly building, its large and unassuming campus is home to just under a million members;[15] estimates are that 5 percent of the city attends this church. While its sanctuary seats only twelve thousand, its many auditoriums seat another twenty thousand, and multiple services over the weekend provide for its attendees, including a Sunday school of thirty-eight thousand. This city is thus the home to the largest Pentecostal (and Presbyterian, and Methodist) churches in the world.

In 1960, there were thirty known Christians in Nepal; today, there are more than 1.4 million.[16] Isolated from other cultures, the country did not allow most foreign missions. Then, some time after 1960, conversions began to multiply, seemingly without strategy or forethought. One link was Britain's traditional recruitment of Nepalese Ghurkas to fight in the British army. Enlisted, many serving abroad heard of the gospel and came to faith. Returning to their families and villages, they told about the Jesus they had met. Soon churches flourished. Another link lay in the relative lack of university training in the country. Most students went elsewhere, where they contacted Christians in the countries of study. After graduating they, too, returned home and, as with the returning soldiers, told their families and friends about Christ. Churches thus began to spring up in this remote country as a result of the remigration of Christianity through these global wanderers.

Latin America. Viewed as the most Christianized continent on earth, the spiritual transformation of Latin America has become a bellwether for Christian witness globally. Roman Catholics arrived with their European masters, forming a religious monopoly that made every effort to prevent Protestants from relocating there. In the twentieth century, however, as the movement of Spirit-empowered ministries circled the globe, Latin American countries felt that same presence.

By mid-century, the Catholic Church in Latin America was in serious decline. So few males were entering the priesthood that most were brought in from abroad. Only 20 percent of its citizens were active participants.[17] Protestant mission, especially by Pentecostals, resulted not only in rapid Evangelical/Pentecostal increase, but also in Catholic revitalization. Drawing from the Gallup World Poll, Rodney Stark notes that in four of eighteen countries,

Protestants make up a third of the population, and in eight others, over 20 percent.[18] The Pentecostal and Charismatic renewal movements triggered within Catholics a remarkable shift in emphasis in worship forms and community address. The gospel message, with its fire and zeal, is capturing the Latin heart.

North America. A recent United States survey triggered headlines that faith is declining: the Boomer generation is being replaced by Millennials, who are less and less interested in church. Such statistics obviously have a political orientation, where the word *Evangelical,* or even *Christian,* is often reduced to a demographic or voting description rather than a faith position. Some read this as "the sky is falling in," but Ed Stetzer disagrees: "Christianity and the church are not dying, but they are being more clearly defined."[19] Over seven years (2007–2014), Pew learned that those who self-identify as Christian dropped from 78 to 70 percent. The percentage of Roman Catholics moved from 23 to 20 percent, mainline Protestants from 18 to 14 percent, and those declaring they have no religious affiliation from 16 to 21 percent. Evangelicals dipped 1 percent from 26 to 25 percent but added in adult numbers by about five million.[20]

Gallup found *actual* weekly religious attendance was about the same as in the 1940s. While those saying they had no religious affiliation grew from 16 to 21 percent in seven years, as Ed Stetzer notes, "Many of these who have been labeling themselves as Christians are starting to feel free to be honest about their religious affiliation, or lack thereof."[21]

New York City pastor Tim Keller of Redeemer Church assesses—in a concerted move to provide places and train people for the gospel story—that today some 5 percent attend a church that has a "high view" of Scripture, up fivefold from 1 percent a couple of decades ago. He champions a strategy to raise that to 15 percent in a decade.[22]

What is surprising is that 50 percent of Christians in the United States continue to self-identify as Evangelical, with over half attending church weekly. And that number has gone up, not down: in the Gallup poll taken immediately before the time of writing, weekly church attenders were seen to rise from 34 to 35 percent. Millennials continue to constitute 21 percent of the Evangelical world.[23]

In decades of serving leadership in the Christian community, I have never seen such communities of spiritual renewal, social concern, and worship as I am seeing today. There is something afoot, both in the land of my birth and in the wider global community.

A country rooted in a Christian heritage—even when that faith has become dormant for too many years—has within it the residual possibilities of renewal and transformation. As each generation takes hold of Christ, and as each of us rises in the morning with the conscious responsibility to immerse ourselves in biblical faith, the Spirit is present, and more than willing, to infuse his people, and by them their society, with a renewed grasp of the truth and life of the risen Lord. The rumor that God had "died" is being discredited, as "the last four decades have shown religious belief also to be a destroyer of dictatorships, an architect of democracy, a facilitator of peace negotiations and reconciliation initiatives, a promoter of economic development and entrepreneurship, a partisan in the cause of women, a warrior against disease and a defender of human rights."[24]

THE DRIVERS OF GLOBAL FAITH

In the coming five chapters we will explore the drivers giving energy to this rise of faith among people who expect God to break in on his creation. I have experienced these drivers personally from years of service in national and international agencies. Recently, I led a team to publish the first-of-its-kind *Evangelicals Around the World: A Global Handbook for the 21st Century*. This examination of our global Christian community gave additional insights into our history and practice of our faith. Visiting with missiologists and speaking with scholars, leaders on the front lines, and agencies immersed in the tough issues of bringing life into dark places have taught me to see our landscape more clearly.

At the forefront of this amazing growth is a church that has come to know and appreciate the person and gifts of the Holy Spirit. In societies overborne by poverty, empty political promises, and inner vacancy, within emerging generations there is a search for spiritual wholeness and societal peace. The rise of Christian witness is enabled by a new and revitalized encounter and infilling of the Spirit. Even though Christians are trinitarian in theology, functionally we have operated on a dual pivot: the Father and the Son. This repositioning of our theology and spiritual practice to a more faithful trinitarian vision is the basis of what we are witnessing today.[25] This is the first driver.

Underlying everything that Christians are and do is our Bible—the second driver. In the early 1500s, the Reformation charged forth in both Germany and England as the Bible was translated into the language of people on the street, giving those who could read the opportunity to engage the text for themselves. William Tyndale, the first to translate the Bible into recognizably modern English from the original languages, said that he did this work so "a ploughboy" could read it. Luther in Germany and Tyndale in England unleashed the power of the Word, enabled by the Spirit.

I was born with a Bible, in my language, in my hand. It has always been with me, without my ever knowing anything different. For people who have never read the Bible in their own language, a translation sensitive to their culture has an echo effect, resonating immediately with the images and concepts in their minds, rather than having to go through the mediation of a translator. The centuries of Bible translation, however, built a foundation on which the current rapid and stunning building of Christian faith rests.

The third driver of this tide-like move is the revolutionary influence of locally grown leaders and ideas. This is not unconnected to the first and second drivers—movements of the Spirit are profoundly indigenizing, as is the power of the written word in one's own language. Great events such as the East Africa Revival, the Harrist movement in West Africa, the Galiwink'u Revival in Australia, and the Pyongyang Revival of 1907 transformed Christianity into a local faith. In each of these, indigenous men and women moved from relying on Western-dominant personnel, methods, forms, and language to those of their own people. As nationals took over, the church changed, sending some mission boards into fits, but these nationals cultivated on their own soil societies receptive to the seed of the authentic and biblical gospel. Indigenous leadership has been critical not only for the astounding growth of the church but also for the church being able to read the gospel in context—that is, in a local language or dialect (vernacular) that expresses what indigenous Christians believe. As missionary Jonathan Goforth noted of the Pyongyang Revival, "Korea made me feel, as it did many others, that this was God's plan for setting the world aflame."[26] Indigenization is one of the gospel's most important strategies for expanding the global church.

Re-engaging the public square—the fourth driver—is, for many, one of the most surprising. Taught for decades, yes for a century, that the gospel was about inner change and eternal redemption, the Evangelical church, both in its sending and receiving, left to others—often secularists, mainline Protestants, and Roman Catholics—the running of government and public service. The shift of Christianity from a privatized spirituality to a wider and more engaged stance is profoundly upsetting for the traditional elites. On the other hand, it also projects into the public imagination of many cultures the shape and role of a new, vibrant, and Christ-centered faith.

"Wholeness"—the fifth driver—is not a new application of the Bible. When I was a child, helping those in need in our community or raising money for those half a world away was embedded in what our church believed and did. Yet, not unlike the withdrawal from the public square, Evangelicals viewed our calling to be one of personal conversion and salvation for eternal life.

Inevitably agencies and societies sprang up, funded by our communities, who helped us see the human person holistically, not just as a "soul" separated from human needs. This more vigorous integration of the whole person—personal transformation, work, education, food, and family—is based on the understanding that the gospel speaks into all of life. This recognizes how injustices are often the fruit of systemic malignancies in the social body. Taking an axe to these roots is a biblical call. In the end, if God says he loves justice, we should too.

◀━━━━━▶

As younger Christians move in and the older move on, change is an essential part of bringing renewal to the life of the church, its witness, and its vision. This new global church is *young*. At the mission conference outside of Cairo noted above, I estimated the average age was around thirty-five to forty. In that least probable of places, young men and women, university students, professionals, parents, and their children were intent on learning and then going out into an insecure world with the belief that what they had mattered more than anything else in life.

For two thousand years, the rise and fall of Christian faith has had much to do with renewal and revival. Stagnation is often followed by a break-in of the Spirit, refreshing the ever-new message of the risen Christ: "God has no grandchildren." Each generation must make its choice. And as demographers observe, one generation can say no to faith and the next yes.

PART II
DRIVERS GROWING AND SHAPING THE CHURCH

TWO

THE AGE OF THE SPIRIT

IN 1954 EVANGELIST TOMMY HICKS was invited to speak at a series of public meetings in Buenos Aires, Argentina. Pentecostals organizing the event were appalled when he suggested they rent a 25,000-seat stadium. He insisted and so was driven to a local stadium where an official, declaring himself in pain, queried Hicks about healing through prayer. Hicks laid hands on him and the man reported himself to be healed. This man was an acquaintance of the president, Juan Perón, and so when Hicks asked to meet the president he got his request. When Hicks met Perón he learned that the president was suffering from a disfiguring skin disease. Taking his hand, Hicks prayed. The skin cleared, and Hicks got his stadium.[1]

But soon, a 25,000-seat auditorium was not enough, and so the campaign was moved to the 110,000-seat Huracán Football Stadium. It too was soon at capacity. In two months, it was reported, some 3 million had attended and three hundred thousand made public confessions of faith in Christ, with reports of many healings. It was an event that changed the nature of the church in

Argentina and opened the door for wider changes in Latin America.[2] The "Catholic continent" was thereafter increasingly opened to a new and vital message of faith, with demonstrations so obvious it was quite impossible to ignore.

This story illustrates how the message of the presence and power of the Holy Spirit affected the global church through the twentieth century. The message was bold and audacious. Those affected by this movement were confident that the Spirit would effect change and so they moved out with an abiding faith in his miracle-working presence.

In Africa, for example, the Pentecostal[3] message encountered local spiritualities that readily absorbed its exuberant forms of worship, deliverance from the demonic, physical healing, and unusual utterances. In Asia, as this new message of the Spirit was embraced, new churches, in South Korea and elsewhere, multiplied and grew to tens of thousands of members. Their reach soon extended throughout the region and north to China.

Why was this new and dynamic Spirit encounter so influential in the rapid growth of churches? To answer that question, we first view the historical context—how the church historically understood the Spirit. From that, three questions emerge: What triggered this major spiritual revolution? What did it produce? Where has it taken us?

HOW WAS THE SPIRIT UNDERSTOOD?

By the end of the nineteenth century, the magisterial churches of Europe had "tamed" the Spirit. Servants of their respective states, they were steeped in a millennium of modest and cloistered theological understandings of the Spirit. Over its 1900-year history, the church had not been particularly good at grasping the person, nature, and gifts of the third person of the Trinity. There were occasional outbreaks of Spirit consciousness, but official reception was marked by a distinct lack of continuity and by a preference for (an often static) Christology.

To be sure, the Father was understood, for we all have fathers. Jesus, God in the flesh, was understood too: four portraits in the New Testament help us visualize him sailing, or healing, or comforting the broken heart of a father who has just lost his daughter. But the Holy Spirit? For many the Spirit was mysterious, a mere shadow in (or even "the forgotten member" of) the Trinity.[4] This "forgetfulness" of the Spirit in the traditional church was quite at odds with what began to unfold in the twentieth century.

For state churches (interested in order and constraint), the Spirit lived on the fringes of the mystical, a topic many even today consider spooky and threatening. From time to time there were Spirit-driven revivals—some (as J. Edwin Orr has noted) very extensive. None, however, proved to be lasting. After such "waves," the church seemed to return to its normal institutional inertia.

Pneumatology (the theology of the Holy Spirit) was thus slow to emerge. As Emil Brunner noted, "The Holy Spirit has always been more or less the stepchild of theology and the dynamism of the Spirit a bugbear for theologians."[5]

In AD 135, a convert named Montanus began to preach that the Holy Spirit gave him direct messages. Controversies resulted that were not resolved until the fourth and fifth centuries, when church councils formulated what they believed was the relation between the divine and human natures of Jesus. The Holy Spirit was merely an extension of this state-sponsored concern with the Son.

The Reformation in the early 1500s opened a window onto the Spirit. Both Martin Luther and John Calvin pointed to the necessity of the Spirit as an illuminator of the biblical text. The English Puritans pointed toward his centrality in conversion and in faithful living. John Wesley (and the Moravians) also evidently exercised belief in the work of the Spirit, but each was cautious about "tongues speaking" because of the unease it created. Dwight L. Moody, while not part of the Pentecostal upsurge, was an important model for the influence of the Holy Spirit on the life of this effective minister. Each of these traditions, however, corralled the Spirit within the limitations of their commitments to one or another vision of a stable society.

As the nineteenth century came to a close, however, a new interest was brewing, a willingness to explore a fresh and more vigorous engagement with the Spirit in life, witness, and human reformation. In 1875 the first Keswick Convention was held in the Lake District in England.[6] Its emphasis was that, in following Jesus, the believer would progress from the experience of conversion to a second work of grace, called "sanctification" or "being filled with the Spirit." It was a Wesleyan theme, yet disconnected from "speaking in tongues" (as Pentecostals would later preach). The Keswick emphasis—driven by the pressing need of home and foreign missions, and the fading power of the institutional church—was on the power of the Holy Spirit to assist one in a sanctified daily walk, and to experience the joy of Christ. Moody, surrounding himself with others of like mind, transplanted Keswick to his Northfield conferences in the United States. The impact on his preaching was notable:

> I was crying all the time that God would fill me with His Spirit. Well, one day in the city of New York—oh, what a day—I cannot describe it, I seldom refer to it; it is almost too sacred to name. . . . I can only say that God revealed Himself to me, and I had an experience of His love [so] that I had to ask him to stay His hand. [After that] I went to preaching again. The sermons are not different; I did not present any new truths, and yet hundreds were converted.[7]

Had gifts ceased?

The rather ambivalent understanding of the Spirit through these centuries had resulted in teaching that served to keep people from considering the Spirit's gifts to his people. A blockage was "cessationism," which argued that gifts ceased after the contents of the Bible had reached final definition (around the fifth century).[8] Spirit gifts, according to this teaching, were solely for the foundation and expansion of the early church, as a way of providing authenticity to the message of the apostles. What was their rationale? Once the actual contents of the Bible had been determined, then the biblically predicted "perfect had come." The Bible now gave a fixed record against which ideas could be compared, measured, and refuted. So, these teachers asserted, with the New Testament in place, and with church bodies in agreement, Charismatic gifts were no longer needed as a means of guidance. Further, while the power gifts of healing and exorcism were important in the launch of the church, after the apostles they were more associated with mystics and "cults."[9]

The emerging interest in the Spirit after Keswick, therefore, ran right into the rising concern of cessationists, such as B. B. Warfield and other Princeton conservatives, about the impact of liberal interpretations of Scripture. Warfield, a leading theologian and influencer among Evangelicals, made it clear in his book *Counterfeit Miracles* that gifts of the Spirit were just for the apostolic age. His Reformed colleague Louis Berkhof produced a widely circulated *Systematic Theology* that gave space for the Spirit only under the doctrine of God. Indeed, as Tennent points out, Berkhof (whose book was studied even in Pentecostal seminaries) said nothing about the work of the Holy Spirit in enabling the church for public witness, overlooking Jesus' admonishment to his followers (just before he ascended) that the Spirit would instruct them (Acts 1).[10]

Warfield and Berkhof were disciples of Calvin, well entrenched in the Dutch and other European Evangelical populations, the migration of which emerged from Calvinist state churches to make the movement a transatlantic phenomenon. Like Calvin, they were suspicious of mystics, who (in Europe at least) were often persecuted; there were plenty of foot soldiers in the heresy-hunting cause. The Calvinist churches would, in later years, remain some of the hardest places for Charismatics. Whether they were mystified by non- or extra-rational experiences, or wary of the mystery of the nature and workings of the Spirit, the inclusion of teaching and conscious engagement of the Spirit seemed constricted to the underground of their church life. They had reason to be: there were excesses. This always seems to be the case when there is an outbreak of spiritual fervor. Spectacular accounts of why the Charismatics were wrong reinforced the mainstream denial of their authenticity.[11]

The church of the twentieth century, however, demonstrates the global pushback. Even with naysayers and legitimate biblical concerns and questions, the gradual maturing and explosive nature of the Pentecostal message has transformed the global church, ushering in a more vibrant life and witness tied to the Spirit's outpouring. In order for these to be born, it would take a sustained series of events to establish major global mission endeavors and in time grow a tree from which the wider influence of this new Spirit awareness would bear fruit.

WHAT TRIGGERED THE REVOLUTION?

William Joseph Seymour—an African American born to exslaves in 1870—was interim pastor in a black Holiness church in Texas. When evangelist Charles Parham brought Frank W. Sandford's emphasis on the Holy Spirit to his own Bible school in Houston, Seymour decided to attend. Because the school was segregated, Seymour had to sit outside the classroom (in the hallway) to hear lectures. It was in a related prayer meeting that Agnes Ozman was reputedly baptized in the Spirit with what she thought was *xeno-lalia*—an ability to speak in a language she had not learned. A woman from Los Angeles visiting family in Houston heard Seymour preaching in a local church. She was so impressed that she told her Holiness church prayer group back home about him, and they invited him to come for meetings. Then they did the best thing possible for Seymour: they tossed him out of the church, forcing him to form his own prayer group on North Bonnie Brae Street. It was the emergence of a catalytic point in what was even then becoming a world movement.

For three days, "cooks, janitors, laborers, railroad porters and washwomen" prayed, writes Foster.[12] Some broke out in tongues, others worshiped powerfully under the influence of the Spirit. From this meeting of the social underclass was born a movement that declared God was no respecter of persons. They eventually found a place at 312 Azusa Street to which people from all over the world gathered. Ridiculed by Los Angeles newspapers, lambasted by clergy, that mattered little to those gathered in this nondescript building to see, hear, and taste of this remarkable Spirit moment. The hinge had been oiled. The door swung open.[13]

THREE FACTORS AT PLAY

This upsurge did not happen in a vacuum. It was born into a wider Protestant world where various elements fostered its advent. It was only later that what might be called the "sacramental" traditions were touched by its overflow.

First, an important factor that nurtured this Spirit outbreak was the Protestant world itself (at a time when Protestants were still predominantly Evangelical). Its beliefs were shaped by an Evangelical theology sprung from Wesleyan/Methodist revivalists. These revivalists had an absorbing interest in the Spirit,[14] as did many of their Evangelical associates, who sowed hunger for a deeper life and a manifest desire for empowerment for service in a world that seemed to be trending away from gospel values. The

Keswick and Mildmay movements, for example, acted as *entrepôts* where the missionary aspiration and "deeper life" convictions of a variety of Protestant Christians mixed together, with global consequences. They would (sometimes against their own explicit desires) go on to have a very powerful effect on faith missions and the emergence of the new "age of the Spirit."[15]

A second factor assisting the breaking free of this pent-up desire to know the Spirit was, surprisingly, a growing rationalism in viewing Scripture (also known as higher criticism). From the 1870s in particular it infiltrated major Western seminaries from its points of origin in Germany and France, inevitably influencing mainline Protestant churches.[16] Its damaging result was a diminishing of trust in the Bible, shifting emphasis from a personal need of salvation to that of social transformation. Jesus was seen as *a* way to salvation, not *the* way. Eternal paradise was not for those "saved" but (in a doctrine referred to as *universalism*) for *all*: after all, a loving and all-powerful God could not be conceived of as *not* wanting to redeem all of creation. This was a theological dustup of no small proportion, a cerebral approach among scholars and clergy that added salt to the broad popular thirst for a Spirit-enabled faith. The more this rationalistic approach became evident among theologians, the more intense became the search for a faith that was *felt* and a spiritual life that touched the life of the believer.

But there was also a third factor at play. Evangelicals were just as much users of the tools of their modern era as their liberal colleagues. While liberals and conservatives ended up at opposite sides of the debate on the Bible, they both employed scientific tools for interpretation and redaction. For both groups, truth was based on the notion of order. Liberals arrived at the conclusion that the Bible was not to be trusted. It was "myth," or "story," made up of texts that could have a moral and uplifting effect but in no way could be considered "inspired" in and of themselves.

Evangelicals ended up on the other side of the fence, concluding that the Bible was to be trusted, indeed *needed* to be trusted in its original texts as *inspired*, lest the distinctiveness of the Christian gospel disappear altogether.[17] Apologetics, the "evidences of truth" approach that had become entrenched in Protestant thought, became a particularly foundational approach to public witness for Evangelicals. Proving the Bible was infallible and inerrant seemed essential to convincing people of the gospel in a rationalistic age. The assumption was this: if it could be demonstrated that the Bible was accurate, this would compel people to believe in the gospel. Belief was what mattered; in time, this made *doctrine* (rather than experience, or even the inner witness of the Spirit appealed to by Calvin)[18] the defining boundaries of Evangelical orthodoxy.

These three factors helped foster an interest in and affection for the mystery and workings of the Spirit. The increasingly rational approach that framed both mainline Protestants and Evangelicals created a gap between their thought leaders and the people in the pew. The old banks could not contain the growing waters of restless souls. These hearts—looking for an inner and life-changing encounter—began spilling out and forming new rivers of faith.

OUT OF STEP

The Pentecostal movement was, by nature and by way of contrast, out of step with the age's need to *verify* by rational categories only. As with Keswick, dry scholasticism and sterile doctrine provoked a search for a deeper Christian spiritual life. Physical healing and other phenomena, while unconventional, were not unknown within the Christian community,[19] especially among missionaries whose stories of demonic exorcisms and answers to prayer continued to circulate. They remained a standing reminder of God's presence and intervention. The more culturally sophisticated churches "at home"—wrapped in the rising tide of universal education, modern medicine, and the claims of science—however, often thought such matters were best left to less educated "foreign fields" where such things could be explained away as the results of superstition or ignorance.

By way of contrast, this turn-of-the-century Spirit outpouring had a natural link to the late-nineteenth-century revivals in Europe and North America, which featured an emphasis on the "deeper life" and divine healing. In seeking for a more authentic life in the Spirit, beyond rational quests too often characterizing liberal and conservative approaches, these revivals sought to go beyond head knowledge to heart knowledge.

This sharp contrast within the Evangelical world between belief in doctrine and the desire for personal empowerment can be seen in the publishing of a twelve-volume set of books (*The Fundamentals: A Testimony to the Truth*) by two wealthy Americans between 1910 and 1915. Its purpose was to restate foundational and "fundamental" Protestant orthodoxy. It contained contributions by sixty leading scholars and preachers from across North America, and some 3 million copies were sent free of charge to pastors and church leaders. Their circulation added fuel to the higher criticism debate, sparking a new and lively liberal/ conservative disagreement on Christian faith around the insistence by these "Fundamentalists" that faith (and in particular the biblical record) was still defensibly rational and could be verified. *The Fundamentals* came (for better or worse) to act as one definitional form for Evangelical theology and doctrine. As valued as this series was, however, one cannot but wonder if—in their focus on logic, argument, and apologetics—the authors missed the inner spiritual dynamics of transformative faith. Of the ninety-one articles in *The Fundamentals*, only one was devoted specifically to the Holy Spirit. Another concerned itself with the Holy Spirit and "the Sons of God."

A return to the miraculous. As these debates continued, many grew fed up with institutions, the noise of liberal theology, the cramped styles of conservative Protestantism, and antagonistic scientism. They sought another way to personal freedom. Harvard theologian Harvey Cox puts it this way:

> Conservatives dug in and insisted that dogmas were immutable and hierarchies indispensable. Liberals tried to adjust to the times but ended up absorbing so much of the culture of technical rationality that they no longer had any spiritual appeal. But the pentecostals, almost by accident it sometimes seems, found a third way. They rebelled against creeds but retained the mystery. They abolished hierarchies but kept ecstasy. They rejected both scientism and traditionalism. They returned to the raw inner core of human spirituality and thus provided just the need of "religious space" many people needed.[20]

Their emphasis on miracles does serve to stereotype many early Pentecostals as "mere experientialists"; this, however, they were not. Many shared the same doctrinal convictions as their Evangelical siblings, but only left their company when, in the 1920s, Keswick and other organizations forcefully rejected them.

And, of course, they did not *invent* the contents of this turn to the miraculous. As Stan Burgess and Donald Dayton point out, earlier Christian movements explored miracles, exorcisms, and mystical contemplation. In the early twentieth century, however, the idea that the gifts of the Holy Spirit were for today opened up new vistas for ministry opportunity. Spirituality was not to be fragmented. The Spirit was not only at work in the human spirit, he engaged in the totality of human life. As the early British pastor-teacher Donald Gee noted in 1928, "Whenever you touch reality in the spiritual realm you touch things which are so vital that any normal, healthy person cannot fail to be moved."[21] The physical, including the darker side of the demonic activity, was the Spirit's concern, and an encounter with the Spirit was the ultimate means of convincing and convicting. Stories of healing and Spirit deliverance were not just for foreign fields, but also for those in the "advanced world." Hunger for an experience in the deeper life prompted exploration in his gifts. This quest transformed into one for a more tangible human transformation.

End times theology. Embedded in the theology of early Pentecostals (and many of their contemporary Evangelical colleagues) was an overpowering view that Jesus was about to return. Indeed, in some ways, their interpretation of the coming of the Spirit was an important trigger for a movement linked to the biblical metaphor of the "latter rain." Such language and its imagery is to be found everywhere in early Pentecostal journals. It was an interest given point by the influence of the Scofield Bible, a King James Version—including notes derived from a British preacher, John Darby, and his theory of Dispensationalism—compiled by Cyrus Ingerson Scofield. Darby's scenario was that the return of Jesus was not only *imminent*—as the church had traditionally expected—but *immediate*. World events seemed to give cause to this theory, sufficient to create a consuming belief that his return was just around the corner. This provided the fuel of urgency for missions to go global, "to bring back the King." The Balfour Declaration and the re-forming of the nation of Israel in 1947 were seen as proof positive of that expectation. Strangely, this attracted two intertwined cultures. On the one hand, it attracted many cessationists, who believed that the gifts of the Spirit had ended. Yet Darby's colleague Edward Irving also believed that the sign of the end times was the restoration of these gifts.[22] Neither position discouraged Pentecostals from adopting this theory of end times into their doctrines and mission.

The Bible, core to identity and practice. Pentecostals believed they were the culmination and end of all things, rejecting Enlightenment rationalism, understanding truth as being held by God but *knowledge* as personal and relative to their own experience, language, and culture. All was useful insofar as it created new openings for the Spirit.

Given this openness to experience and hearing from God, what was their view of Scripture? Alongside the verified truth of the biblical text, Pentecostals held that one could reach out to God and, through experience, by way of insight and intuition, enjoy a life walk in the Spirit. They embrace, engage ,and enter into truth unfolded by their spiritual vision through experience and a "listening" intuition. Yet at the same time the Bible to them is bedrock. Their experiences are wrapped in biblical texts, expressed in biblical metaphors, lived according to biblical patterns. It is the final touchstone of what is true. Whatever is experienced needs to conform to what the Bible says, however much the hermeneutics used might appear to others to be idiosyncratic. Although Pentecostals differ in some interpretations with their Evangelical counterparts, on this they agree: the Bible says what it means, and means what it says. There are many variations today, but the core of their theology and history is centered in a hunger that their faith, practice, and doctrine be framed and anchored in the biblical text and its theology.

Ahead of its time. As ragtag as this early-century group seemed, they were ahead of their time. But life changes. Human paradigms inevitably weaken, adapt, transform. The Western mind moved from the Enlightenment through Romanticism to modernity and is now arcing into whatever is "post." To hold that one of these philosophical paradigms is more hospitable to Christian faith is to cherry pick from various ways of knowing. The gospel works in any context, speaking what God has already spoken, but in ways, tones, images, and references that make sense to its contemporary audience. To say otherwise is to deny two centuries of Evangelical thought about transnational and multicultural mission.

Within the Protestant world, liberal and mainline churches watched with (often dismissive) disregard for what they considered a movement for the socially marginalized and uneducated—people who seemed incapable of understanding the gospel they preached. Fundamentalist, and sometimes Reformed, Protestants were horrified by what they saw as emotional excess and a misreading of the biblical text. Not to be deterred, the message spread globally like a grass fire: missionaries were sent, churches sprang up, and evangelists trekked their way across hill and plain, sailed oceans and seas, with the riveting message that God is here in this place to meet your need. In other places, indigenous rediscoveries of the spiritual potential of Christianity saw local forms emerge. His Spirit, living in you, gives you power and words to tell the story to others. Christ's life flows, as promised in his death—"with his stripes we are healed" (Is 53:5 KJV) is a text absorbed by Pentecostals from their nineteenth-century Keswick forebears to claim the promise of healing. The narrative of God's covenant with the Jews, their failure, and Christ's incarnation, death, and resurrection gave proof that his promise to return was assured. The story was told, simply. The promise was clear, uncomplicated. The abiding presence was promised, experienced. The mandate was straightforward, direct. We had come face to face with the mystical and experienced the power and joy of the mysterious. An open door was enough. No mountain was too hard to climb for this new movement, no ocean too wide to sail. There was no danger so forbidding as to stop it from trying.

WHAT DID THE PENTECOSTAL
MOVEMENT PRODUCE?

In their initial outburst in the first decades, these Spirit movements produced a small but globalized movement of Pentecostal ideas, missions, and denominations. It elicited a growing indigenous response. But with that came a major fault line, especially in the Evangelical world, a chasm that in time the Spirit would bridge.

In the 1950s and 1960s many Evangelicals were suspicious of Pentecostals. Stereotypical descriptions of Pentecostals hanging from chandeliers and rolling down the aisles confirmed the bias of many that they were heretical. Not until the 1960s did these barriers between Pentecostals and other Christian communities begin to fall.

This was a movement concerned with spiritual empowerment. Its divisive characteristics such as glossolalia were evidential and experimental, a means of seeking to *know* that God's power and Spirit ruled. Here was an answer to rationalist doubt, one that (as the mainstream churches came into crisis in the 1960s) would make them important in another key historical moment: the rise of the Charismatic movement.

In the interim Evangelicals, in some cases (as in the formation of the National Association of Evangelicals in 1942 in the US), accepted Pentecostals. But the chasm—especially between Pentecostals and other Evangelical families—was aggravated by the doctrinaire attitude of some Pentecostals toward tongues as *the* "initial evidence" of being filled with the Spirit. A classic question emerged from the presumption that infilling was primarily about power for service: "If Billy Graham hasn't spoken in tongues, are you telling me he isn't filled with the Spirit?"[23]

Pentecostals, however, read the New Testament texts about "baptism in the Spirit" through a deliberative form of rational naiveté. If one were "filled," its evidence was speaking in unknown tongues. This evidentiary logic found yea- and nay-sayers alike. Some replied that "speaking in tongues" was *an* evidence, not *the* evidence, of Spirit indwelling. Many Evangelicals declared it unorthodox, a distortion of biblical texts.[24] Pentecostals replied that their Evangelical cousins were speaking out of experiential ignorance.

These two opposing, but also in a sense mutually reinforcing, notions served to silo the Spirit, containing his work and power to a small (if growing) Pentecostal community and keeping others caught between the two points of view from entering into the overflow of the Spirit. It was as if Pentecostals and traditional Evangelicals both had so much invested in their own hardening views that another way of seeing the question was shut off.

Three primal factors. In time the Charismatic wave began to undermine even the boundaries separating Protestants from Roman Catholics and Orthodox. Its ethos was intensely attractive to people from various walks of faith, vocation, and society. Harvey Cox suggests that there are three emerging factors "in which the unending struggle for a sense of purpose and significance goes on"—primal speech, primal piety, and primal hope.[25] Simple observation suggests that Cox is onto something both particular and general: particular, because it speaks into the actual moment of a Spirit encounter, and general, in that it gives insight into embracing what others see as peculiar.

Whatever their stance on various spiritual gifts, many view it unfortunate that speaking in tongues became the trademark of this resurgence. Even so, is it so surprising that some of the controversy was over language? Spoken language, after all, literally speaks of what is interior: "For it is with your heart that you believe and are justified, and it is with your mouth that you profess your faith and are saved" (Rom 10:10). The unknown factor of speaking in tongues suggests something absurd, false, or so deep that no words are able, in any language, to describe the mystery. Or might it be that communication with God's Spirit is so linked to the inner life that it bypasses the cognitive or, worse, bypasses the official interpreters of the Word, the pastorate? This "language of the heart"[26] (as it was described by the Puritans and Methodists) overflowed the banks of conventional Christianity, leaving unschooled men and women a bold new means of knowing and engaging with God. It seems unfortunate, therefore, that this label of "tongues" remained a stumbling block. Within the streams of spiritual expression and boldness of faith, there was much more than this one current.

If tongues became symbolic of a heartfelt language, showing the movement's unearthing of a primal, new means of God engagement, piety was also primal. In the world in which I grew up, it was clear to us that to be holy was what God expected. It resulted in all sorts of silly and needless forms of legalism, but one could not gainsay this central quality of God's call to "be holy, because I am holy" (1 Pet 1:16). This was bedrock Puritan and Methodist faith. Millions of people around the world who adopted these earlier Protestant spiritualities may, indeed, have represented a great dam of spiritual energy, a pent-up force, building for decades among Pentecostalism's precursors. The global outpouring provided those people with a place to test their inner longings for holiness, with a place to belong. A phrase often used was that the Spirit was "poured out." Along with that picture of plentiful water is the image used by the prophet Joel when he spoke of "the latter rain" (or in the NIV, "autumn rain"), a time when autumn rains gave added nourishment to the final days of the growing grain just before harvest: "Be glad then, ye children of Zion, and rejoice in the LORD your God: for he hath given you the former rain moderately, and he will cause to come down for you the rain, the former rain, and the latter rain in the first month" (Joel 2:23 KJV). A "primal hope" that they were living in the last days caught people up in excitement and a palpable anticipation. This eschatology—a theology of the end of the age, or the return of Christ—acknowledged that the world was winding down, yet was still firmly controlled by a Jesus who pointed to the goodness of eternity on the other side. This spiritual impulse was important, but at the same time, it was only one side of the story. The "Spirit outpoured" emphasized the mandate of going into the world, preaching his gospel. If Jesus was coming soon—and everything in their turbulent world seemed to reinforce this to be true—then the reason for the Spirit's gifts were not about our experience, spiritual holiness, or well-being, but for empowerment to go into the world. Time was short: we needed to "evangelize the world in this generation" because there would be no other. Growing up in this milieu, I can't recall any other verse preached on with such frequency as Acts 1:8: "And you will receive power when the Holy Spirit comes on you; and you will be my witnesses in Jerusalem, and in all Judea and Samaria, and to the ends of the earth."

Residual in these primal realities is a belief that God is here, among us, and at work by his gifts providing healing, deliverance from spirit oppression and economic reversal, restoration to those disabled by disease, and liberation for those enmeshed in the control of spirits foreign to Jesus. This message knew no boundaries except disbelief. Cox sums it up with this phrase: "At Azusa Street, a kind of primal spirituality that had been all but suffocated by centuries of western Christian moralism and rationality reemerged with explosive power."[27] In fact, that primal spirituality was already out of the church "box" in many places around the world by then. Azusa Street merely provided further energy to an ongoing process.

A chasm. The Pentecostal assertion that infilling with the Spirit be "signed" by tongues, however, remained contentious. This emphasis on the particular experience of Azusa Street divided the Evangelical world between Pentecostals who (mostly) insisted that to be considered filled with the Spirit one had to speak in tongues (glossolalia),[28] and cessationists,[29] who said that gifts of the Spirit had come to an end. This linking of gifts and the fullness of the Spirit divided both organizations and broader Evangelical consensus, creating variant rivers of doctrine and generating often-heated public debate.

As the movement grew, its message encircled the globe, emerging in North America (1896, 1904, and 1906), India (1905), Australia (1870), Korea (1907), and the like. Many missionaries returning from China, Latin America, the Subcontinent, the Pacific, or Africa brought with them experiences of the Spirit that their stay-at-home colleagues found hard to grasp. As the center of increasingly global communications, however, it was in the United States that this grassroots spirituality growing even within mainline Christianity broke through into a broader public awareness.

A new way. As the Spirit surprised Peter, leading him to a Roman soldier who would be an agent for Christianity to break through into the Gentile and Roman world (Acts 10), so in our own times the Spirit employed those outside of the two opposing camps to surprise both Evangelicals and Pentecostals.

To those in the Evangelical camp at the time, it wasn't obvious whom the Spirit would use. It turned out to be outliers, those largely outside the Evangelical world, such as Episcopalians and Roman Catholics. It was in the late 1950s that a series of events triggered the Charismatic movement (a word drawn from the biblical Greek *charismata*, "a gift of grace") in the mainstream churches of the West.

For North Americans, the conventionally accepted catalytic moment occurred in a High Church Episcopal (Anglican) parish in Van Nuys, California, in 1960. Father Dennis Bennett at St. Mark's Episcopal parish on Easter, April 3, 1960, reported to his congregation that he had received the fullness of the Spirit and had "spoken in tongues." This created a backlash. Forced to leave that parish, he was assigned to the fledgling St. Luke's Episcopal Church in Seattle, Washington, which became an important center from which the Charismatic movement grew. His now-famous book *Nine O'Clock in the Morning* telegraphed his story and message of Spirit empowerment to the world, catalyzing often preexisting movements in mainline denominations. This resulted in many seeking the experience and consequently joining or forming new churches and movements.

In 1967 the renewal landed in the Roman Catholic community, where Kevin Ranaghan and others formed movements at the University of Notre Dame and Duquesne University, Pittsburgh, from which were launched Charismatic revivals. They swept through churches and religious parishes and communities worldwide. A Catholic scientist visiting from Australia, for example, took the renewal back there, to St Michael's College at the University of Sydney.[30] In turn, from there, it spread to Methodist and Anglican ministers, as well as throughout the Catholic Church in Australia and parts of Asia. In Canada, I found myself in the middle of it while in Montreal. There, renewal was led by Father Jean-Paul Regimbal, a priest who returned from Arizona with "the infilling."[31] He was later sequestered by his bishops and sent to Granby, in the Quebec hinterland (on the mistaken assumption that he could not be heard from there). Gradually, however, the movement gained recognition. In Rome in 1975, ten thousand Roman Catholic Charismatics gathered in front of the Vatican in St. Peter's Square, along with Pope Paul VI. After that, the CCR (Catholic Charismatic Renewal) moved rapidly toward official recognition around the world.

A bridge. The Charismatic movement bridged historic churches, Evangelicals, and Roman Catholics. The speaking in tongues gap was spanned through new ways of thinking and intercommunal discourse. The Spirit gifts, these emerging groups affirmed, actually *were* in play, requiring a new interpretation of biblical texts. Cessationists, the Charismatics said, misread biblical texts and history through the light of their own lack of experience.[32] For Charismatics all the gifts of 1 Corinthians 12:8-10 were for today: wisdom, knowledge, faith, healing, miracles, prophecy, discerning of spirits, tongues, and interpretation of tongues. Unlike Pentecostals, however, being filled with the Spirit did not *necessitate* tongues. While underscoring the importance and biblical legitimacy of tongues, they affirmed it was not *the* but *an* initial evidence. Other evidences there could be—prophecy, gifts of healing, administration, and helps—but, in fact, the whole idea of evidences was probably less a biblical one than something absorbed from the dominant modernist presumptions of the late nineteenth century.

The door swung open. As it did, the Spirit rushed in. The message was caught up throughout the expressions of the Christian church worldwide,[33] eliciting once again forces of resistance. As a consequence, while many stayed, many others left their Roman Catholic, Anglican, mainline Protestant, and Evangelical churches to form independent churches. The story was picked up by the media, adding fuel to the growing blaze, introducing the movement to people hungry for a fresh (and for some, a first) acquaintance with the Spirit in congregational and personal life.

Walls tumbled through the 1970s in particular. One's Christian community—Protestant, Roman Catholic, Orthodox, Reformed, or Holiness, conservative or liberal—mattered not to Charismatics. The wave of Spirit interest immersed people in a new kind of belief, joy, and enthusiasm for life and worship. Contemporary worship had the effect of wiping out differences. The mixing and blending of fundamental assumptions, worship forms, exercising of faith, and believing in God's renewing of the church had became catalytic for broader changes in often-troubled traditions.[34]

This was a radical and transformative change in church life, fueled by an outbreak of Spirit-understanding. Its major consequence was growth, expansion, and new visions for ministry. Activities such as Life in the Spirit seminars, Sharing Our Ministries Abroad (SOMA), and Charismatic community formation spread rapidly around the world.

WHERE HAS THE MOVEMENT BEEN TAKEN UP?

A global force. While best known as the Pentecostal/Charismatic revival, the sweep and message of this movement has unalterably changed the face of global Christianity as a whole. Todd Johnson and others address the issue by referring to this global tapestry of Pentecostal/Charismatic movements as "Renewalists,"[35] a movement growing twice as fast as the global church average. By 2010 it represented 28 percent of all Christians. By 2050 estimates are that it will total upward of 1.2 billion members around the world. Between 1970 and 2020 in Africa, Renewalists will have grown from 18.8 million to 226.2 million; in Latin America from 12.8 million to 203.1 million; and in Asia from 9.3 million to 165.8 million.[36]

In Latin America, as Pentecostals faced an often-belligerent dominant church, they pressed forward, working with both the middle class and the poor, raising up churches and missions, pushing to extend their witness beyond the walls of their places of worship. Even those who opposed them were themselves influenced, a sort of competitive cross-pollination by learning of the Spirit. Roman Catholic Churches discovered within their own liturgies, communities, and pastors new expressions of faith coming from the surrounding revitalized church.

The Spirit wasn't to be confined within either cultures of liturgical compromise or within Pentecostal and Charismatic groups. For example, in all of Latin America in 1960 there were only

4,093 candidates studying for the priesthood in Catholic seminaries. That jumped to 20,239 by 2011.[37] There was a corresponding rise in mass attendance: by 2011, there were thirteen national Roman Catholic Churches with weekly attendance of more than 50 percent of their members.[38] This occurred in countries where Roman Catholic Church attendance had typically hovered around twenty percent.

This spiritual hybrid of Pentecostals and Charismatics moved much of this hemisphere into a new and vigorous Christianity. Brazil in 1970 had close to 6 million Evangelicals: by 2010 this was over 51 million.[39] Guatemala had the highest proportion of Evangelicals in the population (41%), followed by Honduras (39%), El Salvador (39%), Nicaragua (34%), Brazil (26%), the Dominican Republic (24%), Costa Rica (23%), and Chile (20%). This move—from a total membership of fifty thousand in 1900 to some 66 million (12.1% of the population)[40] in 2010, in a Latin American population of 546 million—is evidence that resurgent, pluralized, Spirit-driven Christian faith has managed to float all the Christian ships at the same time.

Christian resurgence in Latin America, moreover, has affected the entire Christian world. *Harmony* is still not a term one would apply here. Division and competition are rife, not only between Protestants and Catholics but also within the Protestant world itself. Yet this movement of faith—regardless of denominational tribe, musical preference, language, or liturgy—has spread (through migration, travel, and mission). As Rodney Stark notes, in describing the value of religious competition in fueling growth, "Latin America has never been so Catholic—and that's precisely because so many Protestants are there now."[41]

A spiritual revolution. Its impact on the entire church over the last century can only be described as a revolution. Phyllis Tickle's periodization provides us with a way of seeing this as one of the "axial" moments in the church's life over the last twenty centuries. Her working thesis is that every five hundred years, on average, the church has had a major revolution that brought discomfort and division yet nevertheless has opened the way for it to grow.[42]

The Council of Chalcedon (AD 451) resolved the church's view of the divine and human nature of Jesus. The Great Schism (AD 1054) was a final, permanent division between the Roman Catholic Church and the Eastern Orthodox. In the early 1500s, Martin Luther set loose the Protestant Reformation, whose children today populate so much of the world.

There are of course other ways to divide church history into periods. Staying with this model, however, if the Council of Chalcedon resolved the nature of Jesus; if the Great Schism served to define the end of Roman imperial Christianity and to establish Catholic orthodoxy as the West's dominant tradition; and if the Reformation brought to the fore a more personal salvation, in time freeing the mission movement to expand into the world; then what is the fourth historical "moment"?

That moment is the Age of the Spirit. For the past century, a new and vital understanding of the nature and gifting of the Spirit has set loose a global spiritual migration of peoples going out from their world, boldly asserting that Jesus is Lord, healer, baptizer, and coming king.

As many Protestants turned away from a liberal theology toward Fundamentalism, those who took hold of a new way of understanding the Spirit chose another course. While steeped in Wesleyan Holiness, their interest lay in living within the expression of the power and gifts of the Spirit-empowered faith, overcoming darkness and bringing relief by healing. They didn't wait for an ecclesiastical authority to grant them permission to go. They just went. As sociologist David Martin notes, they had a will to go "through the exercise of an outrageous religious entrepreneurship,"[43] developing a vast array of voluntary associations, new denominations, and agencies. Built on lay leadership, those without ecclesiastical authority moved out into ministry with "divine permission to speak without certification."[44] Absorbing Luther's vision of the priesthood of all believers, they became the plainly dressed priests of this new order. They reinterpreted "imminence" to mean Jesus would return for his church *at any time*. Meanwhile, they also reemphasized immanence: *he is here now* to empower and fulfill his promises. Thus hope reigned. It was eschatological, rooted in an abiding belief that his coming is soon and he is transformational: he is here, now, in this place, and every place where two or three are gathered.

Churches were planted, some "rafts for the respectable poor,"[45] others connected to emergent denominations or church-planting movements. Most were modest varieties, locally based (often located in storefronts or home Bible studies led by those with little to no education), yet filled with the enthusiasm that recent converts so often express. From those hole-in-the-wall churches to megachurches populating major cities and Charismatic networks spanning the globe, the wide-ranging planting of churches, missions, and multiforms of outreach mark this century as a time of global revolution, as the Spirit has swept along a people fervently desiring this latter rain.

THREE

THE POWER OF BIBLE TRANSLATION

IT WAS A COLD PRAIRIE WINTER AFTERNOON, January 1956. I packed newspapers in my shoulder bag, preparing to head out on my delivery route across snowy trails. My eyes caught a late entry: "Missionaries Killed in Ecuador." This news engaged my young heart.

Jim Elliot, along with his four colleagues, had died in a jungle riverbed while trying to reach the Huaorani in Ecuador, South America. The news riveted our small city community, a shocking picture of the cost some were prepared to pay to take the gospel to distant lands. What power that shining conviction had: no price was too high to get the Scriptures to this tribe. The message of faith expressed through their deaths had a powerful outcome: it provided the impulse for others to create written forms of oral language and the biblical text in their tongue.

Just as the printing press was an essential ground for the Reformation, so the Society for Promoting Christian Knowledge (SPCK) and the British and Foreign Bible Society were grounds for the great nineteenth-century upsurge of Protestant missions around the globe. The sweep of Christian faith we see in our own day continues to be carried by people who, often because of the sacrifice of missionary translators in earlier times, now have the Bible in their own tongue. Without translation, the current explosion of indigenized Christianity would have been unimaginable. It's difficult for Westerners to understand the euphoria many experience when they hold, for the first time, a Bible in their own language. I live where Bibles are in most hotel rooms, where bookstores carry multiple translations, and smartphone Bible apps are downloaded by hundreds of millions. This is not true for the world's majority. Having the Bible in one's own language (the vernacular) is an exquisite privilege. From Augustine to the present, the words "take up and read" (*tolle, lege*), when relating to the biblical text in your own tongue, are wonderfully transformative.

Prof. Agide Pirazzini, who became a leading Hebrew scholar in New York in the early 1900s, had been converted when he saw a Bible in a Rome store window. Reading the open book so affected him that he visited the window every day for weeks, as two new pages were displayed each morning. In time he walked into the British Bible Society store and bought a Bible. Despite living in the intellectual atmosphere of Italy's capital, he had never heard of this wonderful book. It became special to him, and he believed he must have been the only person in Italy to own a copy.[1]

Pirazzini's conversion had enormous impact. He trained hundreds of Italian ministers and evangelists. His new faith influenced his son-in-law, Frank Gigliotti, who went on to play a key role in adding the freedom of religion clause to the constitution of postwar Italy.

Such stories, as scholars Adrian Hastings and Mark Noll note,[2] can be multiplied many times over. So why does the Bible in our mother tongue have such impact? As Andrew Walls notes,

"The proper human response to the divine act of translation is conversion."[3]

EXPANDING THE GOSPEL FOOTPRINT

Bible translation went on to play a key role in planting the gospel. In many places the vernacular Bible is now so universal that its impact can spark a major move to Christian faith. This happens in three ways. Bible translation provides an in-depth understanding showing how Christ speaks into one's own life; it brings written and oral texts into local languages and dialects; and it helps pastors and teachers interpret the gospel in local "language of the heart." The cumulative effect of these three streams has been converging since the late nineteenth and early twentieth centuries, contributing to today's rushing river of faith.

God speaks to us. Within the Bible's stories, songs, poems, prophecies, letters, and histories, one discovers not only remarkable ancient literature but also marvelously simple and descriptive notes on the cosmos and beyond: how the Creator God stoops to speak directly to humans. When we read this grand narrative in the language spoken to us by our mothers or most intimate friends, or in the daily discourse of being ourselves, life (both personal and communal) makes a new kind of sense.

I began, as did many in my generation, with Bible stories at bedtime. Immersed in picture books, I connected to an artist's rendition as my mother read to us. We sang Bible songs at Sunday school and church and were bathed in its stories and parables. There has never been a time when the Bible wasn't in my world.

Places of the coming of the Bible. Thousands of stories from around the world tell how the Bible came to people. To the Oromo people, it came this way. Ethiopia had experienced more than seventeen centuries of continuous Christian witness, stretching back (tradition says) to apostolic times. More recently, though blood-soaked by an oppressive communist government, there was an explosion of Christian conversion. Here, the Spirit took a problem and turned it into an opportunity.

A young Ethiopian named Hika was born in 1856 but lost his father when young. Raiding tribesman stole him from his mother, and after being traded four times he ended up in Massawa on the Red Sea, at a boys' school run by the Swedish Evangelical Mission. He was converted and early expressed his desire to evangelize his own Oromo people.

In a series of bizarre twists and turns, he studied in Sweden and returned determined to minister to his people. He made four attempts, but each time he was refused entry. In one period of uncertainty, he began to translate the psalms and hymns and books of the Bible into the Oromo language. In time he translated both the New and Old Testaments into the Oromo vernacular. For the next seventy-five years this would be the primary Bible for use by his people, and his work was foundational for the eventual spread of Christian faith. The Spirit made way for the Bible, and the Bible laid the basis for the move of the Spirit. Today Ethiopia has one of the most dynamic church movements in Africa.[4]

Mongolia was long under the shadow of the old Soviet Union. When those clouds dispersed, there was a readiness of heart, especially among its young people, to hear the message of Jesus. At the very time it was opening its doors, John Gibbons, a British missionary from New Tribes Mission in Hong Kong, had started in 1972 to translate a Good News version of the New Testament. He worked with Altaa—a Mongolian university student whom he married—from a Russian translation. Thirteen years later, after free elections in Mongolia, five thousand copies sat in a warehouse in Hong Kong with no way of gaining entry to the new country.[5] Then doors opened: in a remarkable stroke of perfect timing, his translation was printed and made available even as missionaries poured in. Tens of thousands of young people—made inquisitive by the sudden vacuum left by a failed and retreating Marxism—now had a Bible ready, printed and on hand. As Philip Jenkins notes, "Once the Bible is in a vernacular, it becomes the property of that people. It becomes a Yoruba Bible, a Chinese Bible, a Zulu Bible."[6] In this case, it became a Mongolian youth manifesto.

The power of translation. The Bible, this book of many books, is held together by a simple unity: the theme of God and his creation. This creative fusion comes about by actual words (text) and the Word (Christ). In short, God is a God who makes himself known in languages we speak and read, and in Christ we have the Word. Both translate. Both incarnate. Translation itself is a form of incarnation, whereby the Word enters into human speech.

As words come into our world, so does Jesus. *Incarnation* is a beautifully rich concept, describing both process and result: he took on humanity and lived among us. We know about him because the Bible tells us so. Children look at Jesus and see God. As a child I hadn't figured out the idea of God. All I needed was to learn of Jesus. He was in my world, my family, my life. God spoke to us and in Jesus became as us. Eugene Peterson reimagines this in his paraphrase of John's statement—"The Word became flesh and made his dwelling among us"—with the words "and moved into the neighborhood" (Jn 1:14, *The Message*).

Putting this written word into the hands of those for whom it has been distant and is now new lights up the proverbial sky. Martin Luther said, "The Bible is alive—it has hands and grabs hold of me, it has feet and runs after me."[7] In effect, when the Bible comes into our hands in our language and its cadence fits our tongue, it evens out the playing field. No longer are those from the North advantaged over those from the South.

For some, this lived experience is not by direct reading. Most audiences in the Majority World listen and remember. They are not necessarily illiterate. Many can read but still prefer to take in information with their ears rather than solely with their eyes. Indeed, 70 percent of the world's population are oral readers.[8] The power of oral cultures, through memory, etches the spoken word indelibly on the mind and in the color and images of their own cultures. Walls notes the importance of translation "so that Christ can live within ... his followers, as thoroughly at home as he once did in the culture of first-century Jewish Palestine."[9]

A FAITH TRANSLATED FOR ALL

Christianity is a translated faith, and a faith translated. Our earliest texts are translations from the language Jesus spoke (Aramaic). That surprised no one in the Greek and Latin worlds. The very idea that God was translated into human form by the incarnation gave credence to the words of Jesus translated into the vernacular. With this as a precedent, it was expected that the biblical text would leap into other languages, being translated again and again in various traditions as it moved across cultural boundaries.

Translators referred back to identified standards—the Greek or Hebrew manuscripts—so that, like a carpenter using a standard rule to measure cuts, each translation stayed on course. Indeed, the release of Erasmus's Greek New Testament was one of the major preconditioners of the Reformation, and the search for better copies of primary-language manuscripts (written closer to the events they describe) has been a major exercise ever since.[10] Faithful translation is critical to the witness of Christ. It matters, as "Christianity seems unique in being the only world religion that is transmitted without the language or originating culture of its founder."[11]

Christianity was born in the Judean hills of the Middle East. One would not be surprised if we had discovered that the apostles wanted to stress the Jewish roots of their teachings. But that was not what they did. As the message spread, their Jewish culture decreasingly defined its content. At times, of course, some tried. The apostle Paul challenged Jesus' disciple Peter for trying to ride two horses at the same time: keeping the Jewish leaders happy by insisting that Gentile (non-Jewish) converts abstain from eating meat offered to idols, while eating such meat himself when out of their range. (This is the conflict behind the story of Peter being instructed to "kill and eat" in Acts 10.)

The message spread quickly through the Roman network as Greek culture shaped its language. This was quite unlike Islam, a cultural religion definitively entrenched in classical Arabic—formed, nurtured, and reinforced by its foundations in the Saudi peninsula, with Mecca as its center. Although many Christians visit Jerusalem, they come as spiritual tourists, an impulse quite different from the mass obedience to the Islamic requirement for pilgrimage to Mecca (*hajj*).[12] There is no such iconic Christian center. Centuries after its founding, "Bible translation enabled Christianity to break the cultural filibuster of its Western domestication to create movements of resurgence and renewal that transformed the religion into a world faith."[13]

Jesus didn't write the Gospels. We have no record, in fact, that he wrote anything. Neither, unlike Paul and other New Testament writers, did he dictate. Instead, Gospel writers took down what they heard, transcribing it into a language he might not have frequently used. (Jesus spoke in Aramaic and they wrote in the common Greek—*Koine*.) While the New Testament cites the Greek Old Testament (the *Septuagint*) 340 times,[14] it is not possible to know whether Jesus ever did so, or whether those who recorded his words later were working from memories shaped by the Greek text. Either way, what we have is a reaffirmation of the incarnation as translation: Jesus, the incarnate Word, is given to us in the Bible as the translated biblical word.

To the original Greek would be added Latin, German, English, and other translations, until today at least a portion of Scripture exists in more than three thousand languages. As the gospel spread across the early post-Jesus world, it found its way into popular languages. It was not to the lofty intellectual heights that Jesus or the disciples preached. Rather, their message resonated among those who lived in the bustle of life, those who wanted to know but whose lack of education kept them at rudimentary levels of understanding. Lack of translation could also be a means of social control. Through the centuries the liturgical nature of the Roman church obscured the Bible from its people, telling stories in its architecture or art for the illiterate but holding on to an archaic Latin text that not even all priests found accessible. Of course, in time that too was broken. Sanneh's metaphor is apt: "Christianity could avoid translation only like water avoiding being wet."[15]

WHAT BIBLE TRANSLATION ACCOMPLISHES

It lives in their neighborhood. One of the inadvertent outcomes of translating the Bible was that it provided tools and skills for national or regional languages and dialects. Adrian Hastings notes that Bible translation was often the first step in creating a national literature, which helped people identify themselves as a nation: "The Bible provided, for the Christian world at least, the original model of the nation. Without it and its Christian interpretation and implementation, it is arguable that nations and nationalism, as we know them, could never have existed."[16] Those without a written script received one as translators devised alphabets and dictionaries, fashioning grammars for teaching. The translators did this, of course, so that people could read and understand the Bible. In the process, however, Bible translation created written language for all sorts of tribes and provided a means for cultural enhancement and renewal. It became a service and facility for all, whether or not they received the gospel for themselves.

Western anthropologists often assume that Bible translators, in engaging cultures without written languages, do harm to indigenous peoples by reshaping their imagination in ways that might be outside their traditions. The Gambian-born Lamin Sanneh, in contrast, sees its effects like this:

> Bible translation inscribes into the cultural imagination a narrative and wisdom tradition that enhances oral and ethnic affinity with biblical stories or creation, covenant, captivity, wilderness, suffering, restoration, hope and abundance. With the added advantage of a dictionary and a grammar, a culture's enhanced capacity to connect and to expand becomes cumulative. Without such advantage, a culture is at risk of stagnation, if not failure.[17]

A second benefit is for people, for they are the object of the exercise. The goal of translation is for them to read the Bible in their own language, enriched by metaphors and pictures of their understanding. Receiving a Bible translation is like a repeat of the Day of Pentecost, when the Spirit descended to create the church: an early step in God's mission to make himself known to a people. It fulfills his incarnation, a divine translation into human reality. What is presented is not a set of doctrines or a theology, but knowledge of a Person. Doctrines and theologies flow from knowing him.

Translation carries with it the implicit assertion that God is at the center of every culture. People of all tribes quickly learn they are beloved and stand on common ground. Culturally some societies seem more sophisticated, more learned or "advanced" (a term once used by global plutocrats). Levels of human distinction rule our social, economic, and political worlds: *here* is where power is assigned and administered. Yet when one engages the language of a people outside of the mainstream, hidden behind "banana leaf curtains," the Bible in their tongue affirms that in God's economy, they are of equal worth. The ideas that permeate the text are as much for them as they are for Shakespearean sophisticates whose knowledge of the text, much used in the history of their language, has been made alive in their culture. Along globalizing pathways, the Bible gives to all people the language of self-respect and "bridging social capital" with which to establish themselves. None then is above another in God's view. To translate is to incarnate. To bring the Bible to a people, in words they embrace, in a language their tongue can feel and articulate, is to say in no uncertain terms that Jesus also lives in their neighborhood. It is revolutionary, even for those who don't consider themselves religious.[18]

It empowers. The Bible also helps Majority World people press back against the dominance of the West and the Enlightenment ideas embedded in scientism: denial of the miraculous and the demonic, and dismissal of the story of God's hand in creation. Some argue that translations skew the original text to suit a philosophical or doctrinal view. Even if that were the case, however, translation is a communal and critical activity. Over time, translations are tested and retested against the early manuscripts, and the evolving translations are then corrected and revised to mitigate any translator's self-interest or bias. For specialist translators such as the Bible Society or Wycliffe/SIL, the power of the text's meaning is overwhelming, inviting readers to participate in the earliest texts in whatever tongue is being used.

A translation in one's own language is resilient and powerful. It brings the reader close to those persuasions and dreams that drove the people of Israel. The process—described by Adrian Hastings— by which the Bible played a role in the rise of European national self-consciousness was repeated around the world in the nineteenth and twentieth centuries. From Ethiopian nationalists[19] who became the founders of modern Nigeria to the Karen Baptist Convention in Burma,[20] the Bible is a fundamental force shaping the modern world. It opens, to people of a different language, prophetic words about God's calling his people to righteousness and justice, forecasting Jesus' coming. It provides (centuries later) that history and recounting of Jesus and the early church.

It brings the gospel into today. Today, people with no idea of the nature or culture of the early church can hold in their hands letters written by apostles and others who guided new Christians (then and now) to explore and understand the gospel. Readers now have that early written text in their own tongue. It is neither subtle nor subversive, but read in the first flush of the discovery of a new world. It doesn't wander into matter-denying Gnosticism. It doesn't hive off the physical world, as if the gospel were ethereal, mystical, and nonmaterial. The written texts of both testaments are as they were written, the same as for those who returned to Jerusalem to await the descent of the Spirit. Letters from the apostles and the four Gospels become for them and for us guidance and counsel, an undergirding that can be relied on, boundaries in which this cosmic faith is to be lived, and unbounded love from its source, the life of Jesus. It is not locked up in Western historicism, as if it were just for those in the first century. A person under a balsam tree in a remote jungle has it to read, as does one on the fiftieth floor of a Manhattan skyscraper. They read it in its sparkling naiveté and clarity and translate the translation into new patterns of apostolicity in their own lives.

Such a man was Francesco Penzotti. Born in Chiavenna, Italy, in 1851, he migrated to Uruguay while still young and came under the influence of Presbyterian merchants and Methodist ministers. After his conversion in 1876, he spent time as a Waldensian pastor in Colonia before taking up the work of a Bible distributor (colporteur) for the American Bible Society. Over his career, through much opposition expressed through stonings, beatings, and imprisonment for being a "propagandist who had the nerve of giving out immoral and corrupt books [i.e., the Bible!]," he personally distributed 125,000 Bibles, and "under his direction more than two million New Testaments and smaller portions were placed in the hands of people in Spanish-speaking lands."[21] He was one of many thousands around the world following the apostolic call of the biblical text, and indeed he has been called "the Apostle of the Central American Church." On such humble, energized, and patient labors were built the explosion of popular Latin American Protestantism a century later.

The Bible's power engages people in life, transforming darkness to light and moral squalor into salvific behavior. Philip invited Nathanael to come and meet the Messiah (Jn 1:45-46). A woman with a notorious reputation, on meeting Jesus, ran to her village and invited the residents to meet a man unlike anyone she had previously encountered (Jn 4:28-30). People obscured and hidden in worlds remote from the "enlightened" of the West can hold in their own hands and read in their own tongue what God has done and will do for them. This is a fire-spreading accelerant!

A Chinese church in Toronto held two morning services, the first in English and the second in Cantonese. During the Cantonese service I turned to the pastor and asked how many in the congregation understood English. "About 95 percent," he responded. "So why don't they come to the earlier service?" I asked. "There is no echo," he said. "No echo?" I wondered. Then it made sense: there is a double power not just in translating, but in translating the words of the Bible into your own language.

The Bible is full of poetry, song, and story. One's mother tongue provides antecedents—rich metaphors, years of hearing and knowing in a language, beliefs and experiences rooted in one's culture, and life-long learning in one's native tongue. Encountering that poetry, song, and story in one's own language eliminates the linguistic "echo" that plagues self-translation from a second tongue into the inheritance of a long and deep knowing. The power of reading and hearing the Bible text in your language removes barriers to plumbing the depths of what God intends us to know.

Every act of translation brings with it a transition into a local "dynamic equivalent." The Maasai of East Africa, for instance, in their creed colorfully use their known world in referring to Jesus' resurrection: "He lay buried in the grave, but the hyenas did not touch him, and on the third day he rose from the grave."[22]

Where it wasn't translated. We also see the power of Bible translation in building a healthy church by viewing countries in which translation was not the norm. In the early Christian era in North Africa the Bible was not translated into the local languages, and Christianity died out when the supportive "Christian" state was removed by waves of Islamic invasion. Berbers in North Africa, for example, had the Bible in Latin but not in their own language, robbing the gospel of a place in the local verbal currency. Without the text in their tongue, the mass migration of the Christian elite and the forcible suppression of teaching under the Muslim conquest effectively degraded the church until it died. Only in the twentieth century, when the Bible was translated into their language (Amazigh or Tamazight)—a job made the more difficult by the many disparate regional dialects—did the church begin to reappear among the Berbers, who have tended to use religious identity to resist first the dominance of Latin under the Romans and now the use of Arabic under the powerful Sunni tradition. The Bible in Berber is thus one important means for cultural survival, even apart from an ongoing Christian witness.

The opposite was true in Egypt and Ethiopia, where it was translated and faith continued despite many trials. Even under the shadow of Islam the Coptic witness remained, because they had the Bible in their language, a working translation that used familiar idioms and metaphors, even when they were subject to harassment, persecution, and even internal heresy.

THE BIBLE'S INHERENT POWER

Why is Bible translation so important to the expansion of the Christian story globally? The answer rests in the inherent power of the biblical word, converting and transforming people to become followers of Christ, the Word. It is not just what they read, but the power of the Bible narrative that shapes and directs lives to a greater good.

Bible translation is ultimately about opening a person to Jesus—not an idea of God, or God as a theophany, but as a person, who took on flesh and (as the book of the Revelation tells us) now bodily still bears the marks of his crucifixion.[23] As missiologist Walls points out, "Christ was not simply a loanword adopted into the vocabulary of humanity; he was fully translated, taken into the functional system of the language, into the fullest reaches of personality, experience and social relationships."[24]

The Scriptures, then, open a person to God's only visitation in human flesh, encountering people in the sordid and complex manners of society, families, and personal life. The Spirit-inspired text attracts readers and listeners to the power of the narrative, to its stories, logic, wisdom, and ideas, and then connects them to the Spirit in ways that transform and renew members of his church.

Jenkins links the Christian "surge" to places where the average age favors the young, an age group full of enthusiasm and boldness.[25] When they believe, it is with a faith rooted in vision and enmeshed in a theology of certitude, ringed by hope. This often happens in countries sideswiped by failing political systems, stormed by economic thuggery, and financially depleted by massive theft of public funds. It is, remarkably for them, a relevant message resting on a foundation for ethical standards.[26] It fuels idealism. In that idealism, Bible stories provide new and future-driven frames, placing Jesus over and against their surrounding societal fictions or the often wild and unreliable promises of their leaders and cultural elites.[27] The Bible instead connects through cosmological concepts to the wider world: creation, economics, vocation, family, sexuality, social experiments. People from traditions in which stories form the basis of memory and history suddenly find themselves walking in believable Bible stories that have stood the test of time and offer solace and truth.

What is it that the world finds so heart-tugging and wisdom-telling in the Bible? For starters, the Bible doesn't deal kindly with the privileged. First-century Palestine had little or no middle class. Though Jesus was a tradesman who worked physically hard every day (probably more in stone than in wood) and was not among the destitute, there was no leisured middle class of the sort that grace the shopping malls of consumer societies. There were the rich and the poor, with little in between, supported by a massive slave population (estimates range from 7 to 20 percent of the total population of the Roman Empire).[28] Today there might be opportunity for enterprise by risk and hard work, giving people space to advance their social and economic well-being. Then, it was not so. In the Transjordan, in the world of Jesus and the Jewish community, to be rich meant you were either born into the right family or you had aggregated your wealth by illicit and unfair means.

Alongside the recent remarkable economic and social lift in some places in Asia, Africa, and Latin America, the attraction of the Bible is not surprising. In Africa most still are poor. Much of Latin America struggles to achieve common standards of fairness, and in Asia, many millions in India, Bangladesh, Pakistan—even in China, a stunning economic story—struggle for daily sustenance. The gospel speaks into their harsh social and economic climates, offering hope in all matters of life. To read the Bible in these contexts is transforming, sometimes revolutionary.

Impact on cultures and societies. Translators have had a profound impact on the emergence of national consciousness, creating paths through written and readable transcripts. By so doing they add richness to their societies, giving them a written language of their own, a cultural asset that is used not just for the Bible but also to keep records of their histories and cultures. "More than 90 percent of these languages have a grammar and a dictionary at all only because the Western missionary movement provided them, thus pioneering arguably the largest, most diverse and most vigorous movement of cultural renewal in history."[29]

Bible translation has enabled countries to free themselves from colonialism. Often it was the first written form for tribes, giving them the means by which they could put in written form demands and concerns, which for most led to disassociation from their European overlords. Not surprisingly, when one looks at the key moments for decolonization or the recognition of indigenous rights, missionaries and translators are often in the picture. In the construction of the Treaty of Waitangi in New Zealand, for example, Colonial Secretary James Stephen (an Evangelical) directed Governor William Hobson along profoundly biblical lines of "sincerity, justice, and good faith." The Māori version was translated by missionary Henry Williams and his son Edward and printed by the missionary printer William Colenso. Though imperfect in some ways, it is often held up as a major distinguisher in the lives, for instance, of Aboriginal Australians just across the

Tasman Sea. *Ngā tohu* became the founding document for a new nation.[30] David Barrett, a pioneer in the statistical analysis of Christian communities around the globe, had lived in Africa. He notes that some churches—who made reading a requirement for baptism—created within tribes a cadre of those who could read and write, the precise skills that tribal chiefs needed to resist and eventually to negotiate with colonizers for their independence. In fact, "as an independent standard of reference; the scriptures have therefore provided African Christians with indispensable guidance at a crucial period at which they would otherwise have been inarticulate. So began the demand of African society for spiritual independence from the religious imperialism of Western extra-biblical ideas."[31]

It was a process that didn't diminish cultural identity or tribal awareness. In fact, it did the opposite. Not only did learning to read the Bible set a baseline for freedom and emancipation; it also gave tools for the development of indigenous leadership. Translation "triggered a much broader process of ethnographic field research and historical documentation to produce a ripple effect on politics, economics, culture, and society, as well as on religion."[32]

Moving from a Hebrew world. Translation is important and powerful, as it takes what is true in the biblical text and transports it into another time, place, and culture. It is axiomatic that Vietnamese fishermen on the coast of the South China Sea read the biblical text through different eyes than Mongolians in treeless hills watching their herds. Such an observation hardly needs noting—and yet it does bear repeating, in part because those who speak English think that *that* is the true normal. As local people read and study the Bible's rules of spiritual engagement, they do so in the midst of their real lives, in places and within social strictures that harness those rules to practical applications in their world. The assumptions of Vietnam or Mongolia are foreign to my world. I live in a world where the demonic is politely restricted from public appearances and cared for in sophisticated health systems. In the hills of Nepal, that realm is more obvious. In Africa, where disease and scarcity abound, their conscious awareness of the demonic shapes how they read the biblical text, a framing within their reality, not mine.

The Western mind reads the text in ways shaped by Greek philosophy and modified by the European moments of the Protestant Reformation, the Enlightenment, and its stepchild, modernity. In today's human rights environment, the individual rules. Liberalism, based on the notion of the autonomous person, places the individual at the heart of society; its laws conform to those rights. This is not so in places where community or family is sacred, where individual rights are not supported by a well-funded public order that enables people to detach themselves from community and family. Societies in the Global South might in fact be closer to the biblical Semitic world, a world in which community is the heart and soul of life. Here the person has rights *because* of community, rather than despite it. When Africans or Middle Easterners read the Bible, they understand and feel the thick culture of the original text more clearly than I, for in their world family is the ruling framework. I've been taught to read God's promises and his provision for salvation as an individual. Writers such as Ken Bailey take me into the Hebrew culture of the biblical text and help me see the intricate weaving of that world, and its meaning to the Gospels, the teachings of Jesus, and the outworking of his call to the Hebrew and Greek world.[33] As the Global South ascends and expresses its take on the Bible, its understanding will press against Western interpretations of individualism, giving us wider and more varied insights into how the text might be read and understood.

GETTING THE BIBLE INTO THE LANGUAGE
OF THE PEOPLE

The more than seven billion people on earth talk to each other through some 6,880 languages. To date 3,255 languages have all or some of the Bible translated. Some 1,432 have a New Testament and 1,145 have portions. Even so, 3,655 language groups, representing 253 million people, still need the Bible. For more than 1.3 billion people, the full Bible is not yet available; 657 million have only the New Testament. For others, portions are in the process of translation. Translators are at work on more than four hundred projects.[34]

Three hundred years after Luther and Tyndale triggered the Protestant and English Reformations by translating the Bible into the vernacular, a cobbler from England set lose a firestorm of translations that in this century remains one of the most sustaining and critical elements underlying the outward move of Christian witness and prevailing faith. William Carey, the father of modern missions, sailed for India in 1793, where he translated the Scriptures into Bengali, Arabic, Hindi, and Sanskrit. What he did subsequently became the basis of a strategy for Protestant missions generally. However, it wasn't until the mid-twentieth century that a global movement devoted to Bible translation was organized.

In 1942, the first Wycliffe Translators organization was formed, bringing together translators already at work. They are now engaged in translations of the entire Bible or New Testament into 890 languages. Of course, it is one thing to translate, but another to get the translation into the hands of people. The numbers are astounding.

In 2014, the United Bible Societies distributed a total of 428.2 million Scriptures around the world. And that is just one Bible society, although it is the largest. *Guinness World Records* reports that 5 billion "units" of the Bible have been sold.[35] By late 2015, the Bible site YouVersion offered 1,200 versions in 868 languages on their digital app. The Faith Comes by Hearing group completed Audio Scriptures in 915 languages and the Jesus Film Project has produced a stunning 1,370 different language versions.[36] OneHope provides Bibles and literature for children, distributing, at the time of writing, 1,032,631,559 copies in 142 languages. Breaking all this down into regions, the countries in which the largest number of Bibles are distributed are China, Brazil, the United States, South Korea, Malaysia, India, and Nigeria. The Bible, once the patrimony of the Greek- and Latin-speaking Roman world, then the foundation of the Western canon, is now the inheritance of the entire world.

What we have learned is that those who give their lives in mission don't take into account the high price of translation. Translators by nature are immune from counting the cost. Intrinsic to translators' "call and response" is the driving ethos that others matter more than self. The Scriptures are of such value that to leave all and go to another place that might be unwelcoming, often without amenities and away from family, is not a price too high to pay. They simply don't consider abandoning their mission. This is what Bible translation requires: sitting for years with people, listening to them speak, gradually forming a written script that, word by word, forms a written vocabulary in a context that previously might not have had its own alphabet. Once in place, translators figure out how the Bible text can be translated so as to configure it within the verbal, metaphorical, and visionary boundaries of that people.

PLACES OF UPSURGE

Where is this Bible translating taking place? It happens where the Bible is central to patterns of worship, personal study, preaching, and teaching. Wrapped around congregational life, or dispersed throughout social gatherings, Bible study is formative for such communities: in business settings, before a sporting event, a morning coffee hour, or an evening church gathering. Typical events are highlighted by the sermon—from twenty minutes to an hour—not so much read but extemporaneous, on what the Scriptures say and how the mind and heart rooted in Bible knowledge makes for a good Christian.

This Bible-centered worship is not organized around religious hierarchy or managed according to printed liturgy. Rather, its self-conscious pursuit is to know not a dictum or creed but the power of God; this worship intentionally is "not ashamed of the gospel, because it is the power of God that brings salvation to everyone who believes" (Rom 1:16). This comes, of course, with risk. All sorts of wild-eyed ideas raise their heads when there are few formal boundaries. The twentieth century is strewn with abandoned religious ideas, failing when held up to scrutiny. Continuing aberrant forms still hold many captive in mild or even radical heresies, or under the persuasive gaze of a charismatic but theologically askew preacher. Within churches where there is that spark of faith, there is also an occasional wildfire—but that is to be preferred to ashes, be they cool or even warm.

Through the mid-twentieth century, the sacramental church (those with longer traditions rooted in Roman, Orthodox, or Anglican communities) also began to feel the impact of a stronger Bible orientation. After Vatican II, in particular, the Bible became more important in liturgical and personal life. Interest in the Bible climbed on both the popular and the scholarly levels.

In 1960, Vatican II (in its *Dogmatic Constitution on Divine Revelation*) allowed for "translations in every language . . . in cooperation with separated brethren."[37] This opened the door not only for Catholics to pursue new translations but also for them to be allowed to work with "separated brethren," a code word for the

Protestant traditions who had done so much to develop biblical scholarship in the nineteenth and twentieth centuries.

As we have seen in Latin America, where the Protestant church experienced persecution, Pentecostals and Charismatics took root and grew dramatically from the 1950s. As Catholic churches, in a sort of divine emulation, embraced newer forms of worship and an increase of Bible teaching, they too experienced renaissance.

Elsewhere, some Protestant churches were heading in the opposite direction. Unsure of biblical authenticity or authority, many mainstream Protestant churches declined precipitously, not only in Europe, Oceania, and North America, but wherever the nineteenth-century missionary enterprise took root. The mainline Protestants in the Global South, however, for the most part rejected their mother churches' liberal biblical bias. The Anglican Church is an example. Much divided, today her largest churches are no longer in England or North America. Fifty million Anglicans (three out of every five) live in Africa, while in England the numbers drop with each passing year.[38]

Disallowing the Bible in an effort to quash Christianity seems to have the opposite effect. Albania, once considered the most restrictive country for the practice of religion, was walled in by President Enver Hoxha for forty-five years. Hoxha's desire for a pure, postreligious Marxist-Leninist state led him to ban the sale or circulation of the Bible. This, however, only drove people to find creative means for getting one. The more denied it was, the more desired it became. Even before the death of the president in 1985 and the collapse of Soviet influence in 1989, the Albanian church was preparing an underground culture for the time of openness and freedom. Just over the border, missionaries such as the Quanrud family had been working with ethnic Albanians in Kosovo, and the European Christian Mission was preparing a popular Bible translation. When the walls came down in 1990, the Bible surged back into Hoxha's sterilized fields to a rapturous reception. In all of Albanian history up until the collapse of Communism, there had been five Bible translations into the vernacular. Since 1990 alone, there have been seven more added to that list.[39]

China, during its most restrictive years, also made it difficult to obtain a Bible. This fueled networks that moved Bibles from offshore, as demand for Bibles drove clandestine delivery methods. Christians mostly met underground, ready to expand outreach once laws made it permissible to gather for worship. Even when public worship was allowed, the government was selective in where Bibles could be bought, reserving that privilege for registered churches. Their objective, which was to decrease interest in the Bible by prohibiting or restricting its access, only increased people's desire to have one. Cut off from the West, the house church movement in China became one of the most self-directed and Bible-centered movements in the world, and grew dramatically, in part due to the proximity that the Bible gave oppressed Christians to their Lord. Today, Amity Press in Nanjing, China, is the world's largest printer of Bibles.

In India, the caste structure embraces almost all, defining who a person is (or is not), their role in life, and where they can (and cannot) move. The structure is more than just about defining a place for *untouchables*—now called Dalits, though untouchable they are. It is about a religious vision of life that gives enormous privilege to 5 percent of society, and favorable status to 25 percent, with 70 percent relegated to being OBC (Other Backward Castes) and Dalits (Outcasts) or no caste at all. This means that over 700 million people are immutably classed as servants or untouchables; the caste strictures thus put an enormous weight on social mobility and shut down the culture's inner capacity to rethink the notion of personhood.

Yet within those social restraints, Bible translation has led the way. The first translation into Tamil took places in the sixteenth century when most converts were from lower castes. With the Bible in Tamil, outcastes redefined themselves as "people of the Scriptures."[40] This mattered, for it was only the upper class, the Brahmans, who could read the Vedas (the Hindu scriptures, written in Sanskrit). Outcastes were banned from reading it. Thus, "the Christian Scriptures gave these believers a particular identity."[41]

This early and focused mission with the Dalits spoke into the heart of the poor and oppressed, offering them a newfound dignity not located in their cultural history or national and tribal religions.

◀━━━━━━▶

Translation activities do not happen in a vacuum. They are done among people who know and are embraced by the contextual meanings of the words spoken. Words matter, telling us not just what something is but who *we* are. The gospel is in the world of real people, in real time. In a sense the gospel can't help itself. It seeks out those who know not Christ, translating the living Jesus into words and ways that make sense. *Indigenous* is the appropriate word. Wherever the gospel falls, it belongs. While imported (for we all have had it imported from Jerusalem), soon it becomes ours, as if it began with us. We own it. It fits, like a coat. It sits well in our speech, its metaphors become ours, and in time we exchange its word pictures for those around us.

The Bible text is made holy when inhabiting other tongues. Located in the world of people, it projects the Christ who too was in flesh, in time, in place, in culture, in personality. He is not some generalized *other*. And it is that essence of him, Jesus of Nazareth, who wills that he be rooted in other cultures. Philippians 2:6-7 tells us that he, though "existing in the form of God, did not consider equality with God something to cling to, but emptied Himself,

taking the form of a servant, being made in human likeness"
(Berean Study Bible). He did so that all may feel his charm and
grace, be offended by his prophetic sharpness, and be healed by his
loving touch. Foreignness is not his nature. If it were, then he could
have spoken from the skies or sent Michael the archangel. Instead,
he is *Emmanuel*, God among us. We've come to see that he fits into
our ethnic or tribal group. He looks like us. That's the power of the
Word of God, brought out of the past but made present by translation into the indigenous, into the local tongue and all that being
a native speaker of that tongue means.

FOUR

REVOLUTION OF THE
INDIGENOUS

It was a Sunday night church service in my teenage years. A tall, poised preacher with a deep South African accent stepped to the pulpit and began to speak with flowing rhetoric and a rich vocabulary. I had never met a black preacher before, nor heard such preaching. Nicholas Bhengu's enduring story is exemplary of how the power and winsomeness, passion and ability of indigenous leaders formulated an understanding of the gospel for Africans. His story points to a critical factor in leadership throughout the Global South: locally grown leaders, supported by their people, generated a unique, compelling, and transformative witness.

A former member of the Communist Party, Bhengu (1909–1985) converted in 1929, in time starting his own denomination. Known for preaching large "Back to God" crusades, he developed into one of the most influential church leaders on his continent as the leader of the first multiracial denomination in South Africa.[1] It was reported that typically, after a gospel service, a truck was required to haul away guns, weapons, and stolen articles returned by penitent sinners.

He and his theology were deeply African. Speaking to the legislature of Ciskei, South Africa, from 2 Chronicles 7:14, he reframed Africa's significance for the global Christian story, drawing on Abraham's travels in Africa, the Ethiopian eunuch's conversion, and the influence of the early North African church father, Augustine. Bhengu left no one in doubt: "I'm not trying to persuade you to accept or adopt a Western God, but the God of our Ancestors, the God of the Bible."[2]

Time magazine wrote of him in the 1950s, "So phenomenal is his power . . . that tributes have been paid to him by Dr. Verwoerd [Prime Minister] and by police chiefs throughout the country."[3] While Bhengu was heavily criticized for not taking an active role in the political issues of South African liberation, Terrance Ranger points out that Bhengu's reason for not getting involved was that it would only give whites further occasion to demonstrate *their* power. Even so, he was well aware of the issues and often likened the condition of African blacks to Israel's captivity in Egypt. His calling was, however, to invite people to faith, and to plant churches.

This social mobilization through church planting would later help wrest power from whites. Ranger evaluates his impact on South Africa: "That he bequeathed a moral and social legacy affecting the future of democracy—indeed, one that helped prepare the way for democracy—is clear. Individuals converted to evangelical Christianity through the Back to God movement populate every sector of black society: teachers, lawyers, traders, clerks, businessmen, gardeners, and even politicians."[4]

As with other indigenous movements, Bhengu chose to build churches without reliance on external funding. By 2000 the Back to God movement (with just under a thousand churches and a million adherents) raised half a million dollars just in selling hand-icrafts.[5] By the time of his death, Bhengu had been directly respon-sible for planting more than fifty congregations and influencing hundreds more. It took a new generation of local leaders after him to grow an indigenous church framed by "Three Self" motifs: lead-ership, propagation, and support.

◀━━━━━━━━▶

At the age when I first saw Bhengu preach, missionary confer-ences were always a favorite. They involved exotic stories of daring and faraway places, artifacts of remote peoples and movies about people and places about which I could only dream. But there was one constant factor: all missionaries were white. They returned every four to five years to tell their stories, but out on the field they were in charge of churches, training schools, medical clinics, and publishing. Stuck in the belief that these self-sacrificing "mis-sionaries knew best," it took Western agencies and denominations time to reverse the picture. For many agencies, therefore, the story of the twentieth century was a race toward handing off leadership to the nationals or else facing revolt. Their national colleagues were not satisfied with being second in charge. As nationalist movements swept the globe, they pressed to pastor their own churches, lead their own denominations, and teach and run their own schools.

This reversion to indigenous or localized ownership is a major driver in today's global witness. It builds off the power of younger, locally grown leadership, and off fresh insight from those who more easily understand the needs of their own people. These generate momentum, for it is they who know the customs, who can speak in common words to the stirring needs of their people, and who are able to lift hearts and voices in praise and faith. This strategic and biblical shift underlies much of what we now witness globally.

Sometimes shifts come through well-thought-out plans and reorganization, but they also come by unexpected social or political earthquakes, or a transitional understanding among missionaries. A missionary friend sat with a Kenyan family in their home in the mid-1960s and looked up in the rafters and saw a set of drums. So he asked the young man to get them down and play them. The young Kenyan was embarrassed: missionaries had taught him that drums were of the devil, used for dances and "unchristian" events. Unable to resist the persuasive entreaty of the missionary, he got them down and launched into a rhythmic beat. Served by their own musical idioms and styles, such African-style worship liberated hearts instinctively tuned to the mystical and the invitation of the Divine.

In time, as the gospel took on the hue of its newly arrived home, the God-given talent of a drummer made it into an instrument of praise. It is now a ubiquitous instrument in modern worship bands worldwide. It was no coincidence that Pentecostalism emerged from the southern United States at just the time when African-influenced jazz was rewriting the cultural song list of Europe. (Indeed, Pentecostalism has been referred to as "jazz spirituality.")[6] When missions understood the power, utility, and genius of indigenized gospel ideas, the ground shifted. It was a tipping point for a truly global Christianity.

INDIGENOUS

What do we mean by the "indigenous church"? David Garrison's definition is helpful. An indigenous church is "generated from within."[7] William A. Smalley expands on this by defining an indigenous church as "a group of believers who live out their life, including their socialized Christian activity, in the patterns of the local society, and for whom a transformation of that society comes out of their felt needs under the guidance of the Holy Spirit and the Scriptures."[8] An indigenous plant finds its environment hospitable—it's at home, not a transplant. You can transplant a banana tree to Canada, but its rate of survival will be zero. To keep it alive requires a year-round warm nursery. Maple trees, on the other hand, are indigenous to Canada: they not only survive bitter winters, they thrive.

This elementary idea, simple in its essence, is ministry altering in its effect, and not only in the Majority World. Its most obvious function is that it provides a community with its own voice. An indigenous church can nurture people within their own culture and ways of thinking and speaking.

The gospel story multiplies by its nature. It reproduces in whatever place, culture, or language it lands. It can find roots anywhere. It will take the form of a banana or a maple tree as required. Its genius is that it doesn't need a "place like home" to survive and thrive.

Paul transplanted the gospel into the Greek world and it soon became Greek. It felt familiar to the Greeks' touch, smelled good to their soul. Its ability to adapt, without losing its essence, gave new Christians everywhere a story of freedom that became theirs. Only when foreign players attempted to exert control was it kept from becoming a transplant. The ingenious pattern of Christ's message of "grace outpoured" fits the hand like a glove, precisely because grace is *poured* out. It is neither moral nor spiritual relativism. Rather, the gospel is dynamic, speaking to needs in ways understood by local cultures, ministering to issues calling for solutions, big and small, to challenges that perplex and block human progress. The incarnation of Jesus established the prototype, in both substance and process. In the gospel, Jesus comes and lives in our neighborhood. It is God who, in humanity, talks, holds, walks, cries, commands, and condemns, saving, healing, and inspiring. I encounter him in my world. I hear and understand him in my language. The bearer of good news is a member of my own tribe. The chimes of the good news resonate.

The old model. The traditional Western worldview, which came to dominate the globe from the eighteenth century, operated with a two-tier world. In post-Reformation settlements, faith had to be formulated by doctrine: what one believed was something cognitive that worked its way into other aspects of life. Conversion— a personal, inward, and behavioral response—was founded on what one believed. Doctrine defined faith. This doctrine-based faith, however, flattened the interlocking of the personal with the Spirit and his gifts. Tennent, speaking of some of the less-productive Protestant missions, notes, "These missionaries were Evangelical in their theology, but when it came to pneumatology applied to real-life praxis, they were functional deists."[9]

What *did* they have to say to questions about demons tormenting a neighbor, or how to interpret a portentous dream? Many were tutored in the assumptions of the Enlightenment and rationalistic nineteenth-century theologians: anything outside of a rational explanation was seen as superstition. Renewalists,[10] on the other hand, welcome these questions, redeeming the mystical impulse in indigenous cultures. They understood that the demonic could be located even in those seeking faith. Here was a harbor of evil that needed to be shaken up and cleansed. For Renewalists, the "unseen world" of animist receiving cultures was an opportunity for the redeeming narrative of the miracle-working Christ, something to be engaged rather than ignored.

When the colonizers finally packed their bags—and when they were reluctant, the bags were packed for them—old imperial dominations tumbled. "Christendom" died in the shadow of Europe's withdrawal from its colonial experiments. A common thread wove its way through the desire of locals to lead: the needs of their people required of them local interpretations and solutions. Ready or not, the functions of giving witness and shepherding the flock were taken over by nationals. Stumbles and fractures were inevitable. Church organizations, previously the fixtures of mission boards and agencies, became doors on broken hinges. The old, even when good and valuable, was often discarded as the church in its national character formulated itself for the future. Even with missteps, however, the necessary transition—from the old to the new, from colonial control to national independence, from foreign missionaries to indigenous voices—was both desirable and achieved.

While it is true that the Majority World is no longer missionary receiving as a passive receptor of a Western message, there is an interest by both sides in new mutual forms of missions. The energy in traditionally receiving countries for missionary sending is striking. As Dario Lopez has noted,[11] in 2006 more than ten thousand Latin American missionaries were working transculturally, many in areas (such as the Middle East) where the more typical (in appearance) Anglo missionary is deemed suspicious. As I write, Todd Johnson and others estimate that there are now almost as many Majority World missionaries as there are missionaries from the traditional sources of Protestant faith. The mission enterprise is not over. It is in transition, moving from "We've got the message for you to believe" to "How can we help you in your vision and growth?"

Today, as nationals are mostly in the lead and hand in glove with the Spirit, this shift moves the scale of evangelism.

An example of the new model. China manifests the power and accelerating influence of locally grown leadership and ministry initiatives. In 1950 its less than a million Christians were subjected to harassment and persecution, outlawed and killed by Mao's communist government. When Mao died (1976) and the country opened up to the world, a vibrant and fruitful church was found to have grown beyond the most optimistic of views. As Mao tried to repress them, his policies of restricting leadership, funding, and proclamation—the basis for his "Three Self" movement—to state-controlled institutions produced the opposite of what he had in mind. He forced the churches to indigenize, which in turn spurred their dramatic growth.

In the late nineteenth century Roland Allen—sent from England to China in 1895 by the Society for the Propagation of the Gospel (SPG)—advised missionaries to base their work on the idea of the Three Selfs. He saw that the church would work best when put into the hands of indigenous "biblical apostolic witnesses"[12] who would self-govern, self-fund, and self-propagate the message. His vision was that "in every market town in China, in every center of population all over the world [there would be] the Church which could grow and expand without any direction from foreigners."[13]

This notion of "faith as local embodiment"[14] serves to drive the church deeper and deeper into the life and times of a people, region, country, tribe, or community. While the West never had "rights" over the gospel, it often acted as if it did, assuming superiority and the global right to define orthodoxy. When Western missionaries were expelled from China in 1949, it seemed to Western mission societies that a bright light had gone dark. Reports of persecution and killings diminished hopes of any ongoing witness. Then, as the Cultural Revolution (1966–1976) waged war against pastors and Christian leaders, sending them out into the countryside for "reeducation," we assumed that the church had been decimated.

Instead, in a realization that produced a "paradigmatic realignment" of missional thinking,[15] Roland Allen was proved right. Even under official oppression, the Three Self approach grew the gospel witness at the grassroots. National leaders such as Wang Mingdao, Allen Yuan, Moses Xie, Watchman Nee, and Samuel

Lamb rooted the gospel story in their own culture, language, and idioms.

Effectively, state policy transferred expertise to nationals and knit them more tightly to popular desires for a different future. Pastors emerged, many of them spontaneously. Some pastors who could afford it sought "religious training abroad, particularly in South Korea, Taiwan, Hong Kong, Singapore and the US."[16] Giving became lessons in generosity. Evangelists sprang up. Repression, in short, became an accelerator for local mission.

One of the outcomes of reading the Bible in Chinese, and often in isolation from Western influences, was to raise the question, "Where do we fit in the story of Acts?" One response was the "Back to Jerusalem" missionary initiative,[17] emerging first in the 1920s, developing and building on a premise that Chinese Christians would complete the westward circuit of the gospel begun in Jerusalem: from the eastern regions of China and on to Jerusalem. The deep commitment of the Chinese church to evangelize at home and abroad is at the heart of this powerfully mobilizing idea. Its fulfillment will take into account possibly the largest missionary force in history, all from a land in which less than a century ago Christians feared their faith was on its last legs. Instead of snuffing out the gospel witness, Mao fanned flames of faith and courage, resulting in a church that was strong, resilient, and creative.

Not only did China explode in Christian faith; in less than a century its indigenous leadership created its own mission-sending force.

THE POWER OF MULTIPLICATION

Historically, Western mission work has been most successful where Western influence opened the doors and gave missionaries access. William Carey could more easily locate in India where Britain had military, economic, and national interests. However, such an advantage was just that, to open doors. Staying and holding on to leadership could result in the opposite: the closing of doors. Control generally came to an end at the same time as the colonial relationships. This freed up the gospel witness to shake itself free from home-country traditions. Colonial attitudes and control were overturned, at which time the mission impulse took hold.

Philip, directed by the Spirit, met a bureaucrat of the Ethiopian queen. After conversion, baptism, and instruction in the Scriptures, Philip left and let the Ethiopian go home alone. We can assume it was *his* witness, not Philip's, that carried the day once home in Ethiopia. Peter (in Acts 10) was led by a dream to visit a despised Roman soldier. Cornelius's conversion was the beginning of another center of spiritual vibrancy. They didn't need Peter to stay with them. Cornelius, around whom a "cascade of supernatural interventions" marks a new turn in salvation history,[18] spread the word in the Roman military and in time might have carried it with him upon his family's return to Rome.

Vietnam. The Vietnamese church multiplied within four social movements that brought change, giving strength to a growing Christian witness. First there was the outflow of boat people who fled following the defeat of the US coalition, settling in Canada, the United States, Australia, New Zealand, and Singapore (among others). As many came to faith in their adopted worlds, they became active in their diaspora, finding ways to carry the gospel back to their homeland, influencing Vietnamese people wherever they went. Then, in the 1990s, the Vietnam government sent students to Soviet-influenced countries: Russia, Ukraine, and Poland. The now-active Vietnamese diaspora, seeing an opportunity, sent missionaries to these countries. Students embraced Christian faith, many returning to their homeland as emissaries of the gospel. The third group was among international workers taking up employment in places such as South Korea. Hearing the gospel, they returned home and helped in building churches, giving witness to families and communities. Finally, students sent overseas to study were swept up in the same story: hearing of Christ, they returned home to lead families and friends to faith in Christ. Today this vital church is growing through the witness of faith by its own.

India. India is the most complex and varied of countries, with a massive population and multiple layers of languages, customs, religious patterns, geographies, and politics. I asked Richard Howell, general secretary of the Asia Evangelical Alliance (formerly the Evangelical Fellowship of Asia), how the gospel advances in a country corralled by the caste system. He referred to "wildfire" movements of faith breaking out with two types of evangelism. First, the gospel advances fluidly: many come to faith without calling themselves Christians. They keep their traditional names, clothes, and customs and meet together in something other than what would be thought of as a "church." These groups include the Allah Abad ("the church meeting" in the Punjab), where about ten thousand people meet on Sundays in a field. The Yesu Darbar has taken to itself the name "The Royal Court of Jesus Christ." Another group called the Yesus Satsang (or "truth seekers") would not be recognized by many as Christian, yet they trust in Jesus and follow his teachings.

Second, the gospel advances by *spontaneity*—that is, gospel initiatives break out in places where it seems there has been neither strategy nor anyone targeting the area for evangelism. These outbreaks of faith are characterized by a strikingly familiar Acts formula: teaching, healing, and casting out of evil spirits.

Persecution also is a factor. Underlying concerns for the future is the fear that India's parliament might pass a bill naming India as a Hindu country, which, Indian Christians fear, would lead to other faiths being penalized, denied opportunities for employment, and burdened with heavier taxation. Today in rural areas, churches are burned, pastors beaten, and Christians intimidated. In 2017 the Indian government disallowed a number of charities—Compassion International being the largest, sending forty-five million dollars a year for child support—from sending financial support.[19]

Prior to the indigenization of missions, numbers could only grow by *addition*. One spoke to one. However, it wasn't a numbers game that caught the attention of missionaries. The training of national leaders set loose the message so that many could speak to many. Changes in leadership didn't always happen easily: some Westerners were pushed out by national leadership tired of foreign control, in places where missionaries had become targets for resentment. Some mission groups heard misgivings from home churches and denominations, who thought the "time for missions" was over. Here was another irony. This inward turn of some in the West had an odd effect. When the missionary enterprise was no longer a foreign transplant, the formula driving Christian growth in the missionary-receiving country switched from addition to multiplication.

MISSIONS IN CONTEXT

Missiologists refine this conversation through the word *contextualization*. This is a conscious examination, by one planning to move to another culture, of costs, risks, and methods. Anything in the intercultural encounter that distorts the message, creates confusion, or blocks understanding is altered or removed. This understanding can also be subconscious, where the two cultures "speak" to one another through lived experiences of people such as migrants, preachers, businesspersons, and other mobile citizens of the global society. Paul, himself a transnational Jew, modeled this when he spoke to the Athenians (Acts 17). He was careful not to offend by denigrating their gods. Instead he put his message in the context of their world. He framed his ideas so they could better understand

and hear his explanation of Jesus. His "on ramp" to the core message was his reference to the *temple* of the "unknown god." They caught it. This approach gave a road down which he could explain his message. He would later reason with such people also in Ephesus, at the Hall of Tyrannus (Acts 19).

An important question is, how far does one go to understand context and shape the message to the receiving culture? A legitimate fear is *syncretism*: the blending (some would say the debasing) of the gospel by merging it with local ideas and beliefs. One is struck when one visits Haiti and the Philippines, for example, where the dominant church tradition (Catholicism) mixes the gospel with local beliefs and practices. African Independent Churches, too, sometimes blend messianic tendencies with the living prophets among their leadership, regarding them as "divine." It is important, of course, to ask the reverse question. As Richard Fletcher and others note, the West itself is not exempt—its Christian traditions have arisen as a series of compromises with emerging national cultures.[20] How much of the gospel, then, is tainted with syncretism in merging local cosmologies, politics, culture, and ruling economic theories? It is convenient to slip in what is appealing to our culture, making it easier to believe and practice.

Some methods of evangelism are inevitably going to be exploratory. Take, for instance, Muslims who confess faith in Christ but continue to attend mosque and study the Qur'an, retaining their Muslim appearance and identity. This allows them to continue uninterrupted within their world, teaching, where possible, the message of Jesus. The same is done in the Hindu world. The emergence of underground churches, of "Jesus followers" in Japan who do not use the name Christian, and of illegal converts in Iran meeting in private houses present (as Rodney Stark notes about the early church[21]) another valid form of witness that, over the longer term, has proved to be an effective means of expanding the church. If the "blood of the martyrs is the seed of the Church" (Tertullian, *Apologeticus*), then surely quiet, persistent Christian communities are its green shoots.

The early church model. From the start, Jerusalem's church elders made it clear that Gentiles did not have to become Jews first to be Christian (Acts 15). This established a primary feature of the gospel. The gospel was carved in neither cultural nor ethnic stone, however much it would always have to find a place based on such bedrock.

In effect, the elders approved of a culture other than one that was Jewish. The power of that decision enabled those who knew little or nothing of the Hebrew faith to embrace Jesus' life and teachings. In turn this gave permission for peoples other than Jews to receive, embrace, and talk about Jesus to others, in language shaped by their cultural insight. As Paul points out, the elders' permission was pleasant, but in a sense only a recognition that the Spirit had already broken out of Christianity's Middle Eastern origins.

As its early missionaries migrated north and west and south, the gospel localized in North Africa, the Middle East, Turkey, Greece, and Rome, holding on to the narrative of God in Christ. The messenger transplanted the message at every turn. This transplanted faith grew in its new soil, and, while centered on the essentials of the Christian story, redefined the message in local and practical terms. Over the longer term, it would begin to transform its host cultures as the initial encounter took on the form of renewed personal and then social values.

The gospel was mobile from day one. This outward mission move by early church evangelists defined its nature. When Jerusalem was besieged by the Romans (AD 70),[22] Jews forced to flee into Gentile territories soon learned that traditional ideas that seemed so important to them weren't held in the same way or with the same force by new converts. Circumcision, kosher dietary rules, even the Torah wasn't as central to many converts who, in a short time, became leaders in the Christian community. The early church steadily expanded to embrace more and more Greeks. Paul told Christians in Corinth that rituals of the old Jewish faith weren't essential for faith. His principle was that no Christian group has "any right to impose in the name of Christ upon another group of Christians a set of assumptions about life determined by another time and place."[23] Andrew Walls identifies a primary assumption in this: the message of Jesus, beginning in a Bethlehem stable, is reborn in each culture into which it is invited. The gospel is a natural fit into diverse cultures, languages, and peoples.

That does not mean the gospel doesn't have an edge or won't challenge practices, values, and cultural mores. Walls uses a helpful picture, the "pilgrim principle," by which he means that, as the gospel comes alongside people, they better understand that they belong to Christ while living within their world. The pilgrim principle "whispers to him that he has no abiding city and warns him that to be faithful to Christ will put him out of step with his society."[24] For no city, country, or people can "absorb the word of Christ painlessly into its system." In effect, following Jesus might "rub people raw."

The gospel is serial. The ability of the gospel to bring transformation and open up inroads to personal and community conversion hangs on its "incarnation" in congregational life. Andrew Walls contrasts this to Islam, which embraces and takes captive peoples and countries by way of law (*shari'a*), language (classical Arabic), or outright conquest. Christianity, on the other hand, has worked least well when it has been imposed as an imperial or ethnic form. It is at its best when it is *serial*—that is, in serial form as transformed people live in congregational life. There is no "family of the prophet" in Christianity. "Christianity has no culturally fixed element, as provided by the Qur'an fixed in heaven, closed traditions on earth, perfection of law in *shari'a*, a single shrine in Mecca, and true word everywhere in Arabic."[25]

The gospel moves in a "serial" way. As the Ethiopian eunuch converted under Philip's ministry and went on his way home, it wasn't part of a strategy for cultural or national takeover. Rather, the gospel was believed by one and transferred to the community, and from that sprang a believing church. The church has no center but is rather a spiritual force always on the move. Jerusalem, while a strong memory, is just that—it's not the place of our identity or where our faith is located. Instead, our faith is found in Jesus and made alive by the ever-present Spirit. As a serial progression, Christianity is vulnerable to human shifts as the church advances and recedes, and as old margins become new centers of witness.

The gospel built on the incarnational Jesus—alive in word and flesh, in the community—lives within individuals and in congregational life. When that ceases, the church becomes vulnerable to a takeover, reduced to a nominal faith or altogether lost, dominated, or absorbed by another. This was the case of most countries of the Roman elements of the Middle East and North Africa. The Christian church is not *inevitable*. It doesn't spring up without the message being carried in by someone. Neither will it necessarily continue. "New churches, or churches in new areas, are not gains to be plotted on the map. That is an Islamic, not a Christian, view of expansion."[26] For Christians, our "holy place" is Jesus, where the believer encounters the God of the universe.

THE RENEWALIST PUSH

The expansion of Renewalist Christianity has gone hand in hand with the rise of indigenous national leadership. The mutual reinforcing of local aspirations—to translate the gospel into words and patterns of faith that resonate with local and national culture—and global Spirit awareness not only generates interest in the Spirit who is God's Presence with us in our diverse locations, but also enables the rise of national identity. This leads into answering the question, why have Charismatics and Pentecostals become so pervasive? As church leadership shifted from Western missionaries into the hands of nationals, Renewalists[27] gave added momentum to the swinging of the pendulum. Most denominations founded by denominational missions end up sounding much like their originating partners: Lutherans produce overseas Lutheran churches, Presbyterians stamp the name *Presbyterian* on the outcomes of their work. Pentecostals, however, instinctively got what Roland Allen meant when he spoke about "apostolic methods." Rather than seeing themselves as birthed in the early 1900s, Pentecostals located their message at the beginning of a renewed apostolic "age of the Spirit." They believe that their message draws from the well of first-century Christianity and brings with it the historic, continuing promise of empowerment. Some Pentecostals carry their labels as well, of course, forming denominations such as the Assemblies of God. The difference was that over time *Pentecostal* ceased to be just a noun, denoting an integrated denomination, and became an adjective, referring to a hybrid of surprising variety. One can have, for example, a Pentecostal Lutheran, or even a Pentecostal Catholic![28]

This is not to suggest that Pentecostals are always more likely to solicit friendship and work cooperatively with others. They, too, covet, and are inclined to stay within their own tribes or hang closely to an identity framed by their leaders and group tradition. Their self-interest is no less evident. But the magnetism of the message that the Spirit *empowers* draws out those who might otherwise stay locked up in their religious enclave. It creates, as Robbie Goh has noted, a "spiritualization of capital" that mobilizes resources, identities, and symbols to cross cultural boundaries in remarkable ways.[29]

Essential to this synergy—indigenous witness and the Holy Spirit—is this: the Spirit takes up residence, alerts the person to their identity as being of Christ, provides a vision attached to Christ's calling, and then provides resources. That is, he gifts and enables the local person to act independently through a variety of spiritual technologies. The mainstay of Evangelical missions has been conversion. However, there is an enlightening moment when the Spirit becomes obvious. It goes further than conversion. It demonstrates the truth of the gospel in ways less apparent in traditional missionary work.

As this demonstration of the Spirit became more public through the twentieth century, it didn't seem to indigenous leaders that foreign mission personnel were quite as necessary as before. Nationals, moreover, steadily became more confident in their own ministries. This dawning of a sense of significance helped them transition from learners to teachers, from associates to leaders. At the same time, they moved from being receivers of another's wisdom to givers of what is wise, from poverty to financial well-being, from dependency to sufficiency, from waiting for health brought by a foreigner to reliance on God in the present. No longer was the gospel a foreign work, but local. It emerges within the laneways of their villages and cities, finding its voice in its own people, speaking their language, music to their ears. In rhythm, cadence, and harmony, they are caught up in faith and joy, resting on this notion that God is not external nor a foreign import. One's land and people have as much right to the storehouse of the Lord as do those of foreign lands.

China's story. Robert Morrison launched Protestant missions in China in 1807. By 1925 there were eight thousand foreign workers (including children). It had been a remarkable century in which the

British, Americans, and Scandinavians poured in people and resources to build a gospel witness, believing for conversions and assisting in medical and social needs. For all the effort, however, mainstream missions had only converted a few thousand. Hudson Taylor, pioneer of the China Inland Mission, chose a different way: he wanted missionaries who wouldn't be seen as foreigners. They lived as closely as they could to the people, using Chinese dress, wearing pigtails. Taylor warned that the identity of the missionary "was not cultural but theological: human beings were first and last subjects of God's redemptive work in Christ, and their cultural state carried no prior moral entitlement or disqualification. The superiority of Western culture was not Christianity's remedy for the inferiority of non-Western cultures."[30] Missions here as elsewhere had founded their work on their home of experience. Though Taylor pressed his people to live as did the Chinese, most agencies were foreign plants.

By the early 1950s, all missionaries had to leave. The communist revolution was on the move. Would the seedlings of missions see the light of day? Transition came suddenly, prompted by the Marxist revolution, with three factors at work: a shift in leadership from foreign missionaries to local pastors and leaders; the power of the biblical Word in the vernacular giving people direct access to the Bible; and ethical implications interpreted through and rising from biblical stories that wove themselves into issues of daily life.

Indigenous pastors could read Bible texts filtered through their cultural impressions. That combination of local leadership with the Bible in their own language or dialect has a stunning effect on the rise and growth of the church. Imagine: what might the influence of Chinese Christians be, as China becomes the country hosting the largest Christian population in the world? Their business and cultural influence is already fanning out worldwide, spreading their influence globally. Even when the Chinese churches abroad were largely populated by exiles and diasporic Chinese, the influence of indigenous Chinese movements (through the thoughts of people such as Watchman Nee) was profound. How they read and interpret the gospel *now*, as their country reaches worldwide superpower status, will further spread that influence as they travel and apply the gospel around the world.

Thailand: A cautionary tale. Thailand presents an opposing case to China. When I met with Thai pastors, educators, and mission leaders, I was asked why, after all the people, money, and years invested, the Christian mission in Thailand was relatively small. After almost two hundred years of missionary work, investments of thousands of lives and millions on millions of dollars, out of a total population of 65 million there are only some 370,000 Evangelical Christians: one half of one percent.

Thailand is one of the South East Asian "Tiger" economies.[31] While looking somewhat like Malaysia and Myanmar (Burma), it is as different from these countries as Canada is from the United States or Sweden is from Germany. Never colonized, in the nineteenth century—unlike Vietnam, Laos, Myanmar, and Cambodia—it negotiated land for freedom to keep itself out of the clutches of France and Great Britain. Today its national tendency is (apart from some sharp border conflicts during the Indochina conflict and occasionally with Burma) to avoid conflict.

Dr. Wiracha Kowae,[32] founder of the Assemblies of God in Thailand, noted that in the past, traditional foreign-dominated mission boards tended to view Thais as unequal to the task of leadership. Missionaries continued to pastor, teach, and lead denominations and missions. When they left or retired, the "preparedness clock" started again with their replacements: those from the sending country would once again have to start with learning the language and customs. It took years for missions to realize that unless they handed it over to indigenous leadership, the church in Thailand would be orphaned, without its own brand or leadership. The foreigners never really made the critical transition in a society that had managed—by avoiding entanglements in regional conflicts—to maintain a very coherent and continuous sense of itself over a long period of time. Contrasting with the Karen people across the border, who live in a sort of transnational, humanitarian space between Thailand and Myanmar, Buddhism remains the dominant cultural and religio-political force in Thailand.

Kowae also points out that Thais came to think that the gospel was "free." "Missionaries assumed we had little so we weren't challenged to give." "We knew the gospel was free, but that obscured the material cost of missions as most of the finances came from offshore." As a result, the spirit and patterns of generosity and self-propagation were not cultivated. Western leaders had resources coming from elsewhere. Without having to make a personal investment, the sense of being a part of the work was diminished among Thai leaders. "By example we learned not to be givers," Kowae reflected.

That is no longer the case, he made clear. "The Thai church is now led by our own people" and has even generated a number of indigenous church movements that have spread elsewhere (e.g., the Hope of Bangkok movement). Resources come from the people and their vision to take hold of their spiritual future, a future rooted firmly in their world, he assured me.

Argentina. The 1980s were a particularly troubling time for the country. Its economy was in a mess, and the Falkland War made it worse. In April 1982 the government invaded the Malvinas Islands, which had been occupied by the United Kingdom since 1841. England retaliated, and seventy-four days later the Argentinean military scrambled for home.

The humiliation was huge. People were stricken not only by economic depression, but now their national dignity had taken a hit. Professor of history Pablo Deiros noted that within that moment there came a wave of Spirit presence from a most unlikely source, altering the trajectory of church life across the land.

A businessman running a nuts-and-bolts factory near Buenos Aires, Carlos Annacondia, began to preach public campaigns in 1982, at the age of thirty-seven. His meetings soon attracted large crowds. His approach was outside of general mainstream Evangelical public decorum: early in each service he would combat evil spirits. This public affront, especially in a large stadium, was seen as odd and extraordinary.

Resulting conversions launched a wave of church planting that might be unique in the history of the global church. The number of new churches was not verified, but reliable leaders speak of thousands in a few years. There in the 1980s, in the valley of public humiliation, the pride of the people—for surely a characteristic of Argentineans is that they are a people of dignity—became a public emotion in which the Spirit caught their attention, and life for them was never the same.

This was taking place in the context of rocky politics, a disreputable government at times complicit with military oppression. Tens of thousands went missing between 1976 and 1983. The "Mothers of the Plaza de Mayo" became a public voice, insistently calling the leaders to account. Into that social and spiritual void, an unsuspecting local believer became the voice and heart for a fresh outpouring of faith and an amazing flourishing of church plants. The gospel, not guns, became the mechanism of Argentinean internationalism.

Migration. Some years ago I hosted a lunch for a pastor from Ghana who had built a church in Toronto and from that had expanded to others. He brought with him four of his associate pastors. I was surprised to see that one was from India, pastoring a church made up mostly of immigrants from his home country. I wondered why an African church was evangelizing those from Asia. It wasn't extraordinary for the Ghanaian pastor; in fact, it was *because* he was from West Africa that he also had a heart for those from India. He had seen need. He knew people from another part of the world were also hungry for spiritual life. That he lived in Toronto really made no difference except insofar as Canadian pluralism provided new opportunities.

Here in microcosm was an example of how growth occurs. Rooted in Ghana, Ghanaians stand in their "Jerusalem," be that Accra or Toronto, and look out to their "Judeas" and "Samarias," then to the uttermost parts of the world. In this case, an African pastor friend had migrated to Canada. Where he *was* mattered little. That he was in his new homeland simply meant his "Jerusalem" had changed its geographical center.

Migration redefines the world. As people move, so moves their message. In going and arriving, many are shocked by what they find in so-called Christian countries and cultures. Instead, they find the gospel in the West stymied by secular attitudes, made gaudy and fractious by a hedonistic tilt, and communities quite ambivalent (if not actively discourteous) to the Christian presence and its values. Once the recipients of the gospel from the West, they are now called to go. The Western decline is thus being answered by new centers of global mission.

◀────▶

I boarded a Canadian-made train in Colombo, Sri Lanka. It pulled slowly away from the crowded train platform, beginning its laborious trip up the mountains to Kandy, site of the annual Youth for Christ staff conference.

It was early in my expanding experience of the world, and a critical encounter with the global expanse of the Christian faith—from the relative abundance of my Canadian homeland to the real poverty of the country of calling of one of my colleagues.

Sitting next to me was Father Arnold, rector of the Catholic Seminary in Kandy. Our conversation gave rise to a newfound friendship, with an offer for me to speak to his seminarians and for him to later visit Canada. However, it was the cementing of friendship with Ajith Fernando that highlighted this visit. Young and energetic in our work among youth, we together set off on a journey, following the Spirit, each in our respective callings.

Thoughtful, passionate, and humble, Ajith's deep spiritual piety inspired me in service. It was obvious to me, back in our early years, that he had uncommon gifts: teaching, writing, leading. He had many invitations to lead internationally, each of which he quietly but firmly refused. His world was to be in his homeland. Through wars and economic upheavals he stayed, even though he frequently "farewelled" many of his countrymen who sailed for places of greater promise. In a society where Christians were a bare minority, paying the price of a formidable anti-Christian persecution, he told me that if he couldn't raise a witness among the youth of his people, what could he say to those of other lands?

Today, the impact of his careful biblical ministry has been the means of transformation for many. I have seen the cost he and his wife Nelun have paid, an eternal witness to the timely application of faith and its collateral benefits of wisdom, a hunger to study, and a risk-taking spirit. They now run a large staff, and ministry programs reaching young people, healing drug addiction, and building interracial bonds of friendship give evidence to a hostile government that the witness of Jesus makes good citizens.

Decades later, I stood with his staff—on the south coast beach just weeks before the Asian tsunami washed ashore—and looked into their faces. They came from both sides of their racial divide: Singhalese and Tamil. They crossed the gender divides. Exuberant evangelists. Studious theologians. Creative missionaries. Caring social workers. Gentle pastors. And how had such an array of gifts been assembled? The Spirit had chosen a young leader. To that invitation, while still young, Ajith resolved to carefully build a biblically informed ministry framed so its ministry would embrace the broken and needy, fueled by a vision that a Christ-centered gospel engaged all of society. His message, shaped by Wesley, was unrelenting in its call for personal holiness, public witness, and service.

He has written many books and ministered at many conferences, yet he stayed in the land of his calling. And that has made all the difference. Christians here are still a minority. Persecution continues to leave its scars. Spiritual darkness intimidates and exacts its price. The gospel, however, is resilient in the lives of succeeding generations, leaving a legacy in his determination to see the witness of Christ carefully and with diligence planted, nurtured, harvested, and "tasted" in Sri Lanka.

FIVE

RE-ENGAGING THE PUBLIC SQUARE

EVANGELICALS HAVE A VARIEGATED HISTORY with public engagement. William Wilberforce, the English Member of Parliament in the late 1700s, fought a long and ultimately successful campaign to abolish the British Empire Commonwealth's involvement in the slave trade. His concern for the well-being of British public life was intermeshed with his Evangelical theology and fervor.[1] He represents, for many reasons, the Evangelical call to public engagement. The actions of the army of lesser-known Evangelicals that he mobilized as an active minority in voluntary societies and pressure groups were central in bringing about laws promoting human health and dignity that, today, we take for granted.[2]

Such personal and corporate conversions of mindset had global impacts. Through the late eighteenth and early nineteenth centuries, the major impulse of the Protestant missionary movement came in large part from England and North America. Their view of how much one should give with regard to Caesar became "gospel" to those they converted. In brief, one can identify in their message a normative understanding of the relationship of Christians to the public square.

Before about 1870, Protestant churches in the West were for the most part unified by an Evangelical theology and easily mixed their witness with public action. The divisions over theological modernism were, however, already apparent, and a reaction set in.[3] The conservative take on the accuracy and unity of the Bible divided Protestants, the more liberal staying in mainline churches and Evangelicals increasingly moving out into new churches, denominations, and ministries. As Markku Ruotsila points out, modernist church leaders tended to ascribe a kind of sacredness to organizations such as universities and the League of Nations, as if they were present evidence of the emerging kingdom of God.[4]

To conservative Christians this was a form of idolatry, resulting in their withdrawing from what they saw as apostate organizations. By so doing they lost much of the social and political traction they had previously enjoyed through their establishment connections.

But along with this schism there came an even more deeply dividing factor. The Evangelical (or "Fundamentalist") emphasis on holy living and separation from the world (with its focus on personal spirituality) set its adherents even more to the margins. This focus on personal salvation separated Evangelicals from "worldly" activities as a primary concern, and instead turned their eyes to preparation for eternity. In effect this kept them away from involvement in public-sector interests.

This ideological tension held sway for much of the first half of the twentieth century. Mainline Protestants and Roman Catholics continued to "manage" society, but they had an unwritten understanding—a kind of social contract—with Evangelicals that Western societies would continue to operate on a generally biblical understanding of values and public ethics. Evangelicals were content with this social contract.[5] It was as if they said, "You run society with this common understanding, and we will do God's work." By the 1960s, however—as the secular increasingly co-opted the public square, and as social and policy trends departed from biblical ideals and classic Christian precedents to serve an increased pluralism—it became obvious that the old arrangement no longer held. Evangelical expectations of their counterparts—that they would manage society based on biblical ideals—eroded. Evangelicals finally woke up to see that absence from the public square effectively cut them off from influence in ways that directly affected their communities, leading to rising taxes, public debt, secularized social services, and a changing moral order. Not being around the table of public opinion meant their views simply were not heard. With this realization, Evangelicals began to embrace a more open biblical vision—that "all of life is the Lord's." The old line of separation was increasingly seen as counterproductive. Dividing Sunday from Monday—that is, dividing church vocation from public vocation, or Christian service from public service—effectively split God's creation in two. This bifurcated cosmology was not only counter to historic Protestant theology but also rendered Christians ineffective in serving as salt and light in societies that increasingly seemed in need of preservation and illumination.

As Western Christians re-engaged with the public sphere, Western missionaries generally continued to teach a bifurcated worldview: the secular versus the sacred. They emphasized that the gospel's concern was primarily to do with personal and inner salvation, "spiritual hygienics" and preparation for eternity. This did not keep them from building schools, creating medical facilities, and helping develop agricultural skills, but their message was nevertheless limited: Christ came to save us from our sins and for eternity. Even if the missionaries didn't say, "Don't get involved in politics," their focus on building churches, evangelizing, and creating a community of Christ followers made their intentions obvious. What needs restating is this: that as problematic as this division of the sacred and secular was, their ministry had a powerful effect, creating communities of faith that would later exert influence on emerging nations.

WHAT WE MEAN BY THE PUBLIC SQUARE

The term *public square* is, like *Main Street* in the language of modern journalists and pollsters, a metaphor that represents public social institutions that, directly or indirectly, shape our lives and influence those sectors out of which public policy, governance, debate, and action flow.

Many towns in Midwest Canada in the 1950s had a literal public square. Around it gathered the town hall, a hospital, a public school, a general store, and often a church. It was where people met, performed their civic duties, swore an oath to the flag, and assembled for public gatherings, often covered by the local newspaper. Each institution on the square served the public, with some of them occupied by publicly elected leaders. Of course, my hometown was typically North American—the churches were off the public square, on a side street.[6] If I had been born in a town of equivalent size in, say, Italy, the church (often a grand cathedral that overshadowed all the other buildings) would also have been on that square (or *piazza*). The questions this arrangement poses, then, are these: In which institutions is the church to have presence and influence? How much of "Caesar" are followers of Jesus to worry about? The responses to these questions are critical, as they help us understand what and where our presence should be in the world of public policy, leadership, and public service. As we are learning, the answer to that depends on time, location, and the issue under debate. For Evangelicals as a whole, there has been no one right answer.

During much of the past century, Evangelicals were minority players in issues of public concern. Many, of course, continued to stand at the forefront of issues of justice, but in the West there was a general withdrawal from political discussions. In places where they were outliers or marginalized by more powerful sociopolitical forces, Evangelicals developed a kind of spirituality that justified being on the margins.[7] Churches such as the Christian Congregation, a large Pentecostal Holiness church in Brazil, still ban their members from taking part in any kind of public political activity.[8]

This was a separation that grew harder to sustain as Evangelicals, Pentecostals, and Charismatics grew in numbers. Their leaders would inevitably get involved in public-policy debates and leadership selection. When power becomes an option, even the most fervent and pious of Christians find it difficult to resist opportunities to fulfill the desire underlying Proverbs 14:34: "Righteousness exalts a nation, but sin condemns any people."

But does this not come with potential danger? Assuredly yes. Mainline Protestantism can teach us what can happen when an emphasis of Christ's call for personal transformation shifts primarily to social categories.[9] While the Evangelical/Pentecostal/Charismatic communities grew in the Global South, at the same time there was both a decline of mainstream[10] churches and a loss of traditional moral consensus in the West. During the twentieth century this was a battleground in many churches, often resulting in divisions over the gospel's relevance as against personal faithfulness. As the twenty-first century progresses, global Evangelicalism is attempting to regather itself and to build consensus on sustainable, effective positions.

As the circles of influence of Evangelicals/Pentecostals/Charismatic movements expand, churches feel they need to say something more about their world. This leads to a wider range and greater depth of social relationships as they explore how they can shape policy, effect changes in the law, and redraw moral patterns. Their sheer numbers in some countries mean they can now "make enough noise" that decision makers can no longer ignore them.

Stories from the Global South show how complex and messy this turn toward the public square can be. Engaging in public issues is freighted with all sorts of legacy issues and unintended outcomes and consequences. Terence Ranger points out that, in Africa, churches are suspicious of getting involved. They remember the failure of mainline churches: as they got caught up in social matters, they seemed to lose interest in the "interior" or existential issues of salvation.[11] As pure and idealistic as their political vision might be, along the way well-intentioned leaders bump into challenges and run up against complex circumstances—from interlocking political constructs to ethics that rule the public forums—that can work to their undoing. As worthy as is the need to challenge corruption, it can lead to the challenger being corrupted.

Nevertheless, the Evangelical movement is increasingly influential in the public square. We are still unsure of the consequences of this major shift in Christian public life. Evangelicals who have long engaged on the welfare and educational fronts are now putting these skills to use in new ways. By so doing, the church will be influenced and altered—and, we must hope, in places and times of engagement their presence will bring health, healing and moral, ethical, and social uplift to people and their societies. The outward expansion from personal spiritual well-being to societal change is, in short, the grand experiment of our times.

HOW WE GOT HERE

Over the centuries the church felt pushed and pulled by the tension in Jesus' statement about what we should "give back to Caesar" (Mt 22:21). What is the extent of our engagement in a public square in which we understand that God establishes authorities (Rom 13:1), in contrast to his call that we not render to Caesar what belongs to God? The Bible doesn't provide a model to emulate or point to a road to follow. Does Jesus tell us how to draft a constitution or write a bill? Even more basically, how are we to regard the public sector, and if we conclude that that this is a place for witness, what is the means by which we translate conviction into action?

Three major ideas have shaped Evangelical interpretations of the Christian call to be citizens in this world. First, "Christendom" is a form in which the church is intertwined with government. Its response to the question, "What do we owe to Caesar, when Caesar is God's vice-regent on earth?" is "Everything."[12] Second, John Calvin and his Reformed community saw that everything in life was to be a concern to God, including public life. When asked the question, "What do we owe to God?," they responded, "Everything!" Third, the Wesleyan Holiness movement kept its focus on salvation and sanctification. When asked that same question, Wesleyans might say, "The two have little in common." These major Protestant movements were, of course, not exclusive. One didn't preclude what the others had to say. Instead, they formed a sort of continuum along which churches and individuals have found a place that suits their history, view of life, emotional range, and doctrines.

Today in the post-Christian West, the Christendom model is not just out of fashion—it is dead. Richard John Neuhaus, writing in 1984, feared that the death of Christendom would result in a "naked public square," a "hard secularist" public space "unclothed" by the language and practice of religion and religious ethics.[13] Neuhaus, however, came from a magisterial (top-down) tradition (first Lutheran, then Catholic) and underestimated the response of conservative Christians, who believed it right and timely to engage in the public sector. Many Christians now sense the Spirit calling them to be present in public forums. That is happening in real time, in the halls of power, in venues of social caring, on stairways of human toil, and among the landscapes of economic ventures.

Over our two-thousand-year history, the church and our gospel witness have experimented with various models in the erratic relationship between Christians and the world. In earlier centuries, the apostles moved about as wide-open travelers of faith. They journeyed through city and country, and from region to region. Wherever they went, by the power of the Word, in preaching and the demonstration of the Spirit's healing and demon-cleansing presence, churches were established. Occasionally public officials (or, as Paul says, "those who belong to Caesar's household," Phil 4:22) were converted, but in these early centuries the church was largely detached from governments and state leaders. This "primitive" church, small and cut off from seeking to influence the public sector, would remain a powerful model for Christian reformers through the centuries.

The Roman Emperor Constantine was the first to legalize the Christian presence in the empire and then to progressively provide it with a formal role in society. Converted to Christian faith, his ideal was of the unity of church and state—the base model for Christendom—in which the church receives official blessing as the state's official religion and it in turn legitimizes (even divinizes) the state. Constantine's raising of the church to official state status led to unexpected consequences: Christendom became an entrenched political and religious ideal, mostly within countries in Europe, Western Asia, and North Africa where Orthodox and Roman Catholics were the majority. At the same time, there were reactions against Christians among those powers (particularly Persia—today Iran) who began to identify Christianity with their enemies. Centuries later, the Holy Roman Empire asserted the reestablishment of this union of church and state, while the

Reformation in Germany, Switzerland, Britain, and other places resulted in a shift more of its focus than its intent. Protestant and Catholic states after the Thirty Years' War remained largely singular religious states that sporadically persecuted religious minorities.

The leaders of the Reformation, however, were divided over whether Christians were to be involved in civic rule in the public square. Martin Luther's "two kingdoms" view differed from that of John Calvin, Reformed theologian and pastor. Luther's notion of the two kingdoms living side by side became the framework for Germany and other European countries (Sweden, for example) where the Lutheran Church was dominant. Calvin removed the dividing line, seeing the entire world as under Christ's kingdom. The neo-Calvinist prime minister of the Netherlands Abraham Kuyper would famously note that "there is not a square inch in the whole domain of our human existence over which Christ, who is Sovereign over all, does not cry: 'Mine!'"[14]

Anabaptists (or Mennonites) crafted an alternate view. Seeing the degrading influence of power and the deteriorating drag of worldly influence, Menno Simons called for Christians to form an alternative community in which they would live out their faith without being subject to the wiles and attractions of power.[15] While this movement was relegated to small groups scattered about Europe and in the Americas, his message resonated with many in creating resistance against participation in war. His message would be rediscovered by the Christian communities that emerged in the 1960s.

The Evangelical revival (in the 1700s) was associated with spiritual renewal movements. John Wesley's core message to his Methodists was about conversion and the sanctifying work of the Holy Spirit. The subsequent Holiness movement shaped large parts of the Protestant world in North America, where the establishment of the republic had drawn an explicit line between religion and state. That division of Christian faith and political rule is today still being debated, especially in the United States.

The collapse of Christendom—the interlocking of church and state—in the face of modernity, and the subsequent collapse of mainline Protestant churches who naively absorbed various forms of modernism, presented the emergent Evangelical and Pentecostal movements in the West with a conundrum. Their most natural inclination was to remain centered on personal salvation. Many early Pentecostals (Holiness people in the United States; Methodists in Queensland, Australia; Salvation Army people in England) left churches where, during the twentieth century, the social gospel overtook a high view of biblical authority and where social science and social action eclipsed the notion of personal transformation.[16] Which would they choose? Or did they have to? In time, what model of political engagement would fit their biblical sense or match their national issues and concerns? It would indeed take time, but new models emerged that emphasized both personal experience and making life better on all levels. Inevitably, the conflict between the policies and public agendas of the day and what Evangelicals and Pentecostals assumed would be their national spiritual heritage so pressed in on their congregations that it was just a matter of time before they entered the political arena.

FROM EXCLUSION TO ENGAGEMENT

Today's global shift is expanding the view of Christians, as they encounter God's concerns not only as eternal realities but also as matters of daily and civic concerns. This reversal from separation to engagement in public dynamics of faith is a key marker in today's Global South.[17] Christians are now running for public office, taking on increased roles in education, serving in critical social and economic public sectors—all out of a growing awareness that the gospel is not a "shaker" in which the potency of salt and its savor is to be contained, or a bushel basket under which light is to be hidden from a darkened world.

For the past few decades, the road on which Christians have traveled in engaging with the public square has been bumpy. This in part is due to a lack of learned political skills, as well as to a natural theology that is at times faulty, or to a misreading of the forces arrayed against them. Even so, Christians are resolute that not to engage is to be unfaithful to the call to kingdom life and fails to offer gospel values to both civil society and civic life. For Christians, God is not simply the God of those who believe in him. He is God of all creation.

Engaging the public square requires Christians to navigate a path strewn with hidden traps. It is also a vocation pocked with vulnerabilities, unintended consequences, inflated egos, graft, corruption, ideological self-righteousness, and the lure of power. Sociologist Stephen Offutt refers, memorably, to one pastor turned politician, so corrupt that he is popularly known in his country as "Pastor Bribe."[18] The church still needs to deal with Efraín Ríos Montt's *junta* in Guatemala, one of the most shameful events to stain the early forays of Pentecostals into the public sphere.[19] Even with such failings, however, this is still God's world. These examples of naiveté and self-interest make even clearer the wisdom of Jesus' warning to be a wise as serpents and harmless as doves (Mt 10:16) and the counsel of Paul that some would "preach Christ out of envy and rivalry" (Phil 1:15).

As Evangelicals enter the jungle of politics, we might ask—given the dangers—why it is inevitable that we engage. Four reasons come to mind: the sheer numbers of Evangelicals, the growing size of our churches, the power of voters' influence in areas of concern, and, oddly, self-interest. When hundreds of thousands take to the streets to celebrate faith, we can be sure that political experts and "players" aren't oblivious to the potential power of such votes.

Young Evangelicals today are better educated, trained, and equipped to live in this world. They refuse to be shut off from sectors of public influence and presence, to allow class, social status, or ethnicity to impose borders on the borderless world that they inhabit. Allow me to illustrate with stories of three women (real people, though the names have been changed).

Eleanor is the third generation of a large Malay-Chinese extended family that has concentrated its business and investment wealth in a significant family trust. A Methodist attending a large Charismatic church, Eleanor went to university and graduated in law. She earned her stripes in private practice, working for multinational corporations, and then came back into the family trust in management. Her values—family, mission, professional, global—drive her success as an investor and advisor both in personal and in family projects. Eleanor is one of those global Charismatic citizens who have made the Chinese diaspora one of the great powers in the world economy and in the story of the extension of the gospel.[20] It is hard to remember that only a couple of generations ago, her people were marginalized players in the emerging racial hegemony of Malaysia.

Linda was born in Australia, the daughter of first-in-family Pentecostals who had come out of the Anglican Church and worked hard to become professionals. Linda grew up in one of the country's fastest-growing churches, became a prominent worship leader and songwriter, and then moved to the United States to complete her doctorate. She spends her days now teaching in a Pentecostal Bible college and promoting the rights of Australian indigenous peoples as an extension of her Pentecostal belief in social justice and kingdom values. She has a growing reputation not just in theological circles but also in the secular media of her country.

Finally, there is Maria, the daughter of Italian migrants, who went to university, trained in industrial relations, and found a job with a national trades union. Working hard, her transparent honesty, intelligence, and passion made a way for her as an advocate and an organizer. As I write, she has been appointed the head of her union, advises at the top national level of industrial relations, and is seen as an increasingly significant figure in her industry sector. Each of these women has risen into positions of influence not *despite* her spirituality, but *because* of it. Each comes, in a sense, from a marginal position, but has, through education, value-driven discipline, and hard work, arrived at the apex of her pursuits. In previous generations, they might have drifted out of Evangelicalism in pursuit of a more "respectable" faith or in reaction to the dominance of men in their denominations. Instead, they represent the new generation of significant leaders.[21]

This shift has entailed a radical change in the range of the worldviews of Evangelicals/Pentecostals/Charismatics. While, in past years, public service was considered important, it was secondary to what we saw as our principal calling; to do anything else but introduce people to Jesus was insignificant. Younger Evangelicals/Pentecostals bridge the divide between Pentecostals and Reformed Evangelicals, a separation that grows out of divergent views of the nature of God's mission held by classic Methodist "salvationism" and Calvinist "reformationism." This emergence of global partnerships over common issues—for instance, with GAFCON[22] in the Anglican Communion, or E21[23] between the significant Pentecostal churches—might be a game changer. There have been some false starts—for example, with the stir of Christian Reconstructionism through the 1970s and 1980s[24]—but, overall, the quality of thought emerging from Evangelical scholars regarding the nature and ethics of social action has markedly improved.

This has been a time for redrafting our worldview. We've gradually erased the dividing line between God's world and "the world," between the church and the workplace, between Christian music and jazz, between calling and vocation, between pastor and congregation. As young people see their worlds without borders, we realize the church is without borders. It is not *axis mundi*—where there is a holy place or location of spiritual ritual such as Mecca or the Ganges River. Instead, the "holy of holies" is wherever the people of God are. The Spirit indwelling means that any place we go, the Spirit goes. And where he is, God is. Not partially, not parenthetically, nor in disguise, but God himself, in his people in the places they are.

But beware. We traverse this landscape enlightened by two thousand years of well-intentioned connections between faith and politics that too frequently have been overturned on the slippery roads of the world, fraught with missed turns or uneven and treacherous trails.

A GLOBAL TOUR

In order to grasp the range of Evangelical/Pentecostal presence in the public square, it is helpful to take into account their expanding presence around the world. To show the change of attitude and actions among Evangelicals we will sample stories from Africa (Kenya and Zambia), the Americas (Brazil), and Asia (South Korea and the Philippines).

Kenya. In Kenya, Evangelicals were present in post-British national politics from the very start of self-government. One Evangelical sat in the cabinet of their first president and another, in turn, became its second president.

Under colonial rule, the Church of England constituted an official Christian presence in Kenya. Evangelicals arrived in the mid-1800s, and the Pentecostal wave washed ashore in the early twentieth century. In time, the ability of Evangelical/Pentecostal churches to grow community organizations made them an appreciable factor in public and faith issues. Churches were built.

Training schools spread across the land. Mission agencies and denominations, especially after the Mau Mau uprisings during the 1950s, shifted their leadership from foreign to local leadership. Conversionist movements, such as the East Africa Revival, continued to have significant political impacts. In a nation where 86 percent of the population claims Christian faith, it isn't a surprise that Christians would be at the center. What *is* surprising is that in its early years as a nation it was an *Evangelical* who served as president for twenty years.

Daniel arap Moi, Kenya's second president, was in office from 1982 to 2002. He was raised in an African Inland Church, a conservative Evangelical community founded by a Western mission agency. Its heartland was evangelism; the idea that an Evangelical would take on the mantle of politics was foreign to its leaders and to the founding North American churches. They saw the notion, at best, as "worldly." At its worst, Evangelical thinkers at the time were still referring to national states as "Moloch" and "Babylon."

Moi, in his *Kenyan African Nationalism* (1986), provided a blueprint of his views on leadership (popularly called *Nyay*). Centering on themes of peace, love, and unity, he concludes, "From my African origins, through my Christian conversion and then during my political profession, all three have recurred—peace, love and unity. . . . I know no other trio: from them stems all else, justice, equity, comradeship, parity of treatment, etc."[25] Criticized both during his presidency and afterward, Moi was viewed by many as an autocrat, perfecting "the art of control over the lives of [Kenya's] citizens."[26] Ironically, he opposed religious groups entering politics, arguing that politics "is an arena exclusively for politicians."[27] As Riedl notes, this was an attempt not to undermine any particular faith, be it Christian or Islamic, but rather to keep religious leaders out of political life altogether and so secure political control. Such approaches were evidence of the embryonic nature of Evangelical engagements with democratic rule. Moi's views were rooted in the social and political structure of an Africa dominated by tribal identities, expectations, and traditional tensions. For Moi, balancing power between the dominant (mostly Christian) Luo and Kikuyu tribes on the one hand and the (mostly Muslim) Digo and Swahili tribes on the other required skill and a fine sense for self-preservation.[28]

Moi followed Kenya's founding warrior president, Jomo Kenyatta, who had pressed Great Britain to leave, had consolidated a new nation under his charismatic influence, and handed off a new, complicated, and confusing tribalized state to the control of an immature and quite unprepared political class. For good or for ill, the Evangelical community was engaged with civil authority, no longer able to stand aside and simply point a finger at others. How to address the challenges of this public sphere divided the Christian community, and Evangelicals in particular. For pastors and church leaders, to grow too close to a ruling president or party meant surrendering their prophetic voice. Yet if they decided to be on the outside looking in, they might be reduced to a whimpering opposition. The Evangelical community in Kenya was a petri dish in the grand experiment of public square engagement.

Zambia. South of Kenya is Zambia (known as Northern Rhodesia during the colonial period). Public engagement there has been even more dramatic than in Kenya. When its second president, Frederick Chiluba, a self-identified Evangelical, gained power in 1991, he proclaimed his country a "Christian country" within a broader framework of religious freedom, creating "a particularly interesting case of state involvement in religion, which has spurred unintended political mobilization and regime consequences."[29] Zambia, like Kenya, is 85 percent Christian. Building grassroots support was essential—as it was in Kenya—for Chiluba to gain and maintain power. Aligning himself with the Christian media, Chiluba drew together support from the Evangelical

Fellowship of Zambia (a member of the World Evangelical Alliance), the Zambia Episcopal Conference (now the Zambia Conference of Catholic Bishops), and the Christian Council of Zambia (affiliated with the World Council of Churches). In his declaratory speech, he offered repentance on behalf of his people

> of our wicked ways of idolatry, witchcraft, the occult, immorality, injustice and corruption. . . . I submit the Government and the entire nation of Zambia to the Lordship of Jesus Christ. I further declare that Zambia is a Christian nation that will seek to be governed by the righteousness principles of the word of God. Righteousness and justice must prevail in all levels of authority, and then we shall see the righteousness of God exalting Zambia.[30]

It was a declaration that did not go down well among some Christians, who accused the president of proceeding without their knowledge or support. It did in time lead to multiparty elections and was a catalyst in forming the Christian Churches Monitoring Group, "which was significant in increasing transparency and conducted elections that were largely free and fair."[31]

Did the audacious move by this president benefit the nation by instilling Christian values? Opinion is divided. Observable benefits may have been twofold. It created debate within the country about this political issue, bringing into the debate those on the margins. In addition, by putting forward a moral vision for Zambia, it raised expectations as to what good government might look like. It gave people markers against which this and other governments would later be evaluated and judged. "In doing so, he mobilized civil society to offer a trenchant critique of his [own] rule in later years."[32]

So, was Chiluba a good president? Was Evangelical engagement good for the gospel and good for the nation? These are important questions we might ask of any country. I visit countries where Evangelicals take on public issues either because they see it as a biblical mandate or out of necessity born from persecution, marginalization, or the disabling problem of not being allowed to register. Those I meet moving into public affairs believe they are called by the Spirit and, further, out of a sense of personal responsibility.

Regardless of the country or person, we are reminded that those entering civil forums are human: both wise and foolish, creative and ill-advised, manifestly spiritually active and humanly corrupt. They are susceptible to personal and corporate sins regardless of their faith, while that faith itself is shaped by the political and social matrices from which they emerge.

Brazil. In Latin America one sees how Evangelical engagement became a catalytic alternative, conditioning the earlier Roman Catholic juggernaut into a more open and flexible Christian pluralism. Newly emerging groups in the mid-to-latter twentieth century demanded and obtained both space and respect for evangelism and public engagement.

Political scientist Paul Freston views Brazil "as a possible trendsetter, a test case where phenomena peculiar to the new mass Protestantism of the 'South' of the globe may first appear."[33] Brazil has 50 million Evangelicals—some 25 percent of the population—making it (along with China) one of the largest Evangelical communities in the Global South. Their expansion has taken place within a country suffering huge political and economic variations in its race for development. Shifting religious demographics create new patterns of voters with changing interests, particularly in the vacuum left by divisions within the old Catholic/elite regime. As the Catholic imperial order lost its political hold in the face of increasing minority distrust, and the more radical Catholic social "option for the poor" lost its hold on the elites, Evangelical churches surged into the gap. That gap, however, was intrinsically political—even if it meant spiritualizing politics, these new churches would need to have an attitude toward the public square. While this Christian community remains a minority, its rapid growth and media influence have made it a constituency that no one in Brazilian public life can avoid or ignore. Further, Evangelicals are particularly active in rural areas and among the *favelas*—areas marked by a high population of the poor, often lacking services such as power and sewerage, and frequently controlled by gangs. It's here that churches have sprung up in great numbers. As Phillips notes, "Many Evangelical pastors work in remote rural areas and in Brazil's violent slums, where the government is often absent. That gives pastors an unrivaled ability to mobilize voters at election time."[34]

Brazil is a helpful country for Evangelicals to study for two reasons. First, there is a continuing disunity between Roman Catholics and Protestants (Evangelicals/Pentecostals), which provides an impetus for Evangelicals to engage politically. Second, a significant indigenous public presence is the Universal Church of the Kingdom of God (UCKG).[35] While the UCKG makes claims to be within the Evangelical tent (partially because all Protestant traditions in Spanish-speaking Latin America are compressed into the term *evengélicos*), many Evangelicals consider prosperity-driven theology heretical. Converted under the ministry of Canadian Pentecostal preacher Robert McAlister, Bishop Edir Macedo leads a church that has grown rapidly since its founding in 1977. Building massive churches in São Paulo (including the famous replica of the temple of Solomon, exactly four times its size) and throughout the land, it exerts (for a non-Catholic church) unparalleled political influence.

The driving force behind that influence is the UCKG's sheer size and the careful positioning of its representatives. The then president of Brazil, former Marxist guerilla Dilma Rousseff, took part in the dedication of the temple of Solomon and (though a dedicated Marxist) quoted from the Psalms, "Happy is the nation whose God is the Lord."

Brazilian Evangelicals, unlike their counterparts in the United States, are not clustered on the conservative edge of the political continuum. In 2014 Marina Silva, an Evangelical and a member of the Brazilian Socialist Party (PSB), came close to winning the presidency. Party lines became a battleground as political debate over issues—from gay rights to abortion—led up to the elections. Pastor Silas Malafaia warned Silva not to vote for same-sex marriage and so, contrary to her own public position, she changed her mind on the matter.[36]

Of 513 seats in the Chamber of Deputies—the lower house of the Brazilian Congress—Evangelicals currently hold eighty-seven, as well as three in the Senate.[37] The Evangelical Parliamentary Front (FPE), a group bringing together Evangelicals, meets regularly, building connections and support. In a recent election, some 270 Evangelical ministers—many made popular by way of the omnipresent Evangelical television programs that operate in the country—ran for office.

Evangelical conviction, however, is not a secure barrier against personal failing, greed, and self-interest. Corruption is almost an operating principal in failing majority states, and even in the relatively progressive Brazilian setting. During the 2016 Olympic Games in Rio de Janeiro, André Moura, a member of the Social Christian Party—an Evangelically based group—became government leader in the lower house but soon fell under suspicion for corruption. That same year, Eduardo Cunha, the Assemblies of God–based president of the lower house of Congress (himself a radio presenter, and married to a leading journalist), was removed from office because he was charged with obstructing an investigation against him for corruption.[38]

While the main reference here in Brazil is about politics, this is, of course, but a part of what it means to participate in the public square. Essential to Evangelical public influence anywhere is its access to media. Brazil is no exception. The second-largest television company in the country is Rede Record, owned by Edir Maçedo, founder and pastor of the Universal Church, who also owns two publishing houses and a free newspaper, *Folha Universal*, with a circulation of some two million. Journalists compare his influence to that of Jerry Falwell, who mobilized the "Moral Majority" during the Reagan era, pressing Evangelicals to re-engage with politics. The difference is that Brazil's Evangelicals are much more spread across the political spectrum and so haven't moved to take power. Instead they press their concerns into public debate, rewriting policies and government decisions, seeking influence on individual issues and through a variety of party groupings.[39]

As Evangelicals move with more confidence into civic service and civil society, they are finding it a complex and tough place to serve in faith. So much of partisan politics is about winning and losing that it incites desperation and exaltation. It promotes self-interest. It is ego inflating. Palms may expect to be greased (indeed, in many countries it is considered the cost of doing business)— many Evangelicals report paying a price for refusing to do so. Hyperbole becomes the norm. Power is an aphrodisiac influence, nepotism a means to rule, self-righteousness a necessary mask. In such settings, Evangelical convictions can be co-opted or turned into just one more ideology among others. Yet the public square is a vital area of God's creation—a tough place of exceeding vulnerability, but God's world nevertheless.

Negotiating with the guerillas. Another story demonstrates the extension of this in the informal sector, in this case among guerillas.

During the last half of the twentieth century, in Colombia, a country of forty-eight million, 180,000 were killed in an armed conflict called *La Violencia.* In the 1990s, mainly in the rural areas, political conflict was rife between right-wing paramilitary groups, left-wing guerillas, and government troops.

Brutalized by wars of nationhood, guerilla chaos, and land-owners' paramilitary bands, along with government armies, Colombia traveled a road of social upheaval, embroiled in struggles against brutal and controlling drug cartels. It is not a country for the faint of heart. Its inner complexities and religious unevenness are part of its fabric, and the conflict was not just because of the cartels. As in many countries with a religious majority, often the minority faces unusual and unfair practices. This was true in Colombia.

I met Pastor Hector Pardo, who had faced guerillas in his own backyard, defending those of faith. In just a few years cartel gangs killed some four hundred pastors. Working alongside the Mennonite Peace Initiative, Pastor Pardo went back into the highlands and met Salvatore Mancuso, second in command of the United Self-Defense Forces of Colombia (AUC) paramilitary group. He wasn't unfamiliar with the gangs, as his father, in the 1950s, had himself been founder of a guerilla movement. As he told me, "I was with them until the Lord rescued me."

He faced Salvatore Mancuso with the question, "Why are you killing our pastors?" "Well, you support the guerillas," was the response. "Why do you say that?" asked Pardo. "Because when they are injured or hurt or their families are in trouble, you are there to help," replied Mancuso. "Ah, now I understand. Of course. That's what Jesus calls us to do. Everyone is made in his image. He died for each of us. He taught us how to love, even our enemies," Pardo reflected.

The two men made an agreement and the pastors were no longer persecuted. But that wasn't the end for Pardo. He wanted to tell his story, so he wrote *From the Other Trenches,* an account of his life, making sure it got into the hands of FARC (the Revolutionary Armed Forces of Colombia). His argument was this: arms were not the way forward. Only Jesus could bring change and peace. The book did what he hoped it would. FARC leader Zacharias Valencia, nicknamed "the Old Man," read the book and made public a confession of faith. Late one evening representatives from FARC, M19, and a guerilla movement arrived at Hector Pardo's home. And what was their request? That Evangelicals support their causes. While they never did get a promise, before they left, Hector led them in the sinner's prayer and they walked away, each with a new Bible.

Finally, in late 2016 a peace accord was signed between FARC and the Colombian government.

South Korea. In my boyhood, South Korean children were icons of war and abandonment who appeared in the newspapers. Today, South Korea has undergone an amazing process of national development. After its liberation in 1945, the Christian community (divided between Catholics and Protestants) found ways of mutually demanding freedom as the country moved fitfully from a postwar footing to an emerging democracy. Evangelicals, fueled in particular by Pentecostal growth, could not be ignored. As in most emerging countries of the Global South, where Western missionaries had been early witnesses of the gospel, the gospel came first, while public service or civic leadership had yet to find a place in their vocabulary.

It took the 1997 national tragedy of the assassination of their president, Park Chung-hee, to shock Evangelicals into accepting responsibility for forging a national democratic voice. It must be noted that in the beginning it was liberal Protestants and Catholics who "offered a haven for the oppressed and an outspoken voice when others were silenced, keeping the democratic spirit alive. [These] Churches were cradles in which other protest movements were formed and nurtured."[40] Professor Hong notes three triggers that pressed Evangelicals to take their place among those calling for freedom.

No event in the past fifty years widened the vision of Evangelicals for civic service and civil society as did the Lausanne '74 Congress. Billy Graham gathered some 2,400 Evangelical leaders from around the world.[41] Challenged (especially by Latin American speakers) to understand the gospel call to include social well-being as part of spiritual transformation, Graham and others agreed to embed a social calling into the global Evangelical consensus.

South Korea was particularly impacted by this new gospel vision. The global reassessment of their role in sociopolitical matters impelled South Korean Evangelicals to view the civic arena as a place for witness and engagement. The spark for their entry into political action was a student protest that led to a massacre. Evangelicals were also deeply affected when President Park was assassinated, terminating his authoritarian eighteen-year rule. The army (in a coup d'état) suppressed student rebellion and in May 1980 declared martial law in the city of Kwangju, where a number were killed. As Joshua Young-gi Hong notes, "Brutal repression of the Kwangju Uprising (or Massacre) left Evangelical consciences burdened."[42]

Evangelicals realized that governments were not to be blindly trusted. Disaffected by constant infringements on sabbath observance and by the building of shrines, along with the student protest and subsequent killings, Evangelicals found that the Lausanne influence provided a theological framework for entering the fight. True to their national spirituality, their first impulse was to pray. Pastors called their people to early-morning prayer meetings. This involved drawing people into thinking and praying about public matters within the spiritual language of prayer. An Evangelical leader said, "We believe that it is wrong for the churches to become political groups which have direct involvement in politics. . . . This is not the inherent role of the church. . . . [But] we, evangelical churches, confess that we have not played a role of the salt and the light in Korean society."[43]

In order to participate in the national and public debate, in 1988 the Yoido Full Gospel Church (which then had a membership of about half a million) established a daily newspaper, the *Kookim*, providing a forum for Evangelical perspectives on public life. In 1993 South Korea elected an Evangelical, Kim Young-sam, as its seventh president. Kim was an activist pressing for democratic reforms, the first self-defined Christian (Chunghyun Presbyterian Church) and indeed the first civilian to be made president of the republic. He said in an interview,

> During the early stages of my life as a politician, many conservative Christians and pastors . . . persecuted me, saying that Christians should not participate in politics. . . . During my house arrest for nearly 3 years, I read the Bible over and over. I could not help reading the Bible. The Bible gave me power and comfort. Christian faith gave me conviction and courage there was nothing to be afraid of.[44]

His government was not without its contradictions. He restricted unions, and the number of political prisoners doubled under his regime. Even though he loudly protested corruption, Kim's tenure was viewed as a time when those in his close political circle personally benefited from their relationship to his rule.[45] On the other hand, when he stepped down, it was the first orderly civil progression of power since the war. He had presided over the most significant anticorruption campaign in the Republic's history; worked hard to eradicate the legacy of his military predecessors; and promoted Korean internationalization and development (under a policy called *Segyehwa*). On the larger scale, though

Evangelical Protestants were a minority, they "may have provided an initial basis for political society in a historically traumatized country where political society was lacking, which makes Evangelicals potentially crucial for democratic consolidation."[46] Again, well-meaning and committed Christians, working with a poorly fleshed-out vision of political and public engagement, were caught in the very self-interest of which they accused their opponents. As in other countries, their ability to keep afloat in the turbulent waters of public leadership while remaining faithful to Jesus is an ongoing journey. Managing the conflicting interests of faith and politics is a defining issue for twenty-first-century Evangelicals.

The Philippines. In struggles against military dictatorship (the Marcos regime, 1965–1986), it was largely Roman Catholics who carried on the fight for democratic rule. Archbishop Cardinal Jaime Sin called his bishops to press for the government to end martial law. At a key moment in this "yellow revolution," Cardinal Sin summoned Catholics to "surround the police and military headquarters in the nation's capital." More than one million Catholics took to the streets, "clutching Bibles and uttering prayers, in an outpouring that shielded anti-government rebels from attack."[47] Though Evangelicals were a growing minority (13 percent of the population) before the revolution that toppled Marcos, they had largely kept to their traditional activities of evangelism, teaching, social and medical work, and church planting.

In 1965 the Philippine Council of Evangelical Churches (PCEC) was formed, making an important choice from the beginning not to be "Fundamentalist-separatist"[48] but to become members of the World Evangelical Alliance. In 1992 in Manila, at the installation of Augustin (Jun) Vencer Jr. as international director, Philippine president Fidel Ramos (1992–1998) was in attendance, the only Protestant president in the country's history. This important gesture signaled to Evangelicals that the community was morphing into having a wider witness, where faith in Jesus included caring about and serving in their civic forums and civil societies.

It took, however, the People Power movements of 1986 and 1999 to bring Evangelicals into play, first in holding prayer rallies and then taking part in public protests.[49] In the public outcry against Marcos and subsequent presidents, however, David Lim sees three primary waves as influencing the Evangelical decision to move toward public engagement.

In the first wave, as missions continued evangelizing Filipinos, interest in scholarship and training grew, especially among those attached to the InterVarsity movement (part of IFES—the International Fellowship of Evangelical Students). From this movement came the Institute for Studies in Asian Church and Culture (ISACC), established in 1978. Second, Evangelicals looked for ways to ameliorate poverty and injustice. While they had shown interest in and concern for the poor, from among whom most Filipino Evangelicals had come, the message of evangelism and the "deeper life" slowed the apprehension of a social justice mandate.

Third, this took place in a "tsunami of spiritual activity" as Pentecostal movements—with emphasis on the gifts of the Spirit—grew rapidly in the Philippines from the 1970s. Amazingly adept in going public, this witness created a public buzz: "Many of their leaders . . . combined evangelistic zeal and political savvy, using mass media and street marches and rallies."[50] Debate over the country's new constitution pressed Evangelicals to take positions both on its contents and later on choosing of presidents. Flamboyant preachers uttered "prophetic" calls predicting which candidate would become president (largely to be proven wrong). Other pastors were more systematic in encouraging participation in elections, all the while seeking to build a theology of public life.

Indeed, the Philippines seems to have developed a remarkable number of pastors and leaders capable of wisely guiding their people into engagement with civic society, to assist associations and agencies as volunteers and to help in funding. Lim concludes that Evangelicals' biggest contribution to democracy building in the Philippines was to cultivate civil society and interface organizations and services, knitting them together into a common society. Anthony Gill points to another contribution of Evangelicalism in such Catholic-majority countries. The mere presence of Evangelical competition in the "religious marketplace" changes the behavior of the Catholic majority: "Catholic Churches in states where competitive religious markets exist are more likely to pressure authoritarian states to democratize. Conversely, Catholic Churches in non-competitive religious markets with a high degree of state regulation of religion are less likely to pressure authoritarian states to democratize."[51] Evangelical pietism, it seems, can have its own sort of political effect!

It would be wrong to leave the impression that re-engagement in the civic forum and civil society is fundamentally altering the focus of Evangelicals on salvation and holiness. There is no single message that defines our theology more than the narrative of God coming in Jesus. People, in whom the *imago Dei* lives, will also live through eternity. Systems, communities, social structures—all will lay their crowns at the feet of Jesus.

The change for many Christians, however, is that we see these social creations as a gift from our Creator and essential in human life. We need social structures. Leadership is a necessity to help those in need, providing the means by which we are all enabled to live in the shalom of his doing. It is the care for *those* realities that Evangelicals are progressively including in their paradigms, through self-conscious plans of witness and service. A useful word for this process is *enfolding*. There is not a turning from one focus to another. Neither is it a *re*focus. It is rather an *inclusion* of those aspects in a vision of his kingdom.

Political re-engagement, though but one activity among many in engaging the public square, is an important driver of contemporary Evangelical social action. The maturing of an increasingly sizeable and global Evangelical church will inescapably lead it down this path. As noted, there are pitfalls and vulnerabilities. It is predictable, however, that Christians surrounded by failing moral and ethical structures will feel compelled to act.

SIX

THE POWER OF THE WHOLE GOSPEL

SOME MEMORIES JUST DON'T FADE. On a sunny day Ron Nikkel, president of Prison Fellowship International (PFI), and I walked into a dark Reclusoria Sur Prison in Mexico City. It holds ten thousand men, all of them sentenced to at least fifteen years. Sections are run by drug cartels, the underworld power of Mexico linked into drug-producing countries to the south. Sleeping space here is often where you can find it, including bathrooms and hallway floors. Yet we walked among the men without fear, many reaching out for a handshake. They knew of PFI, a prison ministry started by Charles Colson—Richard Nixon's hatchet man—following his imprisonment.

We made our way through a maze of corridors, hearing music coming from a chapel. The clean white building, in sharp contrast to the dingy prison, was constructed by inmates and paid for by PFI. Seated inside were 120 inmates garbed in tan prison uniforms. At the front were twenty-five women in red PFI golf shirts, singing, playing instruments, and leading worship. (I admit to feeling some skepticism: Attractive women ministering to male inmates? Hardly the equation for unfettered spirituality, I thought.) Singing progressed and then two women, like a tag team, led in teaching the Lord's Prayer. They were dynamic and the men sat at attention, listening for almost fifty minutes.

Next came a liturgical mass with singers leading in highly spirited songs. While music played, some of the inmates left their seats to take confession with the priest at the side of the chapel, their sobbing clearly heard.

After mass, lunch was distributed, but I couldn't have anticipated what came next. As volunteers passed out bags, inmates moved to another section of the chapel with an evident sense of excitement. I wondered why they had such exuberant joy. It was then I noticed what each man obviously regarded as his precious contents: two rolls of toilet paper and toiletries. They were like excited teenagers at Christmas, for good reason. They had to buy their own toilet paper. And some have no family, no money, and no one to visit them. Without funds, no toilet paper.

In 129 countries, PFI has national ministries, caring for men and women in prison. That morning I watched it minister love and healing—as moving and real a ministry as I've ever seen anywhere. My emotions were on a roller coaster as I saw kingdom life lived out in such pure and unadulterated ways. Going to the forgotten and those deemed unworthy, Christian volunteers gave these men what few did: unbridled love.

David Mensah, a street kid in Bamboi, Northern Ghana, headed up a gang. He was converted by listening to a seventy-year-old who told him of *Yesus*.[1] Hearing of Tyndale University College,[2] he applied and was accepted. He arrived with insufficient documents in the Toronto airport and with only ten dollars to his name. In a story in which only angels make sense, immigration allowed him to enter and a stranger—whom he never saw again—guided him from the airport to the college campus, a college where later I served as president.

He graduated from college and, wanting to build into his homeland a gospel witness, completed a PhD in water, land, and resource management at the University of Toronto. He returned home and moved six hundred miles north of the capital Accra to Janga, a Muslim-majority area. Putting his agricultural skills to work, in time he built twenty miles of tomato farms along a riverside, dug close to a hundred wells, constructed roads, helped create a weekly market, and opened a medical clinic.

This he did for fifteen years without any public Christian witness. Finally, a Muslim chief asked if he would address the people. They were curious, why he—a Christian—was spending his life helping in food production and medical care. David agreed and that very Friday, three thousand showed up to hear him give his testimony. He told them, "We have been sharing food from the same dish for a long time. Now we are ready to share our meat with you. This Good News is our real meat, the best food that we have to offer you."[3]

The Muslim leaders gave him the best of land to build a church. Today David and his ministry, GRID, are opening a hospital—called Carpenter—in Bamboi. Here, he said, it only took them two years to gain the support of the community to build a church and to begin their public witness. Their strategy is simple but profoundly influential: their vision is to give the gospel time to speak in wholeness to all humanity. While David wanted to see people freed from spiritual bondage and become Christian in word and deed, he chose not to begin with a church, but instead to serve the poor, which in time led to planting churches. "We do not limit access to our programs on the basis of religion, but seek to extend God's love to all in need."[4]

Be it caring for the well-being of men caught in the web of crime and endless prison sentences, or creating productive food sources, the globe is marked by countless thousands of ministries of all sorts, rooted in an understanding that there is nowhere the gospel does not reach and there are no people or situation outside of its concern.

THE NAZARENE MANIFESTO

After his temptation in the wilderness, Jesus returned to his hometown of Nazareth. On the Hebrew sabbath he attended the synagogue, using this place in his early days of ministry to announce his intent. He did it by reading a text from Isaiah:

The Spirit of the Lord is on me,
   because he has anointed me
   to proclaim good news to the poor.
He has sent me to proclaim freedom for the prisoners
   and recovery of sight for the blind,
to set the oppressed free,
   to proclaim the year of the Lord's favor. (Lk 4:18-19)

Note Jesus *didn't* say, "I'm here to get you ready for the afterlife," "My death will carry the penalty for your sin," or "My kingdom will take care of Rome for you." While his life would deal a deathblow to sin and give us the gift of forgiveness and resurrection, Jesus unambiguously outlines his mandate with a manifesto about wholeness.

So why, when, and how did we get sidetracked into thinking that "saving a soul" was the sole calling of evangelism? Surely the four portraits of Jesus (the Gospels) give sufficient detail on his life and service to help us see that he went on to do what he said that day in Nazareth.

We suffer at the hands of one-text analysis, teaching, and strategies, and forget (even those of us who have been preachers for many years) that a sermon or an analysis of a text is usually driven by a desire to achieve certain outcomes. In the late nineteenth century, when our modern approaches to preaching were being formed, most Western countries featured large populations of largely nominal Christians. The task, we Evangelicals thought, was to call those people to repentance and stir up a slumbering faith so people would (re)turn to their local church. We forgot that, for a large part of the world, there *was* no local church—or slumbering faith, for that matter. They would come to these words of Jesus in a totally new and fresh way, driven by the need to replace the old beliefs that they were leaving.

In this chapter I show how Christians are awake to the power and importance of the Nazarene Manifesto, not as a pendulum swing discounting personal faith, but as a natural counterbalancing swing, in which the witness of faith produces practical effects in strength and well-being.

Jesus' message of human transformation—spanning health, education, and social and economic strength—drives an expansive vision of the role of global Christian faith. As those enthused with the witness of Jesus look about them, they see tragedies of human waste, killing, underdevelopment, and persecution. They also see opportunity. They *respond* with a healthy (and life-giving) proliferation of faith-based initiatives: Evangelical institutions, NGOs, charities, megachurches, and "mom and pop" organizations at the grassroots. Both locally and internationally, such initiatives lift people, families and communities, not only with relief, but also by putting in place longer-term plans to bring about permanent and sustainable reordering.

My wife, Lily, and I and climbed the rickety steps to the second floor of a building in a Cairo slum to be briefed by a group called Islamic Vision. It is a social agency working with Islamic families. Surprisingly, it is funded by the Coptic Evangelical Organization for Social Service (CEOSS). A national Egyptian Christian ministry, CEOSS has over five hundred staff and five thousand volunteers, with a range of ministry that is amazing. Working with an annual budget of 10 million US dollars, their capacity to serve the poor is remarkable. The director of Islamic Vision told us how Christians helped imams see that female sexual mutilation (FSM) and forced child marriage were unhealthy. Sitting next to me was an imam, so I asked him his story. He described how Christians had helped him understand these issues. He said now in Friday services at the mosque, he preaches a new message: how treating women properly matters. We left with a warm hug.

Just outside of the sprawling and congested city of New Delhi we visited an ashram—a ministry center. As we walked around its campus, I wondered how it came to be. The director was raised as an orphan, and in his youth came to faith. As he saw lepers marginalized and left alone, he was burdened for their needs and in time persuaded the government to give land where they could build shanties. But there was a roadblock. While the government provided subsistence, to get it they had to fill out forms, which most were simply not able to do. So he began to help them complete their forms. Then another problem became obvious. The children of lepers had nowhere to live—so he built a home and school for them. One thing led to another. He noted that challenged women were being abused on the streets, so he built them a home. But then I noticed a new hospital had been built; I asked where the money came for this, assuming he did regular treks to North America or Europe. No, he told me. He didn't even have a passport. Much of his support came from Hindus in the area. That night after I had preached in the church located at the center, many asked for prayer for healing and freedom from evil spirits. The pastor smiled as I finished praying and said, "Welcome to India." This was a microcosm of the global impulse of the Spirit—to offer full-orbed mercy and grace to a world of people in need.

North of Port-au-Prince in Haiti is Dessalines, a regional center. Its only hospital, Claire Heureuse, is mission built and funded. Chaplain Cadet Hyrouance asked me to accompany him on his morning rounds, and to pray. That morning the first three patients included a baby only hours old, a child with severe burns, and a young man who had barely survived a knife wound just above his heart.

For more than thirty years, Ian and Alice Marie Van Norman have been coming to Haiti, sometimes for months at a time, building schools, a hospital, centers of ministry and churches, and now helping with a university. Entrepreneurs in their home country, they give from their resources, at times matched by business friends. As Lily and I drove the dusty roads and walked the muddy streets with them, we watched as the Van Normans were greeted with wide smiles, bear hugs, giggles, and faces alive with recognition, as children sought to hold their hands. They have brought much more than money to Haiti. For over forty years, convinced their calling was to love and assist Haitians, they gave much of their lives to people they came to love.

Jim and Cathy Cantelon were in South Africa speaking at a church conference in the early 2000s. One evening, watching the news, they were profoundly moved with the destructive force of HIV/AIDS. Troubled and stirred, they returned to the church that Jim pastored in Vancouver. He resigned, and they began to help as they could, forming WOW (Working for Orphans and Widows). They traveled about South Africa, Zambia, and Malawi, seeing what they could do. Some ten years later, with an annual budget of a few million dollars, they continue to help national leadership and Africa-based ministries, always with an eye to lifting the stress off families, often bereft of parents, cared for by relatives and grandparents. Seeking to make every church a "Mother Teresa," their vision was to enable congregations to serve especially those with HIV/AIDS. Their strategy is visibly framed by an understanding of the whole human person and creation. Jim's book *When God Stood Up* is a biblical framing of what tens of thousands of ministries globally believe and do for righteousness and justice. Be it locally operated or a multilayered global agency, the ground rules of ministry now incorporate wholeness as essential, biblical and from the heart of God.

HOW WHOLENESS WAS LOST

To follow how this message of wholeness is shaping much of the present gospel witness, it helps to understand how in the past it was lost as a central tenet of Evangelical witness. It is a story parallel to our earlier review of the severing of the gospel message from a role in the public square. The vision of Jesus' kingdom—having come, being present, and being yet to come (as G. E. Ladd wrote, "now but not yet"[5])—is both simple at its core and complicated in its outworking. The stumbling over Jesus' announcement in Luke 4, as if it were a "good idea" but not foundational in his overall strategy, was brought about by caring and thoughtful people who wanted to make known the life and message of Jesus.

With every change of direction, there are contrarians whose paradigm of calling and ministry resists the change, pulling in the opposite direction. As the Evangelical world tended to make personal salvation its prime emphasis, others continued in holding together what some saw as the polar opposites of salvation and social care. Two stand out. The Salvation Army, founded in the slums of London, didn't waver in its commitment to the needy. In

2015, just in the United States, its budget of over 3.5 billion dollars attests to the ability to marry care for the person with a call to personal faith. Second, Mennonites, in their various iterations, have never lost that link of affirming personal piety with defending human well-being. Their faithful insistence that Christians see people holistically, in their current needs, has been a prophetic as well as pastoral kingdom-making ministry.

In retrospect we can see that in the early twentieth century the church was surrounded by storms, distracted, and blown off course.

Reading the Bible requires what interpreters and missiologists call *context*. We see the words through the lens of our immediate surroundings and listen through ears tuned to the language of our people. When a lover of the music of Bach listens to country and western music, what does he or she hear? If one has no experience in appreciating country and western, its sounds and melodies will seem twangy and nasal. The classical hearer will feel urged to return to the contrapuntal interwoven melodies of Bach, music he or she knows and likes. What is needed is an appreciation for music outside of his or her personal listening experience. So it is with reading the Bible. Context provides the tools by which we view and interpret the Bible.

Western missionaries of the early nineteenth and twentieth centuries interpreted the message of Christianity through their home environment. This they took with them in missions, sometimes unthinkingly assuming that their melodies of the Bible were universal. Just as Christ emptied himself, going to other people—into their languages, idioms, history, and culture—requires suspending our own presumption of normality. It helps to recall, then, how we allowed justice and God's concern for wholeness to become a sidebar.

Body and soul. As the gospel moved across cultures, the restrictions on language and mode of thought within those cultures came to bear on how the kingdom was interpreted. In the early centuries of Christianity, a heresy known as Gnosticism taught that matter—including the world around us and the human body—is evil. This early heresy, reinforced by Greek views of immortality, helped to create a view that only the spirit of the person is what is redeemed, while the body (being evil) is not redeemable. Salvation then entailed breaking the imprisoned spirit away from the body.[6] This dividing of body and spirit, with the discounting of the value of the physical, generated a particular understanding of creation, which over time produced theological bias away from considering the body as being of concern to God.

Focus on the soul resulted in the sidelining of the human side of Christ, requiring a series of Councils to define an orthodox understanding of the nature of Christ (Nicaea in AD 325, Constantinople in 381, and Chalcedon in 451). Those who did not agree were hounded out of the Western Church. This reliance on classical (Platonic and Aristotelian) views of the relationship between spirit and matter steadily pushed the Church in its various manifestations to divide up the human person, in effect subordinating the body. If only the nonmaterial soul lives on, why give attention to the body? This had profound effects on how Christians came to think of what was worthwhile in ministry.

Their fallacy was not understanding that the body, God's creation, is also of inestimable value. He created the material world and called it good. God in Jesus became human. Human life, while set into motion by the breath of God at its creation, cannot be sustained without the body. Life is designed as an embodied experience, and it is the body that is resurrected. Nowhere in the Bible (apart from Saul's profound mistake at Endor—1 Sam 28—about which there are endless interpretations) is a person identified apart from having a body. The Hebrew people, by way of contrast, did not distinguish between the spiritual and physical, as if the two lived without each other. The diminishing of the importance of the body in early Greek Christianity contributed to a redrawing of the inclusive nature of God's creation. Evangelicals in the West, too, were inheritors of this tradition.

Dispensationalism. The Evangelical church in the West faced a disabling idea that soon made its way out along missionary networks. The "aristocratic Irish lawyer-turned-priest-turned-peripatetic evangelist" John Nelson Darby divided time into "dispensations," that is, periods or ages, in an interpretation of the decline of the church that he saw all around him in Ireland.[7] His concern, born out of working among poor Catholics, was enunciated in his pamphlet *The Nature and Unity of the Church of Christ* (1828) and rapidly spread around the world. Darby interpreted the current age as the seventh period of biblical history—that is, from the resurrection of Jesus to his second coming—a period that, according to his theory, will end with a thousand-year reign of Christ, after which will come the final judgment. He was not the first to have this idea, but the enthusiastic expansion of his movement tapped into a general despair about the state of the church and trans-Atlantic society. If Jesus is coming—and its proponents argued that Jesus' second coming was just around the corner—then it followed that our only concern should be "getting people saved," ready for his coming.

Further, a mission objective was to press for his return by preaching in all nations. His followers drew on the text of Matthew 24:14—"And this gospel of the kingdom will be preached in the whole world as a testimony to all nations, and then the end will come." The logic was that if the gospel were preached to all "nations," then the church could catalyze Christ's return. The flip side of this logic was that it undermined postmillennialism and implied that any other initiative was futile.[8] Only getting people into the "kingdom" was a valid and worthy activity for Christians.

This contributed to an emerging "perfect storm," at least in the Protestant world. The religious-historical theory of Dispensationalism, and the turbulent and passionate sermons and books that it produced, arose at a time when mainline Protestant churches seemed overly concerned with their relationship with the state and, at the same time, were flirting with liberal views of the Bible that undermined its authority.[9] Their theology of salvation had shifted from people needing "to be saved" to the need for social transformation. This "social gospel"—a term used by Baptist minister Walter Rauschenbusch—raised objections from many Evangelicals. Rejecting the social gospel message, instead they found in Dispensationalism a helpful explanation for what they saw as the beginning of a disastrous decline of the church. For the "social gospellers," as we might call them, the problems they saw were social: people might need conversion (and not all social gospellers were sure of that), but social norms and categories needed it more. On the other hand, Evangelicals—who had earlier been defined by their social activism under William Wilberforce in relation to issues such as slavery—felt they were being given the choice of either defending the authority of the Bible or championing the social gospel. They chose the former.[10]

Two sides in tension. The way theology played out in these two church movements affected the Christian sense of wholeness. Today's Evangelical church is the child of the great eighteenth- and nineteenth-century revivals. As a result, a Wesleyan form of spirituality—"salvationism," in which conversion and sanctification were paramount—came to influence much of the mission-driven church. Its driving agenda was to introduce people to personal faith and conversion. Pentecostals, a branch of this movement, tended to divide the immanent (the "world") from the transcendent ("spiritual life"). Where mainline Evangelicals concentrated on the text, Pentecostals emphasized the miraculous, the Spirit, experience, and the end times. While there was no stated intention to disengage from public life, from civic forums or civil society, actual Pentecostal engagement in the form of street preaching and (under more oppressive regimes, such as in the Fascist period in Europe) civil disobedience tended to move that way rather than toward social action.

On the other side of the traditional tensions in nineteenth-century Protestantism was a Calvinist, or "Reformed," Christianity ("reformationism"). While its focus wasn't so much on personal conversion, it brought a wider vision of what made up kingdom concerns. The problem, however, was that its foundations on Calvin's *Institutes*, the Westminster Confession, and other weighty tomes made it a wonderful faith for the intellectually inclined but, unfortunately, encouraged a tendency to a kind of Christian fatalism (which neither Calvin nor Wesley would have recognized). It was against "hyper-Calvinism," for instance, that Carey had to war in his drive to provoke his fellow Particular Baptists into supporting global mission.

When these two passionate streams—salvationism and reformationism—of spiritual understanding converge, there is enormous power. It is not that matters of passion, spiritual vision, rational understanding, or biblical or vocational skills are more developed or owned by one side over the other. Rather, when these two butt heads or defend their own turf, the forward movement of both is diminished, robbing each community of the influence they could have had together.

At just the time, then, when mainline Protestants were caught up in promoting the social gospel, Evangelicals in the 1920s set sail, especially in the West, onto a sea of faith where matters of social service and human well-being were secondary. This is not to say that Evangelicals were not concerned about ministries of kindness. They were extensively involved in medical, social, and educational outreach and work. In North American cities, they were at the heart of missions to the poor and to alcoholics—with a clear goal, however, that conversion of the person was the ultimate aim of the mission. International missions built hospitals, provided public education, and engaged in all sorts of social programs, again with the salvation of the individual as their goal.

As missionary work was reborn in the example and vision of William Carey,[11] however, there were outbreaks of expression and action to care for the whole person. When Carey went on his first trip to India with his wife, Dorothy, his only other partner was a medical doctor. His concerns were driven by a desire to "give flesh" to the Word: his associates were printers, schoolteachers, and other practitioners. His Serampore College not only trained indigenous ministers but also taught the arts and sciences to anyone, regardless of caste or country. In 1820, he set up the Agri Horticultural Society of India, because God's creation was evident in the flowers of the field.

Ultimately, the life of the Evangelical church was in its pulpits and local churches. It would be true to say that, at the same time, Evangelical influence—especially during the second half of the twentieth century—declined at the institutional level of mainline Protestant churches: many Evangelicals were either ejected from or chose to leave their "liberal" institutions, which they felt were espousing a gospel built on social reconstruction and not spiritual transformation.

It is not an overstatement to note that although Evangelicals were one-sided in their focus on personal salvation, it resulted from a firmly held, high view of Scripture and an equally cherished experience of personally walking in faith. One well might wonder: if Evangelicals hadn't provided this emphasis on personal faith and transformation, who *would* have (and what would the situation in society be like today as a result)? Ironically, as the welfare states of the West became more or less universal, the liberal church traditions found their Christian (social) presence less and less needed. It was surely this strong, Bible-centered faith among Evangelicals, even if at times unbalanced, that in time gave ballast to the ship of Zion, helping the church stay on course so that both the home church and its missions would affirm conversion of the lost as an ongoing emphasis. Indeed, we can draw a line from that emphasis to the rapid growth of the church today.

Justice matters. The point, however, is that Western Evangelicals, as they focused on "spiritual matters," also seemed to lose sensitivity to God's love for justice. If he loves justice, should we not also? If we accept James's definition of "religion that our God and Father accepts as pure and faultless [as] this: . . . to keep oneself unstained by the world," then we also must accept the first clause of his definition: that we need "to look after orphans and widows in their distress" (Jas 1:27 NASB). Here is the point: Evangelicals did have a heart for those unjustly treated. However, as mainline Protestants espoused "social justice," Evangelicals were dissuaded from making it their cause as well. Engaged in fierce infighting with their liberal brethren, they came to conclude that "if you are for social justice, that means you don't believe that Jesus is the only way to God." This reaction generated a misunderstanding and created a tendency to avoid matters of social injustice. Everyone lost. Without the infectious influence of Evangelicals making social concern part of their program, in the push to incarnate gospel priorities in matters of social inequality, the world church lost an important ally.

A TURNAROUND: THE EMBRACE OF WHOLENESS

As noted earlier in this book, however, Evangelicalism has (since the twentieth-century world wars, but more importantly since the 1970s) emerged from its former Fundamentalist segregation. Parallel to this has been a re-engagement of social and justice concerns.

Times have changed: Baby Boomer Evangelicals in particular saw little reason to interpret the Bible as did their Depression-era parents. The debate over the *trustworthiness* of the Bible was largely won by new generations of outstanding Evangelical scholars (from F. F. Bruce to N. T. Wright). Although this debate still rears its head occasionally among liberal and universalist popularizers (such as those associated with the former Jesus Seminar), its public popularity has diminished. Evangelicals are now more confident that one need not commit intellectual suicide to believe in and follow Jesus, and the rising presence of faith and its influence has been matched by a growing and passionate interest in speaking to matters of inequality and injustice.

◀━━━━━━━━━▶

We drove an hour out of Hanoi and walked into a housing area where fifty recovering drug addicts were receiving therapy and spiritual instruction. In recent years, drugs have infested Vietnam, and the government response has been to imprison the offenders. This has exacerbated and deepened the problem. Earlier that day I had lunch with three Vietnamese in their early thirties, all former drug addicts who now run drug-treatment centers and pastor churches. Two were from well-known Vietnamese families. One had even attempted to sell his own child to sustain his drug addiction. Today, they and their colleagues run some forty such centers with fifty people in each, doing what most therapies can't seem to do: release young lives from bondage and addiction. These and programs of all kinds in Vietnam run by Christians offer help to a materialistic and communist-led society. Their civic contribution is huge, as they give evidence that Jesus is the true revolutionary. He doesn't overthrow political regimes but instead redeems those prone to self-destruct, planting seeds of human well-being. When a party official's son is released from his habits and becomes a faithful husband and loving father, ideology bows before such evidence.

What has brought this about? How have both local and global contexts caused Evangelicals to embrace the wholeness of human life and its needs? In my experience, there are seven main reasons.

The darkness of poverty. The first is the economic dilemma. Human needs are infinite, but resources are finite. There aren't many places we can go without running up against poverty, human dysfunction, murderous acts, unfair social and political systems, enormous inequity of incomes, or children abused and pushed to the margin. How long of a list do we need in order to be convinced? Even in our time, and in the West, where self-interest plagues all generations, one can argue that such darkness allows the Light to shine brighter.

Evidence of evil. For students and the young, their culture and media are redolent with sensuality and materialistic overload. The Christian human spirit sees through the stuff of a world bloated from feeding on itself, peering through the hedonistic mist to a surrounding throng of people who long for fairness and opportunity. In a world taught by *Buffy the Vampire Slayer* and in which Lucifer has a self-named program on Netflix, a West that finds it hard to believe in God finds little problem in believing in evil. One doesn't even need to acknowledge that dark forces are at work to see that something is fundamentally wrong. When the Spirit tunes people into those forces, they will be all the more perceptive in seeing.

The need is obvious. Third, as Christians see need, resources are brought to bear: agencies and people groups, on both the giving and receiving sides, provide the information and means by which something can be done. Even before social media became the norm, Christians were linking arms in creating the means by which resources could be carefully and strategically recruited and distributed.

Some of the resulting organizations are among the largest of their kind. World Vision, for instance, is one of the world's largest agencies dedicated to aiding people in need.[12] I met its founder, the late Bob Pierce, at a Youth for Christ meeting in my home city of Saskatoon, Canada. The desire of our small group to help him sponsor children in South Korea was both passionate and, well, *normal*. People in need elicited our concerns. What we didn't realize at the time was that World Vision, along with a number of subsequent related agencies and missions, would not only facilitate our desire to help but, in time, would teach us that we could do more than just provide band-aid solutions. The gospel called on us to act in digging out systemic injustice.

I visited San Miguel in Honduras, a barrio of 98,000, where just two years earlier there were, on average, 115 killings a month. At the time of writing, it was just three or four. During those years of killing, 64 percent of the inhabitants experienced some kind of violence, ranging from extortion to killings. Now that is reduced to 34 percent. This is, in part, how it happened: World Vision brought together nine Evangelical congregations and the Roman Catholic parish in the barrio, along with USAID, to create a social inversion. They deliberately upset the status quo of violence by targeting violence. Today in a youth center, young people learn skills, from computers to music to barbering and cosmetology and physical fitness, introducing a sense of pride that highlights human value.

Honduras was not always so violent. As a land bridge from the drug-producing countries of the south to the United States, it became a crossing point for drug cartels. High unemployment and few vocational or recreational opportunities made crime a juggernaut of domestic life. But determined Christians refused to let this tide of crime and its accompanying violence wash over its people.

Reshaping the Evangelical mind. Fourth, in 1974 Billy Graham brought together 2,500 church leaders, missiologists, theologians, and agency leaders. The Lausanne Congress on World Evangelization (LCWE) was a turning point in Evangelicals' vision, understanding, and acceptance of a new paradigm.

As assistant to the program director, Paul Little, I had opportunity to see developments and debates beyond what was heard on the floor. Two vital factors from that meeting changed the course of the church with regard to an Evangelical understanding of the gospel. First, the public addresses of René Padilla, Samuel Escobar, Emilio Núñez, and Orlando Costas shocked participants. Many for the first time heard a call to social justice from their friends—not from Catholics, not from mainline liberals, but from Evangelicals who shared their view of sin and salvation. As Latin Americans, they had wrestled with liberation theology in their countries, where injustice had proliferated and the poor were being destroyed by neocolonialism, war, and corruption. These were our friends crying out from the depths of their struggle. Their cry, framed around the biblical shalom, was shaped by the actual message of Jesus, a kingdom message that drew a straight line from God's call to living need. I could feel the growing wave of understanding, strange and somewhat foreign at first, and then, "Ah, yes." For some it sounded initially like liberation theology with a thin Evangelical veneer, but in time, as speakers and workshops searched the Scriptures, and as the Spirit caused the message to seep into our collective hearts, it took hold.

While the impact was enormous, its message and actual ethos was transmitted through the pen of John Stott, who was chief architect and editor of the Lausanne Covenant, the informing guide for Evangelical missions over the next half-century. As I now meet Christian leaders in many countries, reference often is made to the sharp turn this conference created, opening minds so that social justice and societal wholeness could be seen as integral to the gospel mandate.

Young Evangelicals' holistic worldview. Fifth, quite simply the old theological divisions between soul-saving and the "social gospel" no longer grip the minds of succeeding generations. Less concerned with doctrine, and more with authenticity, Millennials demonstrate in their speech, in their new forms of church, and in their attitudes toward simple things such as tattoos and body art, that this divide is being bridged. The defensive maneuvers of my generation are irrelevant to them. As noted above, the old fear that caring about social-justice issues would divert one from biblical foundations doesn't exist for them. In fact, the opposite is true. Plenty of young Evangelicals (and those who would not recognize that name, or apply it to themselves) read the Bible. Some movements, such as the University Bible Fellowship, are virtual revival movements spreading around the world. The Bible is neither the icon nor the "problem" for them that it was for previous generations. Instead, the more they study it, the more younger Evangelicals develop a holistic Christian worldview, grasping the truth that as God is saving us, so he is saving his whole creation. People are not a soul without a body, a heart without a mind, a spiritual reality without a stomach to fill. In understanding what the Scriptures say, they are driven to be friends of God, and being his friend means we love what he loves. Human need and injustice unsettle God's intent, upsetting his rule. Given that our lives are linked into the aspirations and ways of his kingdom, what is of concern to him becomes of concern to us.

The power of cooperative vision. Synergy, the outcome of humans working for a total effect hidden in God's thoughts and concerns, occurs in the emergence of a cooperative vision to re-engage the public square for the resolution of human needs through, and as the extension of, Christ's kingdom. This sixth reason connects with the bifurcation of life noted above. Evangelicals have rediscovered that God is not just sovereign in his words: "The earth is the LORD's, and everything in it, the world, and all who live in it; for he founded it on the seas and established it on the waters" (Ps 24:1-2).

The inspiration of a spiritual consensus. Beyond the traditional frictions between Wesleyans and Calvinists, between postmillennialists and dispensationalists, the Spirit has fermented a growing spiritual consensus. People from various doctrinal backgrounds, varied histories and different denominations, each following their own missional methodologies, find themselves together in celebration, observing God at work in new ways. The interlinking of life in the Spirit breaks down divisions, links new friendships, and opens eyes to see needs, brought on by an admission that without the power of the Spirit, words are empty, methods sterile, and lives as empty vessels. Caring for people in need, confronting injustice, is not confined to organizations, agencies, or programs. Mostly, it comes from people moved to do something. This seventh reason is an important ingredient in the understanding of the shift toward seeing wholeness as essential to the gospel. During the Reformation, Luther's notion of the priesthood of believers liberated followers of Jesus to live out the gospel by the power of the Spirit. While priests of the Roman church had a role in ministry, the Holy Spirit, by indwelling each person, now makes *everyone* a "priest," one called and equipped to serve. This not only connects Monday with Sunday, but also frees Christians to be Christ's presence wherever they go. People are propelled into ministry and service, not relying on a church or agency, not requiring formal seminary training and not needing a vocational tag saying that they have been sent. When they see suffering, they step in. When injustice is witnessed, they speak up. When they observe abuse, they find ways to mitigate or prevent. It is learning to see with the eyes of Jesus. He hears with our ears. He feels with our hands. He is touched by our heart and stirred when our emotions encounter the gritty reality of a suffering world.

FACING SYSTEMIC ISSUES

Prior to the 1970s, the readiness of Evangelicals to stand up against social injustice tended to be episodic, one-off, dealing with particular needs and circumstances of the moment. It also focused on important but narrow issues such as religious freedom. Yet we failed to ask, where do these one-off events come from? What is their cause? What those of us who grew up in that time didn't see were the root systems from which injustice grows. Here mainline Protestants had something important to teach us about injustice. From the great issues of the League of Nations that dominated the period (the 1920s) when the mainstream and Evangelicals parted ways, to the writing of the Universal Declaration of Human Rights (1948), to the antiwar and antinuclear moratoria of the 1960s, such actions created a theological language for engaging the public sphere. Evangelicals dipped into that pool when their social conscience reemerged after World War II.

Farmers, in cultivating, seeding, and harvesting their fields, face an annual thistle problem. Thistles are weeds that suck up moisture, overtake land, and create a general nuisance: topped by a colored flower, they are surrounded by a prickly outgrowth. One solution to the thistle problem is to cut them down one by one. Much like dealing with injustice, however, a one-issue, one-time, one-solution approach does not work. Whenever their root system remains intact, thistles keep on growing. The only way to remove their troublesome presence is to pull them up by the roots. Injustice is like that—hence the word *systemic,* a system that continues to supply (or sap) life.

For a Dalit ("untouchable") in India, the caste system is so rooted in culture that even though a few might be freed from their social and economic prison, each year millions more are born into families designated as Dalit. As I wrote this chapter, Gujarat in India was ablaze with protests over the lynching of a Muslim boy and the beating of a number of Dalits accused of skinning and eating a dead cow. Petrol bombings, mass public demonstrations, and the resignation of senior government officials all point to deeper problems.[13] While one might help a few by assisting them with education, health, and social uplift, until the causes are rooted out, systemic injustice will continue to reproduce itself.

Economic wholeness. Economics, Thomas Carlyle wrote, is the "dismal science." That description was never truer than at the present. In our globalized society, the rich are getting richer, as population growth strains resources and expands poverty. Economic theories attempt to discern and advise, while international financial organizations intervene, putting countries on starvation or steroid protocols—depending on their analysis. Economic levers seem to have some role in lifting the poor, but the gap with the superrich seems to be ever widening. There is, however, a small cloud "like a man's hand" on the economic horizon. It might be an indicator of the role faith plays in constructing the future.

Most missiologists, it is true, see economics as an important contextual factor. The abuse of smaller economies by the self-interested mighty is certainly one factor promoting "spiritual capital formation" among the global poor. Few missiologists, however, see economic well-being per se as a church agenda.

A common response is this: What business is it of the church to meddle in the affairs of business? That question makes sense if the gospel is concerned only with personal and *salvational* matters. The emergence of an indigenized Evangelicalism in the majority world, however—what Amos Yong calls a "ferment" in the case of Asian theologies—has pointed out to the West that there is a troublesome disconnect in the way we hold together economics and the gospel.[14] The West, for example, has benefited from evolving democratic ideals and policies, providing its citizenry with opportunity and skills in creating social and financial frameworks in which we can pursue our interests and utilize abilities. It is not automatic, of course. Each of us is born into and raised in a family and circumstances (such as educational opportunities) that can predispose us either to privilege or marginalization. I was raised in a minister's home, and we were poor, although that didn't seem to be a deciding factor. Our tutelage from parents and community was extraordinary. The point is, however, that mingling with our *salvational* experience and doctrines was a trust that the Lord "will meet all your needs according to the riches of his glory in Christ Jesus" (Phil 4:19). In retrospect, it was a relatively easy faith to have in a country, such as Canada, where various government and private resources enabled that supply to occur. We had relative disadvantage in our immediate frame, but nothing like the absolute disadvantage faced by others in the world.

Now take the Evangelical reading of Philippians 4:19 into the life of a family in a West African country. How should they read that same Bible text? Is there any reason why they should interpret God's promises differently, even though the surrounding opportunities for advantage are radically less developed or available? It has taken the West a good while to catch up to the thought, so obvious to Bible readers in the majority world, that economic and social well-being are as much a concern of the Father as our personal spiritual welfare.

Economic well-being and prosperity theology. There is a global issue that we need to address. It has to do with the underlying search for economic sufficiency, a theme too often distorted by popular preachers who use slogans and hype to build their own financial nest eggs. Without being chagrined by their antics, we ask, what is at the heart of people who are seeking a lift in their total life opportunities?

Angst crowds the African soul: economic inequities, social entrapment, governments swallowed by corruption, systemic poverty, powerlessness, deprivation, life cut short by civil wars, the surging desire to better themselves and their families. Why *wouldn't* Africans want a better life?

Underlying the aspirations of Africans is a universal impulse to lift life from squalor and deprivation, opening doors for one's children to live a better life. Fueled by a vital religious faith and experience, encouraged (or in some cases egged on) by populist preachers, such aspirations seek for the ideas and means by which Africans can change the human trajectory of poverty. Pastor Bishop David Oyedepo, Winner's Chapel, Lagos, Nigeria, speaks from a decidedly African perspective when he says,

> Though Africa's input in American's sugarcane plantation as labourers was part of what helped in revitalizing the economy of America, the African is still not considered as any creation of relevance, because the voice of a poor man is not heard, and his wisdom is despised. . . . That is why economic recovery is a must. Our human dignity as a people must be recovered. . . .
>
> You may choose to be part of it or be somewhere else on a slave trade trip and be hearing of what is happening back home. It is a choice you must make.[15]

Some call it "health and wealth" or "name it and claim it." Another, more uplifting, name is "Word of Faith," but most often those who dismiss it call it "prosperity theology."

Before we glibly ignore the grinding realities of faith, however, we might want to see it from the point of view of those looking for a way out. Beyond the get-rich schemes or a reworking of "possibility thinking," if one can get past flagrant abuses or silliness, what is the logic or at least emotive reasoning underlying this rising tidal influence?

The message of Bishop Oyedepo strikes a chord, an aspiration with a tune to which we in the West can hum. Like it or not, this movement has become a lathe on which Christianity, not only in Africa but much of the world, is being shaped. It has released significant people movements and is deeply entrenched in popular religiosity throughout Africa and its diasporas. Regardless of whether one sees it as heretical, cultic, prophetic, or merely a short-term and inconsequential splash, it behooves both antagonists and promoters to take note.

Recognizing the enormous biblical flaws in their rationale, I suggest that we give it space: see it from the bottom up, not from the latest revelation of a megachurch pastor raising funds for a new jet. Of course, it has attracted a deservedly bad reputation. Dismissed for its inordinate fixation on personal wealth by its promoters, it is often used to fleece congregants and turn a profound promise into heresy. Even so, beyond its facile association with the export of American capitalism, the ease with which Word of Faith teachings have fused with indigenous material spiritualities raises a question that calls for our attention.

Let's begin by agreeing that the Bible is not silent about our personal and family well-being. Salvation speaks into our moral faults and human depravity, bringing life into death, light into darkness, and love from hate and self-loathing. New birth is a powerful and apt metaphor. But that speaks not only to our unseen and inner life. It also radiates out into all we do, in all areas of life. As Allan Anderson notes, there is a "realized eschatology"[16] that sees "the 'not yet' as 'already.' Tragically, some in the West view future promises of the 'not yet' as always being 'not yet.'"[17]

However, if Christ's salvation is only for eternity, then we can dispose of this conversation altogether. The danger is that we might inadvertently dismiss this global move among Christians who desire to break out of their poverty and social disablement just because our *seeing* is besmirched by grotesque purveyors of self-enhancing propaganda who stretch God's promise of provision out of shape. It matters that we see, at its basic level, a real and deep surge among the poor, who are looking for a place in God's good world. They, too, desire to become agents of his grace, not buried beneath strata of death-attracting, disease-ridden, poverty-encasing sorrow. Surely we have time to listen to their cry for God's supply, for their longing for opportunity to live in the bonds as his beloved.

Heresy. There is, however, a pattern at play seen often in church history. As the church grows and is revitalized, heresy is almost always a byproduct. Heresy (a distortion of a biblical truth) is usually a twist on a core biblical doctrine, like a prairie fire out on the edge of the Spirit's work. Crazy things go on: extrabiblical activity, usually quite indefensible. As in contemporary debates over economic and social well-being, heresy turns God's promise from "God will supply" to "God will make you rich." Moreover, the long-term pattern is that heresy will often find its way back into orthodoxy. Our fight against heresy might be more productive if, rather than disputation, we engage in interchange and fostering of serious relationships.

In time, promotional hype most often burns itself out. The core element of faith, that God is sufficient—and living in his light, he will supply our needs—proves itself over the longer term. The gong show of "prosperity" and its promoters will in time drift to the edge of the stage and disappear. But what Christians in desperate situations have discovered will not. If such faith and disposition is orthodox, in line with biblical promises, why cannot that find its way into the lives of my brothers and sisters in any circumstance? Such re-emergences of the power of biblical promise can in fact provoke revolutionary results. They might even teach me something about my own faith.

The virtuous cycle and redemptive lift. Bryant Myers is one of those who have outlined just such a quiet revolution among those whom he calls "Progressive Pentecostals."[18] He notes three subtle trends. The first is "scholars taking note."[19] Dena Freeman from the London School of Economics has observed that African Pentecostal churches do not separate religion from development. Here development is not seen as a social, economic, or human rights issue, but "in terms of 'What God wants for Africa.'"[20] Seen as a spiritual battle in which the demonic is the purveyor of lies and misery, the battle lies in overcoming evil. This contrasts with the massive NGO "third sector," for whom the problem is injustice and poverty itself rather than spiritual forces. Obviously there is a fundamental disconnect between a bureaucratized global society—which (even in the case of some of its "faith-based" cadres) organizes itself in rational, secular terms—and those whom they aim to serve.

The second trend Myers points to is that the geography of Africa is undergoing a major shakeup: urbanization and the drift to the cities means that people leave behind the cults of their ancestors and memories of demonic activity. They move to cities, where they encounter faith and experience the power of the Spirit. In brief, they are leaving the old for the new, while continuing to assess the new in terms of the frameworks they bring with them.

Third, this fusion of past experience, change, and new faith means that a new framework is emerging, "a virtuous cycle that is inseparably material, psychological, and spiritual in nature."[21] This includes aggressive evangelistic outreach, using the most modern of technologies. The focus becomes, "What is God's will for you?" This directs one away from that which diminishes economic well-being—gambling and alcohol abuse, for example—into a strategy that depreciates waste, adopts internal disciplines of work and relationship, and enriches families. This new culture gives a new level of care for children, spouses are honored, and the community becomes both a giver and receiver of newfound social, economic, and spiritual wealth. This is the "prosperity" encountered by those who experience "redemptive lift."[22] It isn't a magical formula by which God pours out wealth. It's a newfound bounty of blessing at all levels, requiring change in behavior. No longer can people live as they choose. Often, giving a tithe or "paying back the blessing" is expected, enabling the construction of new institutions.

This virtuous cycle transforms the person, family, church, and wider community. Many of those who have left old assumptions also make a physical change, leaving the home village, where traditional relationships are entrenched. The person now in a church fellowship learns new skills and habits to survive and thrive in the city. This integration of faith, behavior, skills, and relationships speaks to the question, "What does God want for Africa?" Local and community-level wholeness spills over into the politics of development at the national level.

Interweaving through this fabric of wholeness is what people hold to be true for themselves. The change results in new attitudes about self and others and in turn promotes change in communities as people now changed bring about their own well-being. This is a counterpunch to what Myers calls "marred identity," in which a person internalizes "the impact of chronic poverty and sustained oppression, which resulted in reduced agency, risk avoidance, and resistance to change." Identity matters. It defines how we see ourselves and how we map out possible futures. "Suffering from marred identity is a bad thing, but not knowing that this marred identity is not what God intends, or failing to announce that God has a solution for marred identity, is even worse."[23]

Freeman's analysis understands this as "a shift from seeing oneself as a victim to seeing oneself as a victor. Many people, especially the urban poor, first come to Pentecostal churches feeling wretched, despised and hopeless. Their self-esteem is low and they feel powerless to change their situation."[24] In time, through church and prayer and sometimes by physical and spiritual healings, they "begin to see themselves as valued individuals, part of God's people, a 'somebody' rather than a 'nobody.' Most important of all, they begin to move beyond a passive fatalism and come to realize that they have agency in their lives."[25]

Other scholars are also taking this seriously. Nimi Wariboko (who holds a PhD from Princeton, is Walter G. Muelder Professor of Social Ethics at Boston University, and has authored in-depth writings on African issues) admits to the inherent follies in the Word of Faith approach. He goes on to show, however, that African Christians reject "Western binary thinking regarding the spiritual and the material: that is, God is concerned only with the spiritual and not really with material things." For many Africans, he continues, "The material realm, the realm of the bread and butter, must be opened to the spiritual."[26]

Another form of the Protestant Ethic? The "redemptive lift" theory has obvious parallels with Max Weber's "Protestant Ethic" thesis, which held that Christian conversion tended to create economic and social uplift. Weber compared Protestant Northern Europe with Catholic Southern Europe and saw that economic enterprise was stronger among Protestants than Catholics. He formed the view that the Calvinist doctrine of predestination spurred people on so they could give evidence through a productive life that they were among the predestined.

However, political scientist Paul Freston sees the two as having very different reasons behind their biblical rationale. The Evangelical/Pentecostal drive to a life sufficiency (which seems to be a better term than "prosperity") is not taking place within the economic spaces of mainstream capitalism, as was the case for Protestants in Europe. Rather, today's poor live out on the "periphery of established global capitalism." In addition, this drive for economic sufficiency doesn't live under the stress of the Calvinist urge toward evidential predestination. What it does, however, is to energize people "economically by various aspects of their faith (greater optimism and self-belief, new patterns of honesty, sobriety and diligence) and by skills learnt in the church."[27]

David Martin, also eyeing the Latin American world, sees the Evangelical/Pentecostal church as providing a vision of life that cuts them "free from the world of alcohol, of deals in bars, and of football and the weekend male spree ... a faith of the household poised against the seductions of the street."[28]

In barrios and favelas marked by dangerous competition and poverty, the church comes alongside with optimism, fueling hearts with the message that there is a better way. Enmeshed with the promise and gift of the new birth, it begins with the inner life and radiates outward. This is a continuum, beginning there but moving toward a place where the person and family develop new-found faith to trust that this same Jesus and Savior will take them through steps they need so as to not live forever under the grinding heel of an economic warlord, upheld by a blurry promise that the afterlife will be better. Rather than peering beyond death to that "not-yet" eschatology, they wrap their arms about the future and by prayer, fasting, and faith pull it back into today as a realized "now" eschatology.

By their companionship in a community of faith they learn the basics: to be trustworthy; to work hard; to be independent, self-assured, entrepreneurial, and honest in dealing with others. Martin puts it this way: "Evangelicals are part of a psychic mutation toward personal independence and individual initiative dramatized in their sense of 'personal salvation.'"[29]

More than aspirational. This movement that God is concerned with one's economic well-being is young. Its premises are being tested by millions even as I write. There is much that is aspirational about this movement. It is true globally that in the past few decades there has been economic and social uplift. The reduction of households living in poverty went from 44 percent in 1981 to almost 10 percent by 2013, in part, because of the stunning economic lift among the poor in China.[30] Even so, those living in abject poverty and many living just above the subsistence level number over a billion.

But we can go beyond aspirations to a reflective level where this phenomenon is evaluated. Social scientists too are taking this seriously, seeing this movement as more than a blow-hard promise. The South African Center for Development and Enterprise (a think tank) has worked with professors Peter Berger (Boston University) and James Hunter (University of Virginia) to research this "phenomenon."[31]

In their research they note four factors at play. First, there is an attitude that the believers are to be disciplined in their work, deferring gratification to save and build financial capital. Second, because they have lived within a theology that viewed material things as secondary, a countervailing way "relaxes them and releases energy for the same worldly matters. Precisely because these things mean so little to them."[32] Third, their entrepreneurial spirit allows them to be flexible and nimble as they work with a changing world. David Martin calls it "voluntaristic and competitive pluralism."[33] Fourth, their moral discipline counters social decay and issues within communities that act in a debilitating way. Berger notes in the study, "As long as the individual can indeed find meaning and identity in his private life, he can manage to put up with the meaningless and dis-identifying world of the mega structures."[34]

The long-term effect of the vision of wholeness. Western opinion is framed by its experience of accumulated wealth and social safety nets that protect us from ultimate disaster. But in most of the Global South such things don't exist. Most of the poor operate in the informal economy where survival comes from "their priorities in terms of expenditure, and by religiously-founded hope that they will not descend into the abyss of social chaos."[35]

The re-emergence of a vision of wholeness transforms and deepens the church, at least among Evangelicals. The gospel is given larger weight in the total life of the believer as the theology of the whole works its way through congregations, missions, and people. The understanding that the well-being of a person, family, community, or nation is of equal concern to the Father—alongside the call of Christ to repentance and faith—is a source of driving passion.

It also deepens the church, embedding in its strategies an appreciation for all sides of our human faculties and foibles. The environment, a social cause too long ignored by Evangelicals, is now a common point of conversation and action. It is deepening among Millennials who view this issue of wholeness with comfort, embracing these pieces of life—which my generation left out—and seeing them as a concern of Christ.

Wholeness, as a message, has within the Word of Faith movement attracted increased membership. My hope is that its place within the wider Evangelical community will bring it to maturity and so provide us with inroads into desperate human conditions, witnessing to the fullness of Christ. As the Evangelical church becomes a larger part of the global Christian community, it matters that our theology of wholeness shapes our life and witness.

The world needs it. Other Christians want our involvement. Our Christian community needs to hear from its teachers and leaders how the gospel touches every part of life, reflecting on what the Spirit is doing to enable that understanding. The message of wholeness is as old as creation. Embracing a theology of wholeness is the logical extension of Lausanne. It will give resonance, strength, and courage to the people of God engaged in the kingdom life of Jesus Christ.

God is in us and in this, his world.

PART III
JESUS GOES GLOBAL

SEVEN

WHOLENESS

As I write, I'm returning from China after days with the leadership of house churches. The complexity of this population and its rich land is beyond description. The multiple factors shaping today's church in China presents such a crisscross of people, government regulations, personal initiatives, and regions that one struggles to explain the pulsating witness of this remarkable story.

Take that to a global level and the complexity of explanations for the amazing growth of the Evangelical world this past half-century only multiplies.

In the preceding chapters I've identified five drivers I see at the heart of the growth of the church. In this chapter we will observe factors that weave their ways in and out of these drivers. Three factors are *enablers*—prayer, women in ministry, and worship—and two are *issues*—refugees and persecution. None are independent. Their weaving strands contribute to the design and strength of a creative, emergent kingdom construct.

PRAYER MOVEMENTS

Muslim-majority Jakarta was the site of the 2012 World Prayer Assembly, where we joined nine thousand from sixty countries. The facility was owned by Christians, and on the last day, one hundred thousand joined in praying together at the Bung Karno Stadium.

Prayer is tough, when taken seriously. Praying doesn't come easily. It is a discipline. For most prayer is not our first choice. "Getting something done" usually comes first, which presumes that praying is not.

Yet people everywhere are grouping for prayer: in homes, before the business day, online, in parliamentary groupings. Towns, cities, and regions host annual prayer breakfasts. These prayer gatherings are different and varied: noisy and silent, bombastic and reflective. All kinds.

The World Prayer Assembly was a confluence of streams wending their way on a delta of prayer. This one was hosted by South Koreans—well known for their rigorous early morning prayer gatherings—and by Indonesia prayer groups. It was a four-day pep rally on prayer. The music, dance, drama, and un-abashed enthusiasm were awe inspiring.

The genesis of today's World Prayer was in 1984 in Seoul. Von-nette Bright, who with her husband, Bill Bright, founded Campus Crusade for Christ, led the Lausanne Movement in its late-twentieth-century prayer gathering. Here, in Indonesia, they built on that by joining with the Global Day of Prayer, a stream trig-gered by Graham Powers of South Africa.

The underlying mood of the World Prayer Assembly matched my memories of boyhood camp meetings. Joy captured those as-sembled from the troubled spots of the world. Many were living under the heel of a religious or secular majority, despised and per-secuted. I applauded with thousands as six hundred Christians from China stood to be welcomed. Those from Indonesia know what it means to *pray* in a Muslim-dominated country where, on some of its islands, Christians have been killed and churches burned. Within this burgeoning prayer movement, the gospel is unfolding in new ways. Sometimes its message is hopeful, at other times disconcerting in the extreme. Even so, we are in the vortex of a spiritual windstorm. Spiritual activity creates its own spin-offs. Some of these spin-offs will meander in their style or theological assertions. Even so, it should not deter us from tracing over the delta a larger and more profound work of the Spirit.

Hunger for God and an experiential faith knows no bounds. I'm moved as I witness the breathing of the Spirit into peoples, regions, and vocational sectors. Where this is all going, we don't yet know. The wind of the Spirit, as always, blows where it will. However, in this global meeting of prayer I noted five clusters defining today's prayer movements.

Deep personal thirst. Thirsty people will go anywhere to alleviate dryness.

Who are they? They come from all walks of life, from all kinds of life experiences, from profoundly activist religious groups and from lifeless ones. I see old-line Protestants raised on the message, "Be good and that will get you to heaven," desperate for a fresh infilling of the Spirit. Alternatively, I meet Roman Catholic and Orthodox believers anxious to find new streams to quench their spiritual thirst. I speak with Pentecostals tired of hype, following spiritual journeys of the early church fathers, where quietness and silence meet the desire to go deeper. Mainstream Evangelicals, whose spirituality is framed by doctrine, become seekers of the Charismatic. In every group at least some languish in the system at hand, longing not just for what is new, but also for the Spirit life, something that breaks the barriers of deadness and stops the draining of the soul.

Religion offers the potential of two extremes: on one side a tightly scripted doctrine, on the other a watered-down faith, unsure of what can be believed. Either extreme snuffs out life. In the wide middle there is potential for dynamic, life-changing, and God-intervening faith. We see this especially in the Global South, where people actually believe that God will do what he promises. Be it in healing, solving troubling matters, or providing their "daily bread," such people seek an actual, observable action of God.

Evangelistic passion. The drive to pray for the unreached has been part of our eschatology—our doctrine of the end times—for hundreds of years. More recently, focus on what has been called "the 10-40 window" highlights prayer especially for the Muslim world. Heightened by 9/11 and increased awareness of the Islamic world, prayer groups have focused on reaching the unreached.

Engaging the spirit world. Western minds tend to operate as if faith were just an idea. The debate between liberal and conservative doctrine has thus largely been about *ideas.* The notion that spiritual war is waged in the heavenlies seems spooky. However, it doesn't take many conversations with church leaders in Africa, Asia, or Latin America before you understand that their search for spiritual advancement is within the spirit world. We might be uncomfortable in identifying dysfunction or disunity as something other than psychological, but Christians in much of the world think otherwise. It is for them a battle defined as spirit warfare, and is often associated with intercessory prayer.

Embracing culture. Prayer takes on the life and ways of the peoples practicing it. In my first service in a South Korean Presbyterian church, I was convinced I had ended up in the wrong place. When time came to pray, it wasn't that someone did the praying and everyone listened. Instead, as they closed their eyes, everyone prayed out loud at the same time. The noise was deafening. After a few minutes, the minister rang a small bell and everyone stopped. Today, much contemporary prayer is closely linked to praise and worship, forms that fit the cultural world of those praying. While in the past, worship music in non-Western communities was often just a translation of older Western hymns and choruses, today indigenous music, dance, and forms have become the norm.

Every sharp rise in spiritual interest carries with it extremes. Let's be careful not to be too critical of what is new or different. We can too easily dismiss expressions of prayer outside of our experience. We need to evaluate what is going on historically; new waves of spiritual life often carry with them aberrant forms, but most in time do find an equilibrium. Listening to a text of biblical promise in a village void of clean water, and having no seed for spring sowing, will trigger prayer with different intensity and expectation than in a place where our greatest need is finding a new music minister.

◀————▶

As we made our way out from the prayer assembly, I knew we had felt the wind of the Spirit. We had heard the voice of our Lord, and embraced with joy and faith peoples from everywhere.

The earliest churches met around prayer. In various forms, personal and formal, private and public, written and extemporaneous, from invocation to supplication, prayer remains central to the well-being of any Christian community. As much as it becomes a personal request, asking God to resolve a specific need has historically been a prelude to spiritual renewal and visitation. Even in an age of instant global social media, there are sites dedicated to joining Christians in prayer for wide-ranging issues and on up-to-date matters.[1]

Prayer networks include (as noted above) the Global Day of Prayer (GDOP) and the 24-7 International Prayer Movement, sparked by the International House of Prayer (IHOP) and focused on mission and justice. Websites provide prayer resources such as information and guides for prayer, providing information on various peoples, regions, or countries. And then there are special global days for prayer: the Women's Day of Prayer in March, a Day of Prayer and Fasting for World Evangelization, and Pentecost Sunday. In September there is the International Day of Prayer for Peace, in October the International Day of Prayer for the Peace of Jerusalem, in November the International Day of Prayer for the Persecuted Church, and during Ramadan, thirty days of prayer for the Muslim world.

Today, a central source of prayer information is the one-thousand-page *Operation World*, a dense compilation of data on each country of the world. Designed to enable individuals and groups for prayer, it has become a go-to site for enabling focused prayer. Nothing like it has ever existed before. What is important about this resource is that it comes out of a history of Christians believing that prayer is not something one does when you have nothing else to do, or an activity that holds together other items on the agenda. Rather,

> every prayer is a tiny piece of a great cosmic puzzle, which when fitted together will allow for the completion of the grand picture of the Almighty Lord's plan for humanity and the universe. We do not merely pray *about* the many points featured herein, we pray *toward* something, and that something is magnificent—the fulfillment of the Father's purpose and His Kingdom come.[2]

Prayer instead of bloodshed. The transition in South Africa from white minority power (over both the black and colored majority) is a remarkable story.[3] Political apartheid had evolved through the early twentieth century and came to full bloom in the 1960s. As its laws became more repressive and absurd, Nelson Mandela was among the leaders of a spreading underground resistance and was eventually convicted by the white courts. As the resistance grew into rebellion, the government finally realized that the laws needed changing and they eventually consulted Mandela while in prison. They promised him early release and the holding of general elections (held in 1994).

In 1990 the world watched and wondered as Mandela left his prison on Robben Island and boarded a ferry to cross to Cape Town. His peaceful presence, his measured words, his respect for his captors, and his carefully considered convictions showed that he was a leader of a different stripe. His mature wisdom and gracious manner suggested how he might someday govern.

This is the story we all saw and read. Behind it was another story less reported in the media. After decades of harsh rule the oppressed majority could have easily pursued retribution. Yet, their antagonisms were focused primarily on their own people, for the black community was divided. Mandela led the African National Congress (ANC) while Mangosuthu Buthelezi, chief of the large Zulu tribe, led the Independence Freedom Party (IFP). The two sides were at each other's throats, with killings a regular occurrence.

Christian leaders in South Africa saw that conflict was likely to happen and mobilized prayer for a peaceful resolution. At the same time the ANC and the IFP invited Henry Kissinger from the United States and Lord Carrington from Britain to assist in mediation. Adding to the foment was Buthelezi's threat to command a Zulu boycott of the coming election. This would mean that when Mandela was elected—a foregone conclusion—Buthelezi could then declare that the election was illegitimate, since a major tribe refused to participate. This would, in effect, position Mandela as a president without a mandate, an accusation that could rally the troops to further conflict at the very time the white laws of apartheid were crumbling. What was seen as a wonderful transition was turning into a frightful nightmare.

Michael Cassidy, the leader of African Enterprise, saw the futility of high-level mediation without God's intervention. He reached out to Washington Okumu, a Christian professor from Kenya called "the gentle giant," to join in negotiations.

On April 14, 1994, thirteen days before the election, Kissinger and Carrington left, boarding planes home, to the tune of Kissinger's prediction that a million people would die in what he saw as an inevitable civil war.

A stadium was rented in Durban as prayer meetings sprang up all over South Africa. While they were going on, Okumu worked all night with the IFP to find a way to avoid conflict. With an agreement in hand, he sped to the airport in Johannesburg to get Chief Buthelezi's endorsement, but arrived too late. The chief had already left; at least he thought he had. A few minutes into the flight his pilot told him that they had an instrument problem and had to return to Johannesburg.

Washington Okumu got his meeting with Buthelezi.

On April 17, twenty-five thousand people turned out for prayer at the Durban stadium, matched by smaller prayer groups around the country. In the VIP lounge, Washington Okumu and Buthelezi finally forged a settlement with President de Klerk: they hammered out a plan while thousands prayed for a peaceful settlement.

Ten days later, elections were held. The chief allowed his Zulu people to vote. Mandela was elected and not one person died from related intertribal conflict. The *Natal Daily News* led with the headline "How God Stepped In to Save South Africa" and quoted Buthelezi: "It was [as] though God had prevented me from leaving [Johannesburg], and I was there like Jonah, brought back. . . . My forced return was a godsend."[4]

The convergence of leadership, skill, and a will to pray brought change to a nation wracked by decades of cruelty. In the face of a threat so severe that the country could have been torn apart, Cassidy provided Christian leadership. Washington Okumu, a scholar of Christian faith, lent his considerable skill in negotiating. Thousands on thousands reached out in prayer for their nation, believing the Spirit would intervene in ways no one could predict. And God had his Cyrus, Mandela, to lead the people through the coming days.[5]

WOMEN IN MINISTRY

Ruth Thomson[6] stepped into society as a debutante in a white gown at the Governor General's Ball. She was nineteen in 1959, her Rosedale family part of Toronto high society. But her grand entrance and privilege didn't forecast her life.

After graduating from Tyndale University College, then Toronto Bible College, Ruth studied linguistics, and at twenty-five she headed off to the jungles of Brazil with a team of Wycliffe Bible Translators. Traveling by canoe, they settled in a village to begin the long and arduous task of living among the Kayapo, who "had a reputation for killing foreigners who strayed into their territory."[7] Ruth survived a variety of physical challenges: malaria, flesh-eating maggots, electric eels. She even helped bury a man killed by her adopted tribe because he had wandered into their territory. For five years she learned Kayapo words, helping to create a written language.

There is a remarkable story that is embedded in her journey. She has been one of tens of thousands of women, gifted, brave, tough, and resilient, with intellectual abilities and life-giving skills driven by a call to serve people in Christian witness. In an age when women were generally denied ministry status and opportunity by most churches, denominations, and agencies, compelled by vision, a calling of the Spirit, and an indomitable spirit, they found ways to live out their calling and utilize their skills.

Prevented from living out their callings at home, an important arena available to them was global mission. By the 1920s two-thirds of overseas missionaries from the United States were women. Doing an end run around church policy, their contributions to missions made them indispensible. Without them, most missions would have been greatly diminished in personnel and their effective outreach curtailed.

Single women were going to places and living in conditions many married couples would find intolerable, and agencies and church missions soon found they couldn't live without them. Even groups who viewed women in ministry leadership as "unbiblical" devised ways that opened doors without upsetting the male-headship views of churches back home. Ruth Thomson is emblematic of this amazing and potent global force.

By the end of the twentieth century many denominations recognized the reality and instituted public ordination for women. But mission agencies became the go-to place for women choosing full-time service.

A major divide. Debates continue to swirl over the biblical role of women in ministry and leadership. But what is hardly arguable is that from the early church forward women's influence on the presence and message of the gospel has been pivotal. Even though Christian communions have differed on the place of women in ministry, their involvement in mission, especially outside of congregational life and denominational management, has been a change agent in global evangelism.

While mission agencies were primarily run by men, once women arrived on the field—usually overseas from the sending country—they would end up as pastors, overseers, evangelists, field directors, and church planters.[8] Three women in Canada come to mind.

Soon after James and Ellen Hebden arrived from England in Toronto, they bought a building on Queen Street, converting it into what came to be called the Hebden Mission, known for an emphasis on the deeper life and divine healing. Ellen Hebden reported that on November 19, 1906, she received the infilling of the Holy Spirit with the evidence of speaking in tongues. With this modest beginning, Pentecostal groups began to dot the land. From that new outpouring, it can rightfully be said that she was one of the originators of what today is the largest of the Evangelical communities in Canada.

In 1911, evangelist Alice Bell Garrigus traveled from Boston, preaching at meetings in St. John's, Newfoundland. From that early Bethesda Pentecostal Church congregation, the cluster of churches formed a denomination in 1925 that now includes Labrador.

Following on from this influence, Aimee Semple McPherson—who was raised in southern Ontario, attending the Salvation Army with her mother—became perhaps the most famous evangelist of her time. Building the Angelus Temple in Los Angeles, her influence as preacher, helper of those in crisis, and radio speaker launched the International Church of the Foursquare Gospel, a global denomination.

Women and the Protestant missionary movement. In Vietnam, as in other countries, it took personal sacrifice to build the foundation of Christian witness. The Rev. Dang Van Sung and his wife, Mrs. Diep Thi Do, came in 1953 to the Stieng minority tribe in Binh Phuoc province. Just before communist forces captured the area in April 1975, he was taken prisoner and never heard from again. For six years Mrs. Diep went into hiding, unable and afraid to contact any local Christians. Eventually she surfaced, and one day while in the market she met some Christians. Recognizing her, they pled with her to become their pastor.

She did more than that. Battling the government, she pressed the communist state to open closed churches. In time they agreed.

In Phuoc Long she built a church seating two thousand, then the largest church building in the country, and when she died she was overseeing the construction of a three-story-high school building. At her funeral four thousand showed up, a manifest applause for a woman of faith, widow, pastor, and builder who called herself "only a little woman."[9]

Then we might think of Corrie ten Boom and her riveting testimony, the film *The Hiding Place*, and her extensive public ministry. In Haarlem, Holland, she and her family hid Jews from the invading Nazis. Her time in, and eventual release from, a concentration camp made her an example of the power of Christ in women. She became an exemplar of God's grace and mercy in the face of unspeakable evil. Her public presence spoke not only to her courage but also to the importance of women in ministry, be they ordained or not. To argue about those details now seems immaterial.

Outside of ecclesiastical rules and hierarchy, mission agencies emerged as volunteer initiatives unhindered in recruiting and sending those who fit the mission organization. This impulse brought to a fore the role of laypersons, again opening doors for women. Not being subject to the denominational litmus test of either formal theological training or gender, mission societies were free to recruit. Missiologist Tennent notes, "Even though the formal structure of the society had male leadership, women were often the lifeblood of the society in organizing meetings, recruiting missionaries, raising funds, mobilizing prayer, and in time, teaching about missions."[10]

The China Inland Mission (now called Operation Mobilization or OM) was founded by Hudson Taylor of England in 1865. It set the pattern for a new kind of mission program. Not concerned with matters such as ordination, Taylor mobilized as many as he could find.[11] Dubbed a "faith mission," it operated on the basis that one went without financial support, trusting in God for provision. Gender was not an issue. On his initial sojourn to China, of the fifteen missionaries who joined him, seven were single women. This was a pattern followed by a host of other missions into the twentieth century. By the turn of the century there were forty American women's mission societies, and more women were serving in American missions than men.[12]

Such recruitment wasn't driven by gender arguments or "feminist" theology. The debate wasn't over whether or not a woman could be considered a bona fide missionary, but about the heart and will to move out into foreign and difficult places. Some locations required education or medical skills to run schools or hospitals, but again the litmus test wasn't gender—it was the willingness to go and the evidence of being called.[13]

The influence of this mission force was irresistible. Andrew Walls notes that by "the end of the nineteenth century, women had changed the entire face of the Protestant missionary movement by sheer force of numbers."[14]

The missiological debate over the legitimacy of women in church leadership is now moot. As I write, Evangelical churches in Syria are filling pastoral vacancies with women, pulpits left empty by emigrating male pastors.[15] Rola Sleiman, a seminary graduate, was nabbed by the Tripoli Evangelical Church to serve as pastor. It was just seven years ago that the Fellowship of Middle Eastern Evangelical Churches—a group made up of fifteen denominations—agreed that women could request ordination.

PRAISE AND WORSHIP

Singing as an act of worship was woven into the fabric of the church from its earliest days. Gregory the Great, bishop of Rome, initiated what we call today Gregorian chants. Luther and his start-up church in Wittenberg, Germany, reverberated with lusty

bar tunes lifting newly written hymns as both teaching and cele-
bratory features of his Protestants. An enemy was heard to have
said, "Luther's songs have damned more souls than all his books
and speeches."[16] Isaac Watts, a Congregationalist, offered the
Psalms sung in meter. In the eighteenth century in England,
Charles Wesley, brother of John, founder of the Methodist Church,
was prolific, composing some of the songs most adored by Protestants, "And Can It Be That I Should Gain?," "Christ the Lord Is
Risen Today," "Hark! The Herald Angels Sing," "Jesus, Lover of My
Soul," and "O for a Thousand Tongues to Sing" among them.

The blind American songwriter Fanny Crosby injected into the
Protestant church world new material. Known as the Queen of
Gospel Song Writers, she wrote some eight thousand hymns and
gospel songs such as "Pass Me Not, O Gentle Saviour," "Blessed
Assurance," "Jesus Is Tenderly Calling You Home," "Rescue the
Perishing," and "To God Be the Glory."

But it was evangelist Dwight L. Moody and his musical associate Ira D. Sankey—building on the music of Luther, Watts,
Wesley, and Crosby, among others—who revolutionized worship
with a music style, contemporary and populist, bridging mass cho-
rales and intimate songs that could be sung when one was alone.
Their gospel hymns and songs became the standard fare for Protestant churches (especially Evangelicals) through much of the
twentieth century. Just two books, it is estimated, within fifty years
sold up to 80 million copies. Moody remarked that he was able to
give away more money from the Hymn Book Fund than the
wealthiest of businessmen he knew.[17]

Following on the heels, the Charismatic revival produced a new
form of praise and worship that infiltrated, in time, much of the
Evangelical and Pentecostal worlds.

It began first in California as "flower children" of the free-
speech-movement used popular music forms—like Luther had.

A rising cadre of young musicians, many recent coverts in a "Jesus movement" revival of faith, set their lyrics within its various rock idioms. Larry Norman's early song "Why Should the Devil Have All the Good Music?" evinced its typical edginess. A host of writers and singers, such as Bill and Gloria Gaither, merged the Southern gospel quartet format with newer musical versions and a burgeoning file of new songs. In England the Salvation Army *Joystrings* set loose a new stream of musical worship.

Central to this newly crafted music was a notion, first localized in Pentecostal and Charismatic churches, that in worship, extensive time would be given to singing songs and choruses, often repetitively, creating an environment where corporate and personal worship would activate faith. Often couched in subjective language and emphasizing personal encounter, it stresses a primary relationship with God. Absent are formal prayers and the use of creeds. At first it was more spontaneous, with leader and musician(s) able to move from one song to another. In time that moved to a worship or praise band, with multiple instruments (essential are guitars and drums), the team having rehearsed for worship, thus locking into an agenda that structured even spontaneity.

The late church growth professor Peter Wagner, then at Fuller in Pasadena, commented to me as we walked into a church in western Canada for a pastor's seminar, "I can tell by just walking into a church if it is growing or not: if it does or does not have drums." He saw drums as symbolic of whether or not churches had tapped into the popular culture and, on the basis of that, were able to attract younger people as part of a growing church. This was a typical Wagnerian use of metaphor to make a more substantive point.

In the 1980s, the Australian church Hillsong pioneered a form of contemporary worship, around which a music industry emerged linked to a leadership culture, congregational growth, a school for teaching music composition, and eventually church planting initiatives in Australia and globally. Their music seems almost ubiquitous: in North American and African churches, in youth gatherings and Sunday middle-class churches, listened to on iPods and sung in prisons. It is often listed in the top twenty-five songs most sung in countries that report to the CCLI,[18] selling some 11 million records.[19]

This growing-church worship phenomenon is multidimensional. The strength of its continuing growth is, as we've noted, a new understanding of the gifts and person of the Spirit, the revolutionary influence of the Scriptures in one's tongue and contemporary language, along with leaders—and in this discussion, locals—who understand the language, rhythm, cadence, and metaphors of their own world.

The multidimensional factors, not surprisingly, are integrated into the hearing, seeing, and feeling aspects of faith and belonging. The contemporary worship experience—an *experience* it is—is not for all. My wife and I have a Pentecostal worship heritage combined with classical music training. Contemporary music is not always easy for us to absorb, and at times does not seem helpful in faith building. So we too, at times, need to remind ourselves that younger (and other) generations get first consideration on style and form.

A friend asked if I liked or appreciated the worship music of the student-led chapel at Tyndale. I thought the conclusion obvious: to see hundreds of students in worship and praise to the Lord of their lives is more important than accommodation to *my* musical tastes. There are questions about the forms shaped by the many styles and configurations of contemporary worship. Issues of content are primary. What is evident in talking with worshipers and worship leaders is that content matters. The Bible stories and language that was basic to my worship content is in flux. Contemporary worship, focusing, it seems, on communion, interrelationships, and praise, uses language that on the surface might seem banal, but it lifts, embraces, and creates community in an often-hostile world.

All of this is a matter of the global church finding new wineskins from which the Spirit is poured out. As gospel music of past generations mutates into the next, this too will find different forms that fit the application of biblical faith to coming generations. The idea of the *indigenous* is not restricted to Bible translation nor to theology; it is inherent in all aspects of the gospel message and transmission. Jesus indwells, and that includes our forms of worship. He comes into our world, as it is, with media we understand, giving us entry into his holy of holies in a language conversant with our culture and understanding.

A HUMAN TIDAL WAVE: REFUGEES AND MIGRATION

For those who know their New Testament history, the harbor of Mitylene, on the Greek island of Lesbos, is where Paul the apostle landed when he sailed from Assos, Turkey, just a few kilometers across the Aegean Sea (Acts 20:14). Evangelical leader Nik Nedelchev and I traced the refugee highway from its point of arrival on Lesbos, up through Greece and the Balkans and into central Europe. We had already visited Iraq, Syrian refugee camps in northern Jordan, and Syrians and Iraqis in the Bekaa Valley on the Lebanon/Syria border. But here in Greece the arterial system that carried a million refugees in one year was clogged and suffering an uncertain future. As part of the World Evangelical Alliance (WEA), we knew it mattered that we walk their roads, bearing witness to ministries alleviating suffering and serving as a window on this escalating human tragedy.

This buildup of refugees didn't just happen. It has been growing, like a giant surging wave, breaking on the beaches of Europe. For years there has been a trickle of migrants from North Africa and the Middle East up through Greece (and some through Italy) seeking a better life in Europe. Then wars raged, creating not just economic migrants but "war" refugees. Assad began bombing his people, and ISIS infiltrated the heartland of Syria and swept into its clutches large swaths of Iraq. War, hunger, and a bleak future watered a resident seed of hope for a better life and the plant of human aspiration and desperation grew and blossomed.

The word got out—gossip swished down the refugee pipeline with unbelievable speed, enabled by ubiquitous smartphones. Greece was "opening its doors," it was said, allowing refugees who reached its shore to go on through to the north. Germany would make itself home to a million refugees. Anyone wanting to escape their homeland moved quickly.

This human tide funneling through Greece and Italy into central Europe raises tough issues for both migrants and governments. First, governments didn't see this coming. The buildup of refugees exacerbated by wars in North Africa and the Levant expanded into a full-blown movement. But war is only one contributing factor. Those who wanted a better job (or a job at all) or who were longing for a place in which to raise a family dropped everything, risking all.

Second, when waves of people move in vast numbers, who can stop them? The pressure of their presence, the sheer numbers and public picture of desperate people present such a picture that governments find it almost impossible to deny help. When news flashed around the world of a little Syrian boy lying dead on the shore of Lesbos, governments wilted, a picture ironically that became media fodder in the generating of good will.

There had been no such flow of refugees since World War II. This demographic shift will take decades to decipher. The proportion of people on the move not only alters the country they left but those they will inhabit. Core to concerns was infiltration by terrorists, seeking to locate in countries in which they can do harm. While this is a legitimate concern, terrorists probably won't wait around in refugee lines. When humans surge in such numbers, the world has no choice but to accept such a reality and find ways to both accommodate need and mitigate harm.

The stories of refugees are ancient. Hebraic law recognizes the frailty of a refugee. They are desperate, afraid, and vulnerable to abuse and treachery: "When a foreigner resides among you in your land, do not mistreat them. The foreigner residing among you must be treated as your native-born. Love them as yourself, for you were foreigners in Egypt" (Lev 19:33-34).

Jews knew what it was like and so did Jesus, fleeing murderous King Herod, living as a refugee in Egypt. It is not surprising the Hebrew Scriptures link refugees with widows and orphans who deserve and require protection.

Major global population shifts are altering our planet. People are on the move everywhere. The Internet has made the world known. News of where one might go and how to get there is known in a flash. Hopes and dreams are powerful drivers, and with the sharp divide between the quality of life from nation to nation, people will endure unimaginable conditions to reach their desired goal.

I asked a Greek guard in full riot gear, guarding the gate from Greece into Macedonia, how he saw the situation: "Hope always rules," he noted. I then asked him about solutions. "Fences never solve problems," he wisely reflected. A diplomat could not have been so exact or judicious.

The "hows" and "wheres" of refugee settlements are sociopolitical decisions governments will make. Most of us won't have much to say about that. What we can do is follow the biblical call. Not only are we called to give special attention to refugees, but this also provides the opportunity to care for them, and in the love of our Lord build goodness and truth into their lives. The Spirit takes our offer of friendship and by so doing makes known the Savior who called us to attention with the two great laws: love God with everything you have and your neighbor as yourself.

A caveat. Here feet and hands do the talking. In desperate situations, it is telling who shows up. In the places we visited on the refugee highway, the missions we met included Euro Vision (a humanitarian service of Hellenic Ministries), Samaritan's Purse, Child Evangelical Fellowship, Agape (a ministry of Campus Crusade), the Seventh-day Adventists, Caritas, Youth With A Mission (YWAM), World Vision, World Relief, and many local church ministries. While most refugees on this highway are Muslim, Islamic agencies seemed almost absent, except in Macedonia, where Muslims make up 20 percent of the population. The Office of the United Nations High Commissioner for Refugees was impressive in their organization, presence, and quality of service.

Two dividing factors shape this conversation. First is how it affects me and my family, community, and country. If population movements are seen as a threat, they become offensive, something to prevent or avoid. In December 2015 I met in Wheaton, Illinois, with some 150 leaders of mission agencies and church denominations as the refugee issue was boiling over. I had just followed refugees north from Lesbos through Greece, some of whom got across the border into Macedonia, then Serbia. As the only non-American, at first I didn't understand the evident dissonance I sensed in the room. Speaker after speaker told of challenges they faced. Canada, with its new prime minister, had just days before met a Syrian family at the airport, welcoming them to their new country. Our country was in a kind of euphoria over the thirty thousand arriving refugees. But in this meeting I understood these leaders were taking it on the chin from their churches and constituencies over housing refugees. In their localities it had become a threat. Their dilemma was how to reframe the issue from one of national concerns—over not enough jobs or terrorist threats—to a biblical call to care for the stranger.

It wasn't that Canada is more hospitable in nature than the United States; both began and continue to be domiciles for immigrants. And with our low birth rates, we both need sizeable immigration to maintain our populations. However, in that time, US citizens and the Christian (in this case Evangelical) community were unprepared for receiving those out of the Syrian conflict. There was a critical difference. Americans had experienced 9/11. Canada hadn't.

Two stories recall the two-sided face of this migration of peoples. A mom and dad sat in a tent on the north side of the Greece/Macedonia border. Because they were from Syria, they had been allowed through the exit gate of Greece, onto a refugee trail that would eventually land them in one of the countries that had opened their doors. They had sat the entire night but were content. The memories of killing, fleeing, leaving behind everything they owned, including other family members and friends, was, for the moment, held at arm's length by the increased promise that they were finally on their way. Their future seemed hopeful, at least in light of their flight from the only land they had known.

A day earlier I had stood at the other side of the gate, on the south side, just inside Greece, and spoke with a father from Cameroon, Africa. He introduced me to his wife and the seven children he had brought with him. They had traveled up across Africa, moving north through Chad, Libya, Egypt, Jordan, Syria, and Turkey, then across the Aegean Sea into Greece. Three months it had taken. But they were now stuck. Not being designated "war refugees"—which meant being from Syria, Iraq, or Afghanistan—they were refused exit from Greece, which meant they were not allowed to settle in a country in Europe. He had used every kind of transportation he could find and finally in Turkey had bargained with smugglers to get them across the sea in an inflatable raft to a Greek island—all to no avail. They couldn't go any farther.

Which claim is more legitimate? With the hundreds of thousands of refugees, it is difficult to find a just and fair answer. What we do know is that people today are on the move, and as I learned from this Cameroon father, neither cell nor fence will stop them. This is the context for ministry in the global age.

PERSECUTION

Persecution made front-page stories as ISIS murdered its way across Iraq and Syria, exploding suicide bombs that were both targeted and yet indiscriminate. Human-rights groups, governments, and Christian communities are vigilant in putting before the world this bitter reality.

In this context we ask Tertullian's question when he was defending Christians to his provincial governor in the late second century—is the blood of the martyrs really the seed of the church? So we again ask today, is persecution and martyrdom a deterrent to the spread of the gospel, or an accelerant?

Glenn Penner of Voice of the Martyrs notes, "It would be naïve to say . . . that persecution always leads to church growth or an openness to the gospel."[20] We can only really say that the outcomes are almost never as the persecutor intends.

A century ago, 25 percent of Turkey was Christian. Today that figure is less than one percent. The blood of Christians seemingly trickled away, hardly offering itself as "seed" to the church. Yet in Albania, where not only Christians but also Muslims were persecuted and religion was outlawed completely, today the church thrives. The same case can be made for countries such as China and Cambodia.

Identifying martyrs in today's world. There are two methods used to identify the numbers of Christians martyred for their faith. The Center for the Study of Global Christianity estimates that each year ninety thousand Christians are martyred. Their definition of a martyr is "believers in Christ who have lost their lives prematurely, in situations of witness, as a result of human hostility."[21] The important phrase is "in situations of witness." For example, in the

Armenian genocide, where a million and half were killed in the early part of the last century, most victims were Orthodox Christians, and they died because of their Christian faith and thus are to be considered martyrs. This basis leads to the estimate that up to a million Christians were killed in the decade from 2000 to 2010.

The top ten countries on the most recent Open Doors World Watch list of Christian martyrdom are Nigeria (2,073), Syria (1,479), Central African Republic (1,115), Pakistan (228), Egypt (147), Kenya (85), Iraq (84), Myanmar (33), Sudan (33), and Venezuela (26).[22] These numbers from 2014, representing a recent sixteen-month period, are conservative, registering only confirmed deaths. Many more occur without being reported.

The other method to identify martyrs are those put on trial, killed by a mob, or targeted for death because they stood for their faith, and because of that offense were killed. Using this more narrow definition, it is quite impossible to give statistics. Even so, estimates are that up to ten thousand Christians are killed in a year because their faith makes them targets.

While martyrdom is the ultimate form of persecution, persecutions come in a variety of forms and at varying degrees. For a working definition, Penner of Voice of the Martyrs puts it this way: "Where Christians are repetitively, persistently and systematically inflicted with grave or serious suffering or harm and deprived of (or significantly threatened with deprival of) their basic human rights because of a difference that comes from being a Christian that the persecutor will not tolerate."[23] The countries with the most extreme persecution, again from Open Doors World Watch, are North Korea, Somalia, Afghanistan, Sudan, Syria, Iraq, Iran, Yemen, and Eritrea.[24] The United States Commission on International Religious Freedom (USCIRF) has listed Russia as one of the worst violators against religious freedom. Its recent report notes its sharp curtailing of "religious minorities, missionaries and evangelists."

They also identify sixteen countries as "countries of particular concern" (CPC).[25]

Why this increase of persecution and killings? In the past fifty years there has been a global religious whiplash: communism collapsed and Christianity and Islam rapidly expanded to make a cumulative two-thirds of the world's population. Escalating conflicts between these faith communities is a mark of today's world, with increased tensions, increased persecution and, tragically, the killing of Christians.

Kinds of persecution. Persecution is not an occasional annoyance inflicted by media, government, or neighbors, but rather a systemic, ongoing harassment that deprives Christians of the ability to live out their faith. This is quite different from what those of us in Christian-majority countries might face, where growing secularity makes it difficult to express our faith outside of a church or Christian community. The persecution we speak about here goes beyond that of discomfort to a more insidious offense.

Jesus did warn us of this. In sending his disciples, he told them of the various levels of persecution they would face, from modest to extreme: they would be prevented ("will not welcome you," Mt 10:14). They would be rejected ("or listen to your words," Mt 10:14), detained ("handed over . . . arrest you," Mt 10:17, 19), abused ("flogged," Mt 10:17), pursued ("persecuted," Mt 10:23), and even killed ("kill the body," Mt 10:28).[26] Follow this short list of contemporary matters affecting Christians:

- ▶ A pastor in Turkey told me that to have your own place of worship matters in a Muslim country. People wonder what you believe if you don't have a place in which to worship. The government's refusal to allow for the building or buying of buildings for churches in effect is a very real form of persecution.

- ▶ A man in Egypt whispered to me of his faith in Christ, but said that if his family knew, it would destroy them.

▶ In countries such as Egypt, Syria, Iraq, and Yemen, churches are burned to the ground, and without a police investigation their insurance will not be paid.

▶ House churches in Hangzhou, China, were forced to close to make ready for the meeting of the G20 in 2016 and not allowed to reopen. They in time found other places for worship.

▶ Often it will be a mob that attacks a church in countries such as Pakistan and Egypt, Nigeria and Syria; groups driven by fanaticism bomb, burn, or chase out Christians.

▶ In other countries such as Iran, the courts intimidate, charge, or imprison pastors, generating fear among congregations and sending a powerful signal to others—don't have anything to do with Christians.

We do not even have numbers for North Korea, the most closed of countries, where the estimated three hundred thousand Christians are frequently subjected to concentration camps.

Different forms of persecution. Along with the levels of persecution noted by Jesus, there are various forms of oppressive personal experience.

▶ *Communism.* Five countries continue under this ideological banner—North Korea, Laos, Vietnam, China, and Cuba. There is an uneven application of government laws restricting freedom to minister, with North Korea being a special case. Pastors and congregations are aware and careful, having learned the ways and means of their political masters, seeking peaceful ways to effect witness.

▶ Some countries of the old Soviet Union occasionally ratchet up laws and rules making it difficult for churches to register and dangerous for Christian witness. Kazakhstan leaders have for years tried to establish their center of Bible training, yet the government raises all sorts of regulations, while at the same time requiring their pastors to hold credentials from a recognized school. Because they can't construct one in their home country, they're forced to graduate from a school in Moscow.

▶ *Religious nationalism.* Countries such as Turkey are driven by the politics of national identity and religious consciousness. Being a Turk is increasingly synonymous with being a Sunni Muslim. The same is true in India, where laws are being introduced that make it difficult for Christians and Muslims to operate in free discourse of their faith. India's BJP party seems fixed to intensify its pressure on creating provinces in which Hindu nationalism rules.

> ▶ This is not restricted to non-Christian faiths. Evangelicals and Roman Catholics in Greece and Russia labor under restrictions and inconveniences as these states, in lockstep with the Orthodox Church, create a national identity so that to be Greek or Russian, one is automatically Orthodox.

▶ *Extreme Islam.* Countries such as Iran, Iraq, Pakistan, and Saudi Arabia are oppressive, to the point of criminalizing Christian faith and its exercise. They go beyond national identity. They embrace the extreme, so that if one is outside of their strict and narrow interpretation of Islam, you can be considered an *infidel.* There are other less extreme countries of Islamic majority such as Malaysia and Indonesia. Even so, Christians in Malaysia cannot use *Allah*, the Arabic word for God, as used by Muslims.

▶ *Secular intolerance.* Separation of church and state, as a chosen secular innovation, has moved up the scale to increasingly mean that faith has no place in the secular square whatsoever. The increased intolerance within social and civic arenas, public universities, and publically owned media intensifies exclusion, offering a form of intolerance that in some cases can be seen as crossing the line.

The effects of persecution. I arrived in Cairo, Egypt, just days after ISIS had beheaded twenty-one Egyptians in Libya. To the surprise of the Muslim community, mothers of the slain men went on television and offered forgiveness to the killers of their sons. Pastors said that the next week Muslims attended their churches, women in their customary clothing, intrigued to know why Christians were so forgiving. Story after story surfaced of young Muslims, humiliated by the radical conclusions of their fellow believers, inquiring with interest about the gospel. Here tragedy, faced by loving and gracious Coptic mothers, opened doors beyond what any form of evangelistic initiative might have achieved.

What implications and effects will persecution have on the witness of Christ? While it might seem callous to review the *benefits* of persecution, given its historical and ongoing reality, we want to understand its effect on the role of witness and faith. As the churches in the Middle East understand, martyrdom and suffering are intrinsic to the witness of Christ in the world.

▶ It fosters a believing heart. Christians, caught in a myriad of imposed don'ts, learn instead to practice the presence of Jesus. This discovered dependence could lead to an intimacy that those of us in places of privilege know little about.

▶ It can create a servant's heart, a deep recognition that as Jesus came to serve, so in the midst of oppression and opposition one learns to live that out in their constraining world. The antithesis of confrontation, it can deflate the assumed sense of right projected by those in control. It is the powerful, transforming note of providential irony. I observed a young pastor in a communist-country church, most visible to the party, with obvious cordial relations. I wondered how this came about. After his appointment as pastor, he found the party official assigned to oversee his church was offensive and derogatory. So one day he asked, "Why do you oppose everything I do? You are so mean to me. Why is that?" This opened a conversation. The communist official told him of serious difficulties in his family and the pressure he was getting from his superiors. From this conversation came a new relationship and freedom for ministry in the city, and from there, across the country.

▶ It deepens trust in the Spirit. What one can't do when in prison or when restricted by groups surrounding one's witness, the Spirit is at work, doing even things we might never learn of.

▶ As we saw with the expulsion of missionaries from China in 1948–1949, it nurtures an inner-dependent church, as congregations learn how to foster personal and confidential bonding. Radical isolation gave the church roots so deeply planted that surrounding restrictions only served to fuel growth.

Surprising resources. It wasn't unexpected, so when the secret police arrived asking for Paul Negrut, he knew his time had come.[27] When some of his Christian friends had been swept up in Nicolae Ceauşescu's nets, Paul knew for him it would just be a matter of time.

It was in the 1980s. The general secretary of the Communist Party in Romania was modeling his regime after Stalin, creating what was considered the most repressive country in Europe.

What Paul didn't know was that scores of people, even among the closest of his colleagues and friends, were linked into the surveillance network of the Securitate, informing on him.

One day, after six months of incarceration, a senior guard showed up asking Paul, "Who do you know higher up?" Not knowing why the question was asked, Paul said, "I have God." The official retorted, "Don't give me any of that. Who do you have on your side in Bucharest?" Again Paul simply said, "God." He barked, "Well, get your things, you are leaving." He arrived home, but the "why" of being released was unanswered. As often happens, prayer was at work.

Several months earlier, a Canadian working in Romania had heard of Paul's arrest and went to their apartment asking Paul's wife for a photo of him. Composing a letter to Canadian prime minister Brian Mulroney, he described the stifling oppression and lack of religious freedom, never sure if his letter would ever reach the prime minister's desk in Ottawa.

Canada was the producer of the Candu nuclear reactor being built in Romania, which required professionals to move back and forth between Canada and Romania. Bilateral talks necessitated President Ceauşescu's visits to Canada. On one occasion, the prime minister in private reached into his briefing file and pulled out the picture of Paul that had been sent to him and asked, "Why is this pastor in prison?" Unnerved by this unexpected confrontation, within hours Ceauşescu sent a curt message to Bucharest: "Get Negrut out."

EPILOGUE

Global Reflections

THE WORLD I KNEW IN MY EARLY YEARS is no longer with us. Waves of change continue to wash around the globe, bringing what prophets of any sort could never have foreseen. We've examined two monstrous tides that hit with unpredicted force: secular assumptions—which continue to affect much of life in the West—and the rise of personal faith and its impact on society, shifting much of the landscape in the Global South.

This southward move of Christian witness is reshaping the church, bringing new ideas, challenging ethics, renewing faith in some places, and introducing the gospel message and presence to new areas. The shift of the center of gravity of the global church to Timbuktu—a place many are surprised to learn is a real city, and not just a metaphor for remoteness—is a sharp reminder that the West is no longer the center and source of Christian ideas and leadership. As church movements grow and expand increasingly through sub-Saharan Africa, Latin America and Asia, the center of density will shift even farther south from Timbuktu.

What this means for the church might not seem obvious to most today, but as Africa, Latin America, and Asia grow in Christian concentration, from those centers will emerge insights and understanding of the biblical message that will enrich, upset, and in some cases rub raw against centuries-old assumptions of the Western church. As the Spirit inspires and enlightens our brothers and sisters, they will help us see what those from European origins and cultures never saw. Their nuancing of the biblical story, birthed through their own experiences and cultural ethos, will enrich the entire church. Like it or not, the global shifts will bring them and their Christian witness back into our worlds. May we in the West exercise humility as we learn from them!

The growing power of nations in the Global South creates new pathways—economic, educational, and political. The former military masters are no longer unquestioned by those they once dominated. Along these pathways Christians from those nations will make their way, bringing with them not only their cultural assumptions, engrained patterns of life, and ways of seeing the world, but also their witness of Christ. Imagine what the church will look like in fifty years as the Christian communities in countries such as China, Brazil, and Nigeria grow, become more influential in their respective worlds, and push their way out from their centers, driven by that same missionary impulse that drove historical missions. They read the same Scriptures, are filled by the same Spirit, and live within the same grand story of Christ coming to buy back a lost world, a world he is carrying into the great and final day. Indeed the relative newness of this gospel in their worlds seems to invigorate and motivate them more than those whose cultures reside comfortably in the presence of the historical church. Like new converts alive in newfound faith, their enthusiasm and commitment to tell others is unbounded. That's what much of the Global South feels like.

Missions will continue, but now in the manner of mutually enriching, globally mobile partnerships, helping build up indigenous leadership and funding agencies of all sorts. Some newer mission-sending countries will soon learn, if they have not already, that simply dropping their own national patterns into another setting won't work. Indigenized leadership will look different, as countries mix their populations by way of migration. The location of the Global South will also change, with urbanization and the emergence of global elites. There are parts of the United States, the Rust Belt for example, where life experiences might be closer to some places in Africa than they are to New York. For the increasing number of humans who are migrants of one sort or another, their *next* generations, knowing only the place of their growing up, will themselves be the new "indigenous ones." The role of mission changes as it has since the apostle Paul set out from Jerusalem. But because its inherent impulse is biblical, driven by the Spirit, it will continue in different variations. We can expect that by the overall growth of the church, mission will have even more presence and force.

Living in the midst of this resurgence, we can't help but wonder: will it carry on? Spiritual enthusiasm undulates, rising and falling, moving from a high and slipping into indifference. Heat seems inevitably to cool, passion to fade. But given that the growing element of Christianity today is within the Pentecostal and Charismatic community, and that renewal and revival are part and parcel of its makeup, we might well ask, are we on the cusp of something new and different?

As the force of the Spirit is felt through so much of the world, the future of Christian witness in the West can be seen in three possible ways: as a victim of growing secularization, as the first fruits of revival, and as a renewal of today's generations as occurred in the Great Awakenings or an awakening of the next generation. Economic and social upheavals have ways of returning people to spiritual reflection, embracing its message. Who can predict? The intensity of growth of the last hundred years might slow but then accelerate in places and ways we can't anticipate. Theorists such as Arjun Appadurai, for example, think that one of the hidden surprises of globalization is the emergence of unexpected local Christianities. As the Word reaches more people through its continuing translation and via indigenous churches and ministries, we can expect new and vigorous ideas and pervasive grassroots movements.

Inevitably, serving in the public sectors of nations will act as an aspiration both for vocational opportunities and, increasingly, as a venue for expressing faith and its contingent influence on society. Of course, by the very nature of the contemporary church, there will continue to be aberrations as well. As we've already seen, life in the public square is a minefield. We must seek to be wiser than previous generations—learning from their mistakes and catastrophes, understanding the particular dynamics of the public square. We must learn how to discern and promote God's will for the country and the role of the Christian community without trying to enforce a Christian mind or meld the gospel with nationalism. It behooves us to remember Jesus' metaphors, which outline how we should live in society: as salt and light.

Increased concern over the well-being of people is becoming embedded in churches and in missions. A heart for those in need and the importance of developing strategies and creating sustainable realities for ongoing life is mushrooming beyond what most of us have ever imagined. The Evangelical church's absence of hierarchy and its structures modeled on horizon-based networks mean there are fewer borders or constraints. This surely creates more factions, anomalies, and manifestations that might cause some to squirm. Yet its freedom and openness is also its strength:

a group believing they are led by the Spirit need not wait for permission from its "Vatican" to proceed.

Jesus has always been global. This is his world. He is everywhere. The early message, released from Jerusalem, in time traversed to all regions of the world. The nature of his going global is incarnational. The difference today from that early first-century going is that the witness of Jesus is now located in most peoples and tribes. Going global—and continuing that going—is the inherent nature of the message of life framed by the gospel, the good news made known by Jesus of Nazareth.

.

ACKNOWLEDGMENTS

I CANNOT COUNT the many whose ideas and influences have shaped my faith, directed me vocationally, and inspired me to pursue an active role in the public witness of Jesus Christ. In writing this book, I draw on memories and readings, attempting to faithfully record sources, quote excerpts, and identify those I have relied on in working out the arguments for this global account of contemporary Christianity.

As the bibliography shows, there are many whose ideas and insights have fueled my thinking. Let me note a few whose scholarship has been especially foundational: David J. Bosch, Philip Jenkins, Lamin Sanneh, Timothy T. Tennent, and Andrew F. Walls.

I am grateful to the Missions Commission of the World Evangelical Alliance, in recent years chaired by William D. Taylor, Bertil Ekström, and David Ruiz. This commission links missiologists, scholars, and practitioners in their research, critical to work of contemporary missions.

I want to give particular thanks to Mark Hutchinson for his invaluable suggestions on content, his remarkable resourcefulness in research, his editorial skills in helping smooth out the text, and for his companionship in making this book more readable. We had worked together on an editorial team that produced *Evangelicals Around the World: A Global Handbook for the 21st Century*, and I came to learn of his amazing knowledge of the Christian world, its history, people, movements, and trends.

Bert Hickman has been so very helpful in providing research, checking facts, assisting in finding sources and contacts, and providing editorial assistance.

I also thank Todd Johnson for his careful reading of the manuscript and for his suggestions.

Al Hsu, editor at InterVarsity Press, together with his colleagues posed questions that helped unleash new ideas and a more thorough reflection. Mark and Janet Sweeney not only oversaw the placement of the book with InterVarsity Press, but offered substantial help in creating the structure, choosing a title, and being friends along the way.

During the past years in serving the World Evangelical Alliance, my assignment as global ambassador has allowed me to take globally what I had been learning in my home country. I'm especially grateful to its senior leadership, Secretary General Bishop Efraim Tendero, for his encouragement in research and writing.

Lily has been faithfully supportive. To her I express my thanks for a like-minded heart, which has allowed us for decades to live out our dreams and vision in service together.

Through my years of service, friends have provided support for ministry and investment in projects and opportunities. Without your encouragement, this quite remarkable opportunity to work with leadership globally could not be undertaken. My deepest thanks for your belief in the worthiness of ministry and for your gracious and generous support in our journey together.

With that, I accept responsibility for what has been written.

NOTES

PREFACE

[1]As quoted in Jason Mandryk, *Operation World* (Downers Grove, IL: Inter-Varsity Press, 2010), 6.

1 FAITH IS ON THE RISE

[1]This and the next paragraph are adapted from Brian Stiller, "Human Tidal Wave," *The Christian Post*, January 27, 2016, http://m.blogs.christianpost.com/dispatches-from-the-global-village/human-tidal-wave-27131/.

[2]Tara Brian and Frank Laczko, *Fatal Journeys*, vol. 2, *Identification and Tracing of Dead and Missing Migrants* (Geneva: International Organization for Migration, 2016), 5.

[3]"Majority of Americans Report Experience of God's Love Leads to Increased Benevolence," Religion News Service, December 18, 2012, http://religionnews.com/2012/12/18/majority-of-americans-report-experience-of-gods-love-leads-to-increased-benevolence/.

[4]Todd M. Johnson and Kenneth R. Ross, eds., *Atlas of Global Christianity* (Edinburgh: Edinburgh University Press, 2009), 53.

[5]Peter Berger, "A Bleak Outlook Is Seen for Religion," *New York Times*, April 25, 1968, 3.

[6]Peter L. Berger, ed., *The Desecularization of the World: Resurgent Religion and World Politics* (Grand Rapids: Eerdmans, 1999), 2.

[7]Ibid., 2.

[8]E.g., Vincent Pecora, *Secularization and Cultural Criticism: Religion, Nation, and Modernity* (Chicago: University of Chicago Press, 2006).

[9]For an academic survey of this movement, see Preston Shires, *Hippies of the Religious Right* (Waco, TX: Baylor University Press, 2007).

[10]Lucy Battersby, "Census Change: Is Australia Losing Its Religion?," *Sydney Morning Herald*, August 28, 2015; Daniel Burke, "Millennials Leaving Church in Droves, Study Finds," CNN, May 14, 2015, www.cnn.com/2015/05/12/living/pew-religion-study/index.html.

[11]Pew Research Center, "America's Changing Religious Landscape," Pew Forum, May 12, 2015, www.pewforum.org/2015/05/12/americas-changing-religious-landscape/.

[12]Gina A. Zurlo, "Introduction to Regional Graphics," in *Evangelicals Around the World: A Global Handbook for the 21st Century*, ed. Brian C. Stiller et al. (Nashville: Thomas Nelson, 2015), 235.

[13]John C. Kerr, "Evangelicals in Southern Africa," in Stiller et al., *Evangelicals Around the World*, 255.

[14]Fenggang Yang, "When Will China Become the World's Largest Christian Country?," *Slate*, www.slate.com/bigideas/what-is-the-future-of-religion/essays-and-opinions/fenggang-yang-opinion.

[15]It has developed churches in the city and suburbs that many left the mother church to attend. The central church now is closer to six hundred thousand.

[16]This paragraph is adapted from Brian Stiller, "Nepal: A Nation with More Than Mountains," *WEA News*, October 16, 2012, http://worldea.org/news/4106/nepal-a-nation-with-more-than-mountains-by-brian-stiller.

[17]Rodney Stark, *The Triumph of Faith* (Wilmington, DE: ISI Books, 2015), 67-68.

[18]Ibid., 72-73.

[19]Ed Stetzer, "Survey Fail—Christianity Isn't Dying," *USA Today*, updated May 14, 2015, www.usatoday.com/story/opinion/2015/05/13/nones-americans-christians-evangelicals-column/27198423/.

[20]Pew, "America's Changing Religious Landscape."

[21]Stetzer, "Survey Fail."

[22]Timothy Keller and Max Anderson, "A Conversation with Tim Keller on Gospel Movements," *Timothy Keller Sermons Podcast by Gospel in Life*, podcast audio, July 25, 2016, https://itunes.apple.com/us/podcast/timothy-keller-sermons-podcast-by-gospel-in-life/id352660924?mt=2.

[23]Pew Research Center, "Millennials Are Increasingly Driving Growth of 'Nones,'" May 12, 2015, www.pewresearch.org/fact-tank/2015/05/12/millen nials-increasingly-are-driving-growth-of-nones.

[24]Monica Toft, Daniel Philpott, and Timothy Shah, *God's Century: Resurgent Religion and Global Politics* (New York: W. W. Norton & Company, 2011), 8.

[25]This is the position also of leading theologian Amos Yong (*Discerning the Spirit(s): A Pentecostal-Charismatic Contribution to Christian Theology of Religions* [Sheffield, UK: Sheffield Academic Press, 2000]), who notes the impact that a repositioning toward the study of the Spirit has on ecumenical and global engagement.

[26]Jonathan Goforth, *By My Spirit* (Grand Rapids: Zondervan Publishing House, 1942), 28.

2 THE AGE OF THE SPIRIT

[1]See Seth N. Zielicke, "The Role of American Evangelist Tommy Hicks in the Development of Argentine Pentecostalism," in *Global Pentecostal Movements: Migration, Mission, and Public Religion,* ed. Michael Wilkinson (Boston: Brill, 2012), 140-41. See also Tommy Hicks, *Millions Found Christ: History's Greatest Recorded Revival* (Los Angeles: International Headquarters of Tommy Hicks, 1956), xx. Many reports provide varying details to this story.

[2]Wilma W. Davies, *The Embattled but Empowered Community: Comparing Understandings of Spiritual Power in Argentine Popular and Pentecostal Cosmologies* (Boston: Brill, 2010), 95.

[3]T. David Beck, *The Holy Spirit and the Renewal of All Things: Pneumatology in Paul and Jürgen Moltmann* (Cambridge: James Clarke, 2015), 1.

[4]Ibid.

[5]Referenced by Samuel Escobar in *Changing Tides* (Maryknoll, NY: Orbis Books, 2002), 102, from Emil Brunner, *The Misunderstanding of the Church*, trans. H. Knight (London: Lutterworth, 1952).

[6]See John C. Pollock and Ian Randall, *The Keswick Story: The Authorized History of the Keswick Convention* (Fort Washington, PA: CLC Publications, 2006).

[7]Lynn D. Kanaga, "The Ministry of the Holy Spirit in Church History, 1550 to 1900 A.D. (Part 2)," *Enrichment Journal Online*, Summer 2011, http://enrichmentjournal.ag.org/201103/201103_000_Holy_Sp.cfm, quoting William R. Moody, *The Life of D. L. Moody* (New York: Fleming H. Revell, 1900), 149.

[8]The best book on this remains the remarkable work of Jon Ruthven, *On the Cessation of the Charismata: The Protestant Polemic on Postbiblical Miracles* (Sheffield, UK: Sheffield Academic Press, 1993, with subsequent updates).

[9]Much of the scholarship after the 1970s provided fuel for many to reconsider this position. See, e.g., Chris Forbes, *Prophecy and Inspired Speech in Early Christianity and Its Hellenistic Environment* (Tübingen: Mohr-Siebeck, 1995); Ruthven, *On the Cessation of the Charismata*; Stanley M. Burgess, *The Holy Spirit: Ancient Christian Traditions* (Grand Rapids: Baker Publishing Group, 1990).

[10]Timothy Tennent, *World Missions: A Trinitarian Missiology for the Twenty-First Century* (Grand Rapids: Kregel Publications, 2010), 419.

[11]See Carroll Stegall Jr. and Carl C. Harwood, *The Modern Tongues and Healing Movement* (Denver: Western Bible Institute, 1950) and W. G. Broadbent, *The Doctrine of Tongues* (Paeroa, New Zealand: Eldon Press, ca. 1950).

[12]Richard J. Foster, *Streams of Living Water: Essential Practices from the Six Great Traditions of Christian Faith* (New York: HarperCollins, 2001), 116.

[13]Authors such as Donald W. Dayton (*Theological Roots of Pentecostalism* [Grand Rapids: Baker Academic, 1987]), Edith L. Blumhofer (*Restoring the Faith: the Assemblies of God, Pentecostalism, and American Culture* [Urbana: University of Illinois Press, 1993]), Grant Wacker (*Heaven Below: Early Pentecostals and American Culture* [Cambridge, MA: Harvard University Press, 2003]), Barry Chant (*The Spirit of Pentecost: The Origins and Development of the Pentecostal Movement in Australia, 1870–1939* [Lexington, KY: Emeth Press, 2011]), Allan Anderson (*An Introduction to Pentecostalism: Global Charismatic Christianity* [Cambridge: Cambridge University Press, 2014]), and Mark Hutchinson and John Wolffe (*A Short History of Global Evangelicalism* [Cambridge: Cambridge University Press, 2012]) have demonstrated a rising tide of pneumatological practice—if not among the theologians, at least among those concerned about the decline of the church in the face of a secularizing West.

[14]David Hempton, *Methodism: Empire of the Spirit* (New Haven, CT: Yale University Press, 2005).

[15]Joel A. Carpenter, *Revive Us Again: The Reawakening of American Fundamentalism* (New York: Oxford University Press, 1999), 81-82.

[16]For a sense of its global impact, see D. N. Livingstone and R. A. Wells, *Ulster-American Religion: Episodes in the History of a Cultural Connection*

(Notre Dame, IN: University of Notre Dame Press, 1999); Steven Maughan, "Imperial Christianity? Bishop Montgomery and the Foreign Missions of the Church of England, 1895–1915," in *The Imperial Horizons of British Protestant Missions, 1880–1914*, ed. Andrew Porter (Grand Rapids: Eerdmans, 2003), 32-57. For studies of one of its key centers in the USA, see James H. Moorhead, *Princeton Seminary in American Religion and Culture* (Grand Rapids: Eerdmans, 2012) and D. G. Hart and R. Laurence Moore, *The Lost Soul of American Protestantism* (Lanham, MD: Rowman & Littlefield, 2004).

[17] Ronald F. Satta, *The Sacred Text: Biblical Authority in Nineteenth-Century America* (Eugene, OR: Wipf and Stock, 2007), 7-8.

[18] Kevin J. Vanhoozer, *Is There a Meaning in This Text? The Bible, the Reader, and the Morality of Literary Knowledge* (Grand Rapids: Zondervan, 2009), 316.

[19] Stanley M. Burgess, ed., *The Holy Spirit: Medieval Roman Catholic and Reformation Traditions* (Grand Rapids: Baker Books, 1994).

[20] Harvey Cox, *Fire from Heaven* (Cambridge, MA: Da Capo Press, 1995), 105.

[21] Donald Gee, "The Emotions of God: A Sermon Preached in Richmond Temple on Sunday Night, May 6, 1928, by Pastor Donald Gee," *Australian Evangel*, July 1928, 2, http://webjournals.ac.edu.au/ojs/index.php/AEGTM/article/view/6980/6977.

[22] Tim Grass, *Edward Irving: The Lord's Watchman* (Milton Keynes, UK: Paternoster, 2011); David Malcolm Bennett, *Edward Irving Reconsidered: The Man, His Controversies, and the Pentecostal Movement* (Eugene, OR: Wipf & Stock, 2011).

[23] Arthur H. Matthews, *Standing Up, Standing Together: The Emergence of the National Association of Evangelicals* (Carol Stream, IL: National Association of Evangelicals, 1992).

[24] Wayne A. Grudem, ed., *Are Miraculous Gifts for Today? 4 Views* (Grand Rapids: Zondervan, 2011).

[25] Cox, *Fire from Heaven*, 81-82.

[26] Ibid, 82.

[27] Ibid., 101.

[28] There were, of course, exceptions to this. Some proto-Charismatics saw the baptism as a third work of grace rather than a second, while others added other signs as alternatives to tongues. The largest Pentecostal denomination in the world, however, the Assemblies of God, represents a core emphasis on the initial evidence of tongues.

[29] Such as B. B. Warfield at Princeton Theological Seminary.

[30]Mark Hutchinson, "'Going the Other Way Around': Catholic Contributions to the Emerging Pentecostal Norm in Australia," *PentecoStudies* 12, no. 1 (Spring 2013): 32-61.

[31]James Hanrahan, "The Nature and History of the Catholic Charismatic Renewal in Canada," *Sessions d'étude—Société canadienne d'histoire de l'Église catholique* 50, no. 1 (1983): 318.

[32]Tom Smail, Andrew Walker, and Nigel Wright, *Charismatic Renewal: The Search for a Theology* (London: SPCK, 1993).

[33]See, for instance, Rhodian G. Munyenyembe, *Christianity and Socio-Cultural Issues: The Charismatic Movement and Contextualization of the Gospel in Malawi* (Luwinga, Malawi: Mzuni Press, 2011); Michael Poon and Malcolm Tan, eds., *The Clock Tower Story: The Beginnings of the Charismatic Renewals in Singapore* (Singapore: Trinity Theological College, 2012); Edward L. Cleary, *The Rise of Charismatic Catholicism in Latin America* (Gainesville: University Press of Florida, 2011).

[34]See, for instance, the work of Peter Hocken, particularly *Streams of Renewal: Origins and Early Development of the Charismatic Movement in Great Britain* (Carlisle: Paternoster Press, 1997) and his more recent *Azusa, Rome, and Zion: Pentecostal Faith, Catholic Reform, and Jewish Roots* (Eugene, OR: Pickwick Publications, 2016).

[35]Todd Johnson, "The Global Demographics of the Pentecostal and Charismatic Renewal," *Sociology* 46 (2009): 479-83.

[36]Center for the Study of Global Christianity, *Christianity in Its Global Context, 1970–2020: Society, Religion, and Mission* (South Hamilton, MA: CSGC, 2013), 7-8.

[37]Rodney Stark, *The Triumph of Faith* (Wilmington, DE: ISI Books, 2015), 77.

[38]Ibid.

[39]Pablo A. Deiros, "Evangelicals in Latin America," in *Evangelicals Around the World*, ed. Brian Stiller et al. (Nashville: Thomas Nelson, 2015), 290.

[40]Statistics taken from Jason Mandryk, *Operation World* (Downers Grove, IL: InterVarsity Press, 2010), 46-48.

[41]Stark, *Triumph of Faith*, 83.

[42]Phyllis Tickle, *The Great Emergence* (Grand Rapids: Baker Books, 2008), 16.

[43]David Martin, *Pentecostalism: The World Their Parish* (Oxford: Blackwell Publishers, 2002), 1.

[44]Ibid., 6.

[45]Ibid., 24.

3 THE POWER OF BIBLE TRANSLATION

[1]Enrico Sartorio, *The Social Religious Life of Italians in America* (Boston: Christopher Publishing House, 1918).

[2]Adrian Hastings, *The Construction of Nationhood: Ethnicity, Religion and Nationalism* (New York: Cambridge University Press, 1997); Mark Noll, *In the Beginning Was the Word: The Bible in American Public Life, 1492–1783* (New York: Oxford University Press, 2015); Nathan O. Hatch and Mark A. Noll, eds., *The Bible in America: Essays in Cultural History* (New York: Oxford University Press, 1982).

[3]Andrew Walls, *The Missionary Movement in Christian History* (Maryknoll, NY: Orbis Books, 1996), 28.

[4]Jörg Haustein, *Writing Religious History: The Historiography of Ethiopian Pentecostalism*, Studien zur Außereuropäischen Christentumsgeschichte (Asien, Afrika, Lateinamerika) 17 (Wiesbaden: Harrassowitz, 2011).

[5]Hugh Kemp, *Steppe By Step* (London: Monarch Books, 2000), 486.

[6]Quoted in Rodney Stark, *The Triumph of Faith* (Wilmington, DE: ISI Books, 2015), 114.

[7]Philip Jenkins, *The New Faces of Christianity: Believing the Bible in the Global South* (New York: Oxford University Press, 2006), 19.

[8]"Orality," Lausanne Movement, www.lausanne.org/networks/issues/orality; "Who Are Oral Learners?," International Orality Network, https://orality .net/about/who-are-oral-learners/.

[9]Walls, *Missionary Movement in Christian History*, 29.

[10]Hilmar M. Pabel and Mark Vessey, eds., *Holy Scripture Speaks: The Production and Reception of Erasmus' Paraphrases on the New Testament* (Toronto: University of Toronto Press, 2002); Geoffrey R. Treloar, *Lightfoot the Historian: The Nature and Role of History in the Life and Thought of J. B. Lightfoot (1828–1889) as Churchman and Scholar* (Tübingen: Mohr Siebeck, 1998).

[11]Lamin Sanneh, *Whose Religion Is Christianity? The Gospel Beyond the West* (Grand Rapids: Eerdmans, 2003), 98.

[12]Simon Coleman and John Elsner, *Pilgrim Voices: Narrative and Authorship in Christian Pilgrimage* (New York: Berghahn Books, 2003).

[13]Sanneh, *Whose Religion Is Christianity?*, 130.

[14]Gleason L. Archer and Gregory C. Chirichigno, *Old Testament Quotations in the New Testament: A Complete Survey* (Chicago: Moody, 1983), 25-32.

[15]Sanneh, *Whose Religion Is Christianity?*, 99.

[16]Hastings, *Construction of Nationhood,* 4.

[17]Sanneh, *Whose Religion Is Christianity?,* 111.

[18]Ibid.

[19]Badra Lahouel, "Ethiopianism and African Nationalism in South Africa Before 1937," *Cahiers d'études africaines* 26, no. 104 (1986): 681-88.

[20]Clifford Kyaw Dwe, "Tha Byu, Ko," in *A Dictionary of Asian Christianity,* ed. Scott W. Sunquist (Grand Rapids: Eerdmans, 2001), 829-30.

[21]Sidney H. Rooy, "Penzotti, Francisco G. (1851–1925)," in *Biographical Dictionary of Christian Missions,* ed. G. H. Anderson (New York: Macmillan Reference USA, 1998), 526.

[22]Sanneh, *Whose Religion Is Christianity?,* 60.

[23]"Then I saw a Lamb, looking as if it had been slain, standing at the center of the throne, encircled by the four living creatures and the elders," Rev 5:6 NIV.

[24]Walls, *Missionary Movement in Christian History,* 28.

[25]Jenkins, *New Faces of Christianity,* 26.

[26]Godwin N. Toryough, "The Biblical Ethics of Work: A Model for African Nations," *Verbum et Ecclesia* 31, no. 1 (November 23, 2010), available at www .ve.org.za/index.php/VE/article/view/363/479; J. M. Vorster, "Managing Corruption in South Africa: The Ethical Responsibility of Churches," *Scriptura* 109 (2012): 133-47.

[27]See Edward Oyugi et al., "A Tale of Unfulfilled Promises: Kenya, National Report," Social Watch, 1999, www.socialwatch.org/node/10657.

[28]Walter Scheidel, "The Roman Slave Supply," in *The Cambridge World History of Slavery,* vol. 1, *The Ancient Mediterranean World,* ed. Keith Bradley and Paul Cartledge (Cambridge: Cambridge University Press, 2011), 291-92.

[29]Lamin Sanneh, *Disciples of All Nations* (Oxford: Oxford University Press, 2008), xx.

[30]Claudia Orange, *The Treaty of Waitangi* (Auckland, NZ: Bridget Williams Books, 2015).

[31]David B. Barrett, *Schism and Renewal in Africa: An Analysis of Six Thousand Contemporary Religious Movements* (Nairobi: Oxford University Press, 1968), 129.

[32]Sanneh, *Whose Religion Is Christianity?,* 25.

[33]Kenneth E. Bailey, *Poet & Peasant and Through Peasant Eyes* (Grand Rapids: Eerdmans, 1976); *Jesus Through Middle Eastern Eyes* (Downers Grove, IL: InterVarsity Press, 2008).

[34]"Key Facts About the Bible Access," United Bible Societies, 2017, www .unitedbiblesocieties.org/key-facts-bible-access/. Figures are as of December 31, 2016.

[35]"Best-Selling Book of Non-fiction," Guinness World Records, www.guinness worldrecords.com/world-records/best-selling-book-of-non-fiction/ (last accessed January 2, 2017).

[36]José Chambilla, "Progress of Bible Translation," www.jose-lisa.com/main /index.php/ministry/progress-bible-translation.

[37]Second Vatican Council, *Dogmatic Constitution on Divine Revelation* Dei Verbum *Solemnly Promulgated by His Holiness Pope Paul VI on November 18, 1965* (English translation), chapter 6, article 22, www.vatican.va/archive /hist_councils/ii_vatican_council/documents/vat-ii_const_19651118_dei -verbum_en.html.

[38]Todd M. Johnson and Gina A. Zurlo, "The Changing Demographics of Global Anglicanism, 1970–2010," in *Growth and Decline in the Anglican Communion: 1980 to the Present*, ed. David Goodhew (New York: Routledge, 2017), 46-50. The exception to this statement is in London, where migrant Charismatic churches are strong, and in those areas where deliberate Charismatic/Evangelical "overplanting" has taken place.

[39]John Quanrud, *Besë, shpresë dhe dashuri* (Tirana, Albania: Kartë e Pende, 1996); other data compiled from the website of the Institute for Albanian and Protestant Studies, http://instituti.org/blog.

[40]Richard Howell, "The Hindu Missionary Movements and Christian Missions in India," in *Global Missiology for the 21st Century*, ed. William D. Taylor (Grand Rapids: Baker Academic, 2000), 413.

[41]Ibid.

4 REVOLUTION OF THE INDIGENOUS

[1]Allan Anderson, *Bazalwane: African Pentecostals in South Africa* (Manualia Didactica) (Pretoria: Unisa Press, 1992).

[2]Terence O. Ranger, *Evangelical Christianity and Democracy in Africa* (New York: Oxford University Press, 2008), 208.

[3]Ibid., 209.

[4]Ibid., 212.

[5]Ibid.

[6]Douglas Field, "Pentecostalism and All That Jazz: Tracing James Baldwin's Religion," *Literature & Theology* 22, no. 4 (December 2008): 436-57. This is not to say that the connections were direct—merely that they swam in the same ocean and there is evidence of convergence.

[7]David Garrison, *A Wind in the House of Islam* (Monument, CO: WIGTake Publishers, 2014), 244.

[8]William A. Smalley, "Cultural Implications of an Indigenous Church," *Practical Anthropology* 5 (1958): 55. Missiologists would go on to redefine *indigenous* using *contextualization* to expand the idea to be more inclusive of the cultural effect on message, person, and outworking. Smalley was an American linguist, anthropologist (at Bethel College in St. Paul), and missionary to the Hmong.

[9]Timothy C. Tennent, *World Missions: A Trinitarian Missiology for the Twenty-First Century* (Grand Rapids: Kregel Publications, 2010), 425.

[10]*Renewalist* is a term referring to classical Pentecostals (including denominations), progressive Pentecostals, Charismatics, hyphenated Charismatics such as Charismatic Catholics, and independent churches.

[11]Quoted in Mark Hutchinson and John Wolffe, *A Short History of Global Evangelicalism* (Cambridge: Cambridge University Press, 2012), 234.

[12]Roland Allen, *The Spontaneous Expansion of the Church—and the Causes Which Hinder It* (Eugene, OR: Wipf and Stock Publishers, 1997), 42.

[13]Quoted in Sidney J. W. Clark, *The Indigenous Church* (London: World Dominion Press, 1928) and noted in Lamin Sanneh, *Disciples of All Nations* (Oxford: Oxford University Press, 2008), 233.

[14]A phrase used by Sanneh, *Disciples of All Nations*, 234.

[15]Steven Rutt, "An Analysis of Roland Allen's Missionary Ecclesiology," *Transformation: An International Journal of Holistic Mission Studies* 29, no. 3 (2012): 200.

[16]Jillian K. Melchior, "Leading China's Christian Awakening," *Wall Street Journal*, February 21, 2012, www.wsj.com/articles/SB100014240529702033 58704577234813382139048.

[17]Tobias Brandner, "Trying to Make Sense of History: Chinese Christian Traditions of Countercultural Belief and Their Theological and Political Interpretation of Past and Present History," *Studies in World Christianity* 17, no. 3 (2011): 216-36.

[18]Rick Strelan, *Strange Acts: Studies in the Cultural World of the Acts of the Apostles* (Berlin: Walter de Gruyter, 2004), 155.

[19]Ellen Barry and Suhasini Raj, "Major Christian Charity Is Closing India Operations amid a Crackdown," *New York Times*, March 7, 2017, www.ny times.com/2017/03/07/world/asia/compassion-international-christian -charity-closing-india.html.

[20]Richard Fletcher, *The Barbarian Conversion: From Paganism to Christianity* (Berkeley: University of California Press, 1999).

[21]Rodney Stark, *The Rise of Christianity: A Sociologist Reconsiders History* (Princeton, NJ: Princeton University Press, 1996), 95-98.

[22]N. Ben-Yehuda, *Theocratic Democracy: The Social Construction of Religious and Secular Extremism* (Oxford: Oxford University Press, 2010), 91.

[23]Andrew Walls, *The Missionary Movement in Christian History* (Maryknoll, NY: Orbis Books, 1996), 8.

[24]Ibid.

[25]Ibid., 13.

[26]Ibid.

[27]This includes classical Pentecostals and Charismatics in the Protestant, Roman Catholic, and Orthodox traditions.

[28]Tennent, *World Missions*, 423.

[29]Robbie B. H. Goh, "Christian Capital: Singapore, Evangelical Flows and Religious Hubs," *Asian Studies Review* 40, no. 2 (April 2016): 250.

[30]Sanneh, *Disciples of All Nations*, 219.

[31]The next three paragraphs are adapted from Brian C. Stiller, "The Difficulty of Evangelizing in Thailand," *Huffpost*, May 8, 2013, www.huffingtonpost .com/brian-c-stiller/the-difficulty-of-evangelizing-in-thailand_b_3237160 .html.

[32]Personal interview, Bangkok, 2013.

5 RE-ENGAGING THE PUBLIC SQUARE

[1]William Wilberforce, *A Practical View of the Prevailing Religious System of Professed Christians, in the Higher and Middle Classes, Contrasted with Real Christianity* (New York: American Tract Society, 1830), 6.

[2]Joel Majonis, "William Wilberforce and Thomas Chalmers: Development of Evangelical Christian Thought and Practices into Methodical Charities," *Journal of Religion and Spirituality in Social Work: Social Thought* 26, no. 2 (June 2007): 63-89.

[3]Markku Ruotsila, *The Origins of Christian Anti-internationalism: Conservative Evangelicals and the League of Nations* (Washington, DC: Georgetown

University Press, 2008); Neil Southern, "Evangelical Journeys: Choice and Change in a Northern Irish Religious Subculture," *Journal of Contemporary Religion* 28, no. 3 (October 2013): 542-44.

[4]Ibid.

[5]The language of "contract" is an explicit one in much American literature, though obviously the Rousseauian concept of the social contract has European roots. For "breaches" of the contract, and resultant changes in Evangelical voting patterns, see Allen D. Hertzke and John David Rausch Jr., "The Religious Vote in American Politics: Value Conflict, Continuity, and Change," in *Broken Contract? Changing Relationships Between Americans and Their Government*, ed. Stephen C. Craig (Boulder, CO: Westview Press, 1996), 183-85.

[6]Notable exceptions to this rule are (the older) towns in New England and the Southwestern United States, where the church (Congregational and Roman Catholic, respectively) held a prominent place in both individual and corporate life.

[7]Ronald Sider, *Just Politics: A Guide for Christian Engagement* (Grand Rapids: Brazos, 2012).

[8]Paul Freston, *Evangelicals and Politics in Asia, Africa and Latin America* (Cambridge: Cambridge University Press, 2001), 14.

[9]Pew Research Center, "America's Changing Religious Landscape," Pew Forum, May 12, 2015, www.pewforum.org/2015/05/12/americas-changing -religious-landscape/.

[10]Some authors see the term *mainline* or *mainstream* as now outdated and unrepresentative of the religious profile in the West. Mainline Protestantism remains a strong tradition in northern Europe, but is gradually losing its presence in the USA and many other countries, often rendering Protestantism increasingly as Evangelical in nature.

[11]Terence O. Ranger, ed., *Evangelical Christianity and Democracy in Africa* (New York: Oxford University Press, 2008), 10.

[12]J. F. Haldon, *Byzantium in the Seventh Century: The Transformation of a Culture* (New York: Cambridge University Press, 1990), 441.

[13]R. J. Neuhaus, *The Naked Public Square* (Grand Rapids: Eerdmans, 1984).

[14]Abraham Kuyper, inaugural address at the dedication of the Free University. In *Abraham Kuyper: A Centennial Reader*, ed. James D. Bratt (Grand Rapids: Eerdmans, 1998), 488.

[15]Owen Chadwick, *The Early Reformation on the Continent* (Oxford: Oxford University Press, 2001), 381.

[16]See M. Hutchinson, "Westbrook, George Gordon (Don) (1898–1966)," *Australasian Dictionary of Pentecostal and Charismatic Movements*, http://web journals.ac.edu.au/ojs/index.php/ADPCM/article/view/230/227; Grant Wacker, *Heaven Below: Early Pentecostals and American Culture* (Cambridge, MA: Harvard University Press, 2003).

[17]Angela Tarango, *Choosing the Jesus Way: American Indian Pentecostals and the Fight for the Indigenous Principle* (Chapel Hill: University of North Carolina Press, 2014); Adoyi Onoja, "The Pentecostal Churches: Spiritual Deregulation Since the 1980s," in *Religion in Politics: Secularism and National Integration in Modern Nigeria*, ed. Julius O. Adekunle (Trenton, NJ: Africa World Press, 2009), 262-73; Rosalind I. J. Hackett and Benjamin F. Soares, eds., *New Media and Religious Transformations in Africa* (Bloomington: Indiana University Press, 2015).

[18]Stephen Offutt, *New Centers of Global Evangelicalism in Latin America and Africa* (New York: Cambridge University Press, 2015), 33.

[19]Virginia Garrard-Burnett, *Protestantism in Guatemala: Living in the New Jerusalem* (Austin: University of Texas Press, 1998); and Garrard-Burnett, *Terror in the Land of the Holy Spirit: Guatemala Under General Efrain Rios Montt 1982–1983* (New York: Oxford University Press, 2011), 3.

[20]Heidi Dahles, "In Pursuit of Capital: The Charismatic Turn Among the Chinese Managerial and Professional Class in Malaysia," *Asian Ethnicity* 8, no. 2 (2007): 89-109.

[21]Shane Clifton and Jacqueline Grey, *Raising Women Leaders: Perspectives on Liberating Women in Pentecostal and Charismatic Contexts* (Chester Hill, NSW: Australasian Pentecostal Studies, 2009).

[22]A global Anglican community founded on the Jerusalem Statement, and the Declaration of 2008; www.gafcon.org.

[23]Empowered21 (E21): http://empowered21.com.

[24]Michael J. McVicar, *Christian Reconstruction: R. J. Rushdoony and American Religious Conservatism* (Chapel Hill: University of North Carolina Press, 2015).

[25]Ranger, *Evangelical Christianity and Democracy in Africa*, 85.

[26]Rachel Beatty Riedl, "Transforming Politics, Dynamic Religion: Religion's Political Impact in Contemporary Africa," *Africa Conflict and Peacebuilding Review* 2, no. 2 (2012): 41.

[27]Ibid.

[28]David W. Throup and Charles Hornsby, eds., *Multi-party Politics in Kenya: The Kenyatta and Moi States and the Triumph of the System in the 1992 Election* (Oxford: James Currey, 1998).

[29]Riedl, "Transforming Politics, Dynamic Religion," 44.

[30]Freston, *Evangelicals and Politics in Asia, Africa and Latin America*, 158.

[31]Riedl, "Transforming Politics, Dynamic Religion," 44.

[32]Ibid., 45.

[33]Freston, *Evangelicals and Politics in Asia, Africa and Latin America*, 11.

[34]Dom Phillips and Nick Miroff, "In Brazil's Political Crisis, a Powerful New Force: Evangelical Christians," *Washington Post*, May 26, 2016.

[35]There is debate as to whether or not the "tent" of Evangelicals is wide enough to include this church and its heresy-tending doctrines or its accumulation of large sums of money, some of which is owned directly by its senior pastor Edir Maçedo.

[36]"Brazilian Elections: Marina Silva Opposes Gay Marriage," Telesur, August 31, 2014, www.telesurtv.net/english/news/Brazilian-Elections-Marina-Silva-Opposes-Gay-Marriage-20140831-0015.html.

[37]"Poder, religião e preconceito. A ascensão política dos evangélicos" (Power, religion and prejudice: The political rise of Evangelicals), *Agência Pública*, March 20, 2017, http://apublica.org/2017/03/poder-religiao-e-preconceito-a-ascensao-politica-dos-evangelicos/.

[38]Marcos Simas and Carlos Fernandes, "Brazil's Presidential Drama Reflects Political, Denominational Divides," *Christianity Today*, July 15, 2016.

[39]Phillipps and Miroff, "In Brazil's Political Crisis, a Powerful New Force."

[40]Joshua Young-gi Hong, "Evangelicals and the Democratization of South Korea," in *Evangelical Christianity and Democracy in Asia*, ed. David H. Lumsdaine (Oxford: Oxford University Press, 2009), 189.

[41]See "Reshaping the Evangelical Mind" in chapter 6.

[42]Hong, "Evangelicals and the Democratization of South Korea," 190.

[43]Ibid., 191.

[44]Ibid., 209.

[45]Freston, *Evangelicals and Politics in Asia, Africa and Latin America*, 67.

[46]Hong, "Evangelicals and the Democratization of South Korea," 215.

[47]Peter J. Schraeder, "State Regulation of Religion and the Role of Catholicism in Democratic Transitions and Consolidation in Predominantly Catholic Countries," in *Democracy, Culture, Catholicism: Voices from Four*

Continents, ed. Michael J. Schuck and John Crowley-Buck (New York: Fordham University Press, 2016), 302.

[48]David S. Lim, "Consolidating Democracy: Filipino Evangelicals Between People Power Events, 1986–2001," in Lumsdaine, *Evangelical Christianity and Democracy in Asia*, 239.

[49]Donald E. Miller and Tetsunao Yamamori, *Global Pentecostalism: The New Face of Christian Social Engagement* (Berkeley: University of California Press, 2007), 127.

[50]Lim, "Consolidating Democracy," 242.

[51]Noted in Schraeder, "State Regulation of Religion," 302-3.

6 THE POWER OF THE WHOLE GOSPEL

[1]David Mensah, *Kwabena: An African Boy's Journey of Faith* (Belleville, ON: Essence Publishing, 1998).

[2]Then called Ontario Bible College/Ontario Theological Seminary.

[3]Telephone conversation, December 2016.

[4]"Church Growth" GRID & NEA website, https://grid-nea.org/what-we-do/church-growth/.

[5]See, e.g., George Eldon Ladd, *A Commentary on the Revelation of John* (Grand Rapids: Eerdmans, 1972) and *A Theology of the New Testament Gospel of the Kingdom: Scriptural Studies in the Kingdom of God* (Grand Rapids: Eerdmans, 1974).

[6]Roger E. Olson, *The Story of Christian Theology: Twenty Centuries of Tradition and Reform* (Downers Grove, IL: InterVarsity Press, 1999), 88-90.

[7]Mark Sweetnam and Crawford Gribben, "J. N. Darby and the Irish Origins of Dispensationalism," *Journal of the Evangelical Theological Society* 52, no. 3 (September, 2009): 569.

[8]Postmillennial doctrine operated from the assumption that Christ would come after a thousand-year period, during which the gospel witness would advance and the kingdom of Christ be established on earth.

[9]Reforming theologians, such as F. D. Maurice, wrote between "the 1830s' high water mark of the Newman-led Tractarians to the later impact of Darwinism." C. Brad Faught, review of *Maurice and the Crisis of Christian Authority*, ed. Jeremy Morris, *Anglican and Episcopal History* 75, no. 4 (December 2006): 612.

[10]What the Evangelical "biblical" defense missed in opposing Darwin was that the twentieth century would unfold within the context of a biological

revolution. Darwin, Evangelicals might engage or ignore. But what they could not ignore was mass death in the World Wars, the discovery of penicillin and its countless ensuing medical innovations, or the discovery of DNA and the consequences of the Human Genome Project. These completely changed the context of speaking about relevance and truth in this century.

[11]William Carey went to India in 1793 after writing the great conspectus for Protestant world mission in his *Enquiry into the Obligations of Christians to Use Means for the Conversion of the Heathens.*

[12]In its 2015 Annual Report, World Vision International notes expenditures of more than US $2.4 billion for "community development, humanitarian and emergency affairs, advocacy and other programmes" (30). Available online at www.wvi.org/sites/default/files/20161030_WVIAnnualReview .pdf.

[13]Express News Service, "In the Name of the Cow: Murder, Flogging, Humiliation of Muslims, Dalits," *The Indian Express*, August 5, 2016, http:// indianexpress.com/article/explained/gujarat-dalit-protests-una-gau-rak shaks-mohammad-akhlaq-modi-govt-2954324/.

[14]Amos Yong, *The Future of Evangelical Theology: Soundings from the Asian American Diaspora* (Downers Grove, IL: InterVarsity Press, 2014), 49.

[15]*Winning the War Against Poverty*. Quoted in Katherine Attanasi and Amos Yong, eds., *Pentecostalism and Prosperity: The Socio-Economics of the Global Charismatic Movement* (New York: Palgrave Macmillan, 2012), 42.

[16]This sees future promise as being for today. If one sees everything as "not yet"—that is, in the future—it may be the same as seeing the future promise as never coming to pass.

[17]Allan Anderson, "Pentecostal Approaches to Faith and Healing," *International Review of Missions* 91, no. 363 (October 2002): 530.

[18]Bryant L. Myers, "Progressive Pentecostalism, Development, and Christian Development NGOs: A Challenge and an Opportunity," *International Bulletin of Missionary Research* 39, no. 3 (July 2015): 115-20.

[19]Attanasi and Yong, *Pentecostalism and Prosperity*; Dena Freeman, ed., *Pentecostalism and Development: Churches, NGOs and Social Change in Africa* (Basingstoke: Palgrave Macmillan, 2012).

[20]Freeman, *Pentecostalism and Development*, 2.

[21]Myers, "Progressive Pentecostalism, Development, and Christian Development NGOs," 117.

[22]Meaning that the effect of the gospel message in changing people and their behaviors brings about a moral, social, and economic lifting of life and well-being.

[23]Myers, "Progressive Pentecostalism, Development, and Christian Development NGOs," 117.

[24]Freeman, *Pentecostalism and Development*, 12-13.

[25]Ibid.

[26]Nimi Wariboko, "Pentecostal Paradigms of National Economic Prosperity in Africa," in Attanasi and Yong, *Pentecostalism and Prosperity*, 41.

[27]Paul Freston, "Prosperity Theology: A (Largely) Sociological Assessment," Lausanne Movement, October 2, 2015, https://www.lausanne.org/content/prosperity-theology-a-largely-sociological-assessment.

[28]David Martin, *Pentecostalism: The World Their Parish* (Malden, MA: Blackwell Publishers, 2002), 72.

[29]Ibid., 73.

[30]Max Roser and Esteban Ortiz-Ospina, "Global Extreme Poverty," Our World in Data, 2013, revised March 27, 2017, https://ourworldindata.org/extreme-poverty/.

[31]*Under the Radar: Pentecostalism in South Africa and Its Potential Social and Economic Role*, Centre for Development and Enterprise, March 2008, www.cde.org.za/under-the-radar-pentecostalism-in-south-africa-and-its-potential-social-and-economic-role.

[32]Ibid., 31.

[33]Martin, *Pentecostalism*, 170-71.

[34]Peter Berger, *Facing Up to Modernity* (New York: Basic Books, 1977), 177. Quoted in *Under the Radar*, 32.

[35]Martin, *Pentecostalism*, 73.

7 WHOLENESS

[1]See J. Edwin Orr, "The Role of Prayer in Spiritual Awakening," 1976, www.kneillfoster.com/articles/RevivalTruths/roleofprayer.html.

[2]"Understanding Prayer in Light of God's Kingdom," Operation World, www.operationworld.org/understanding-prayer-light-gods-kingdom. Operation World gives current material on a variety of topics, country by country.

[3]This section is adapted from Brian Stiller, "An Untold Story Behind Mandela—Dispatch from South Africa," *WEA News*, May 20, 2014, http://

worldea.org/news/4393/an-untold-story-behind-mandela-dispatch-from
-south-africa-by-brian-stiller.

[4]*Natal Daily News*, May 2, 1994.

[5]Brian Stiller, *An Insider's Guide to Praying for the World* (Minneapolis: Bethany Publishers, 2016), 20-23.

[6]Joe O'Connor, "Debutante in the Jungle," *National Post*, http://news.national post.com/features/when-the-debutante-met-the-tribe.

[7]Ibid.

[8]Timothy C. Tennent, *World Missions: A Trinitarian Missiology for the Twenty-First Century* (Grand Rapids: Kregel Publications, 2010), see 270-74.

[9]Reg Reimer, *Vietnam's Christians: A Century of Growth in Adversity* (Pasadena, CA: William Carey Library, 2011), 59-60.

[10]Tennent, *World Missions*, 271.

[11]Ibid.

[12]Ibid., 273, quoting Ruth A. Tucker, *From Jerusalem to Irian Jaya: A Biographical History of Christian Missions* (Grand Rapids: Zondervan, 1983), 288.

[13]Andrew Walls, *The Cross-Cultural Process in Christian History: Studies in the Transmission and Appropriation of Faith* (Maryknoll, NY: Orbis Books, 2002), 231.

[14]Ibid., 231-32.

[15]Griffin Paul Jackson, "Female Pastors Bring Hope to War-Torn Middle East Churches," *Christianity Today*, May 1, 2017, www.christianitytoday.com /women/2017/may/female-pastors-bring-hope-war-torn-middle-east -churches.html.

[16]Kennedy Adarkwa, "The Role of Music in Worship," *Modern Ghana*, July 24, 2015, www.modernghana.com/news/631897/the-role-of-music-in -worship.html.

[17]Donald Hustad, "D. L. Moody and Church Music," in *Mr. Moody and the Evangelical Tradition*, ed. Timothy George (New York: T&T Clark International, 2004), 113.

[18]CCLI, https://us.ccli.com/. Christian Copyright Licensing International links churches and copyright owners around the world, relating to copyrights of Christian worship songs.

[19]Hillsong Music/Shout! Music, "Who Is Hillsong Music Australia?," https:// distribution.hillsong.com/help/about.

[20]Glenn Penner, "Is the Blood of the Martyrs Really the Seed of the Church?," Voice of the Martyrs Canada, www.vomcanada.com/download/seed.pdf.

[21]Todd M. Johnson, "The Case for Higher Numbers of Christian Martyrs," Gordon-Conwell Theological Seminary, www.gordonconwell.edu /resources/documents/csgc_Christian_martyrs.pdf.

[22]"Nigeria Tops Christian Persecution Violence List: New Open Doors Report," Open Doors, June 3, 2014, www.opendoorsusa.org/take-action /pray/nigeria-tops-christian-persecution-violence-list/.

[23]"Persecuted Nations Defined," Voice of the Martyrs Canada, www.vom canada.com/restricted-nations-defined.htm.

[24]"World Watch List," Open Doors, www.opendoorsusa.org/christian -persecution/world-watch-list/.

[25]Kate Shellnut, "For the First Time, Russia Ranked Among Worst Violators of Religious Freedom," *Christianity Today*, April 26, 2017, www.christianity today.com/gleanings/2017/april/uscirf-ranks-russia-worst-violators-religious -freedom-cpc.html.

[26]Marvin Newell, "In the Context of World Evangelism," in *Sorrow and Blood: Christian Mission in Contexts of Suffering, Persecution, and Martyrdom*, ed. William Taylor, Antonia van der Meer, and Reg Reimer (Pasadena, CA: William Carey Library, 2012), 92.

[27]A conversation the author had with Paul Negrut.

BIBLIOGRAPHY

Allen, Roland. *The Spontaneous Expansion of the Church—and the Causes Which Hinder It*. Eugene, OR: Wipf and Stock, 1997.

Anderson, Allan. *Bazalwane: African Pentecostals in South Africa*. Manualia Didactica. Pretoria: Unisa Press, 1992.

———. *An Introduction to Pentecostalism: Global Charismatic Christianity*. Cambridge: Cambridge University Press, 2004.

———. "Pentecostal Approaches to Faith and Healing." *International Review of Missions* 91, no. 363 (October 2002): 523-34.

Archer, Gleason L., and Gregory C. Chirichigno. *Old Testament Quotations in the New Testament: A Complete Survey*. Chicago: Moody, 1983.

Attanasi, Katherine, and Amos Yong, eds. *Pentecostalism and Prosperity: The Socio-Economics of the Global Charismatic Movement*. New York: Palgrave MacMillan, 2012.

Bailey, Kenneth E. *Jesus Through Middle Eastern Eyes*. Downers Grove, IL: InterVarsity Press, 2008.

———. *Poet & Peasant and Through Peasant Eyes*. Grand Rapids: Eerdmans, 1976.

Barnett, Mike, ed., and Robin Martin, asst. ed. *Discovering the Mission of God: Best Missional Practices for the 21st Century*. Downers Grove, IL: InterVarsity Press, 2012.

Barrett, David B. *Schism and Renewal in Africa: An Analysis of Six Thousand Contemporary Religious Movements.* Nairobi: Oxford University Press, 1968.

Barrett, David B., and Todd M. Johnson. *World Christianity Trends, AD 30–AD 2200: Interpreting the Annual Christian Megacensus.* Pasadena, CA: William Carey Library, 2001.

Barry, Ellen, and Suhasini Raj. "Major Christian Charity Is Closing India Operations Amid a Crackdown." *New York Times*, March 7, 2017. www.nytimes.com/2017/03/07/world/asia/compassion-international -christian-charity-closing-india.html.

Battersby, Lucy. "Census Change: Is Australia Losing Its Religion?" *Sydney Morning Herald*, August 28, 2015.

Bauman, Stephan. *Seeking Refuge: On the Shores of the Global Refugee Crisis.* Chicago: Moody Publishers, 2016.

Beck, T. David. *The Holy Spirit and the Renewal of All Things: Pneumatology in Paul and Jürgen Moltmann.* Cambridge: James Clarke, 2015.

Bennett, David Malcolm. *Edward Irving Reconsidered: The Man, His Controversies, and the Pentecostal Movement.* Eugene, OR: Wipf & Stock, 2011.

Ben-Yehuda, N. *Theocratic Democracy: The Social Construction of Religious and Secular Extremism.* Oxford: Oxford University Press, 2010.

Bloesch, Donald G. *The Future of Evangelical Christianity: A Call for Unity and Diversity.* Colorado Springs, CO: Helmers and Howard, 1983.

Blumhofer, Edith. *Restoring the Faith: The Assemblies of God, Pentecostalism, and American Culture.* Urbana: University of Illinois Press, 1993.

Borthwick, Paul. *Western Christians in Global Mission.* Downers Grove, IL: InterVarsity Press, 2012.

Bosch, David Jacobus. *Transforming Mission: Paradigm Shifts in Theology of Mission.* Maryknoll, NY: Orbis Books, 1991.

Brandner, Tobias. "Trying to Make Sense of History: Chinese Christian Traditions of Countercultural Belief and Their Theological and Political Interpretation of Past and Present History." *Studies in World Christianity* 17, no. 3 (2011): 216-36.

Brian, Tara, and Frank Laczko. *Fatal Journeys*. Vol. 2, *Identification and Tracing of Dead and Missing Migrants*. Geneva: International Organization for Migration, 2016.

Broadbent, W. G. *The Doctrine of Tongues*. Paeroa, NZ: Eldon Press, circa 1950.

Bruce, F. F. *The Spreading Flame*. Eugene, OR: Wipf and Stock, 2004.

Burgess, Stanley M., ed. *Christian Peoples of the Spirit: A Documentary History of Pentecostal Spirituality from the Early Church to the Present*. New York: New York University Press, 2000.

———. *The Holy Spirit: Medieval Roman Catholic and Reformation Traditions*. Grand Rapids: Baker Books, 1994.

———. *The New International Dictionary of Pentecostal and Charismatic Movements*. Grand Rapids: Zondervan, 2003.

Burke, Daniel. "Millennials Leaving Church in Droves, Study Finds." CNN, May 14, 2015.

Cantelon, James. *When God Stood Up: A Christian Response to AIDS in Africa*. Toronto: John Wiley and Sons, Canada, 2007.

Carpenter, Joel A. *Revive Us Again: The Reawakening of American Fundamentalism*. New York: Oxford University Press, 1999.

Center for the Study of Global Christianity. *Christianity in Its Global Context, 1970–2020: Society, Religion, and Mission*. South Hamilton, MA: CSGC, 2013.

Centre for Development and Enterprise. *Under the Radar: Pentecostalism in South Africa and Its Potential Social and Economic Role*. March 2008 www.cde.org.za/under-the-radar -pentecostalism-in-south-africa-and-its-potential-social-and -economic-role/.

Chadwick, Owen. *The Early Reformation on the Continent*. Oxford: Oxford University Press, 2001.

Chant, Barry. *The Spirit of Pentecost: The Origins and Development of the Pentecostal Movement in Australia, 1870–1939*. Lexington, KY: Emeth Press, 2011.

Cleary, Edward L. *The Rise of Charismatic Catholicism in Latin America*. Gainesville: University Press of Florida, 2011.

Clifton, Shane, and Jacqueline Grey. *Raising Women Leaders: Perspectives on Liberating Women in Pentecostal and Charismatic Contexts*. Chester Hill, NSW: Australasian Pentecostal Studies, 2009.

Coleman, Simon, and John Elsner. *Pilgrim Voices: Narrative and Authorship in Christian Pilgrimage*. New York: Berghahn Books, 2003.

Cox, Harvey. *Fire from Heaven*. Cambridge, MA: Da Capo Press, 1995.

Dahles, Heidi. "In Pursuit of Capital: The Charismatic Turn Among the Chinese Managerial and Professional Class in Malaysia." *Asian Ethnicity* 8, no. 2 (2007): 89-109.

Darko, Daniel, and Beth Snoderly, eds. *First the Kingdom of God: Global Voices on Global Mission*. Pasadena, CA: William Carey Library, 2014.

Davies, Wilma W. *The Embattled but Empowered Community: Comparing Understandings of Spiritual Power in Argentine Popular and Pentecostal Cosmologies*. Boston: Brill, 2010.

Dayton, Donald. *Theological Roots of Pentecostalism*. Grand Rapids: Baker Academic, 1987.

Doughrity, Dyron B., and Jesudas M. Athyal. *Understanding World Christianity: India*. Minneapolis: Fortress Press, 2016.

D'Souza, Joseph. *On the Side of Angels: Justice, Human Rights, and Kingdom Mission*. Colorado Springs, CO: Authentic Publishing, 2007.

Escobar, Samuel. *Changing Tides*. Orbis Books, 2002.

———. *The New Global Mission: The Gospel from Everywhere to Everyone*. Downers Grove, IL: InterVarsity Press, 2003.

Fanning, Don. *Trends and Issues in Modern Missions*. Forest, VA: Branches Publications, 2011.

Field, Douglas. "Pentecostalism and All That Jazz: Tracing James Baldwin's Religion." *Literature and Theology* 22, no. 4 (December 2008): 436-57.

Fletcher, Richard. *The Barbarian Conversion: From Paganism to Christianity*. Berkeley: University of California Press, 1999.

Forbes, Chris. *Prophecy and Inspired Speech in Early Christianity and Its Hellenistic Environment*. Tübingen: Mohr-Siebeck, 1995.

Foster, Richard J. *Streams of Living Water: Essential Practices from the Six Great Traditions of Christian Faith*. New York: HarperCollins, 2001.

Freeman, Dena, ed. *Pentecostalism and Development: Churches, NGOs and Social Change in Africa*. Basingstoke, UK: Palgrave Macmillan, 2012.

Freston, Paul, ed. *Evangelical Christianity and Democracy in Latin America.* New York: Oxford University Press, 2008.

———. *Evangelicals and Politics in Asia, Africa and Latin America.* Cambridge: Cambridge University Press, 2001.

———. "Prosperity Theology: A (Largely) Sociological Assessment." Lausanne Movement. October 2, 2015. www.lausanne.org/content /prosperity-theology-a-largely-sociological-assessment.

Fulton, Brent. *China's Urban Christians: A Light That Cannot Be Hidden.* Eugene, OR: Pickwick Publications, 2015.

Garrard-Burnett, Virginia. *Protestantism in Guatemala: Living in the New Jerusalem.* Austin: University of Texas Press, 1998.

———. *Terror in the Land of the Holy Spirit: Guatemala Under General Efrain Rios Montt 1982–1983.* New York: Oxford University Press, 2011.

Garrison, David. *A Wind in the House of Islam.* Monument, CO: WIGTake Publishers, 2014.

Gee, Donald. "The Emotions of God: A Sermon Preached in Richmond Temple on Sunday Night, May 6, 1928." *Australian Evangel,* July 1928, 2. http://webjournals.ac.edu.au/ojs/index.php/AEGTM/article/view /6980/6977.

Gerson, Michael L. *City of Man: Religion and Politics in a New Era.* Chicago: Moody Publishers, 2010.

George, Timothy, ed. *Mr. Moody and the Evangelical Tradition.* New York: T&T Clark International, 2004.

———. *Pilgrims on the Sawdust Trail: Evangelical Ecumenism and the Quest for Christian Identity.* Grand Rapids: Baker Academic, 2004.

Gnanakan, Ken. *Learning in an Integrated Environment.* Bangalore, India: Theological Book Trust, 2007.

Goforth, Jonathan. *By My Spirit.* Grand Rapids: Zondervan, 1942.

Goh, Robbie B. H. "Christian Capital: Singapore, Evangelical Flows and Religious Hubs," *Asian Studies Review* 40, no. 2 (April 2016).

Golf, Paul, and Pastor Lee. *The Coming Chinese Church: How Rising Faith in China Is Spilling over Its Boundaries.* Oxford: Monarch Books, 2013.

Granberg-Michaelson, Wesley. *From Times Square to Timbuktu: The Post-Christian West Meets the Non-Western Church.* Grand Rapids: Eerdmans, 2013.

Grass, Tim. *Edward Irving: The Lord's Watchman.* Milton Keynes: Paternoster, 2011.

Greenman, Jeffrey P., and Gene L. Green. *Global Theology in Evangelical Perspective: Exploring the Contextual Nature of Theology and Mission.* Downers Grove, IL: InterVarsity Press, 2012.

Grudem, Wayne A., ed. *Are Miraculous Gifts for Today? 4 Views.* Grand Rapids: Zondervan, 2011.

Gushee, David P. *A New Evangelical Manifesto: A Kingdom Vision for the Common Good.* Danvers, MA: Chalice Press, 2012.

Hackett, Rosalind I. J., and Benjamin F. Soares, eds. *New Media and Religious Transformations in Africa.* Bloomington: Indiana University Press, 2015.

Hague, William. *William Wilberforce: The Life of the Great Anti–slave Trade Campaigner.* London: HarperCollins Publishers, 2008.

Haldon, J. F. *Byzantium in the Seventh Century: The Transformation of a Culture.* New York: Cambridge University Press, 1990.

Hamalainen, Arto, and Grant McLung. *Together in One Mission: Pentecostal Cooperation in World Evangelization.* Cleveland, TN: Pathway Press, 2012.

Hanrahan, James. "The Nature and History of the Catholic Charismatic Renewal in Canada." *Sessions d'étude—Société canadienne d'histoire de l'Église catholique* 50, no. 1 (1983).

Hart, D. G., and R. Laurence Moore. *The Lost Soul of American Protestantism.* Lanham, MD: Rowman & Littlefield, 2004.

Hastings, Adrian. *The Construction of Nationhood: Ethnicity, Religion and Nationalism.* New York: Cambridge University Press, 1997.

Hatch, Nathan O., and Mark A. Noll, eds. *The Bible in America: Essays in Cultural History.* New York: Oxford University Press, 1982.

Haustein, Jörg. *Writing Religious History: The Historiography of Ethiopian Pentecostalism.* Studien zur Außereuropäischen Christentumsgeschichte (Asien, Afrika, Lateinamerika) 17. Wiesbaden: Harrassowitz, 2011.

Hempton, David. *Methodism: Empire of the Spirit.* New Haven, CT: Yale University Press, 2005.

Hertzke, Allen D., and John David Rausch Jr. "The Religious Vote in American Politics: Value Conflict, Continuity, and Change." In *Broken Contract? Changing Relationships Between Americans and Their Government,* edited by Stephen C. Craig, 183-207. Boulder, CO: Westview Press, 1996.

Hertzke, Allen D., and Timothy Samuel Shah. *Christianity and Freedom.* Cambridge: Cambridge University Press, 2016.

Hesselgrave, David J., and Ed Stetzer. *MissionShift: Global Mission Issues in the Third Millennium.* Nashville: B&H Publishing Group, 2010.

Hocken, Peter. *Azusa, Rome, and Zion: Pentecostal Faith, Catholic Reform, and Jewish Roots.* Eugene, OR: Pickwick Publications, 2016.

———. *Streams of Renewal: Origins and Early Development of the Charismatic Movement in Great Britain.* Carlisle: Paternoster Press, 1997.

Howard, David M. *What I Saw God Doing.* Self-published, 2012.

Howell, Richard. "The Hindu Missionary Movements and Christian Missions in India." In *Global Missiology for the 21st Century,* edited by William D. Taylor, 407-20. Grand Rapids: Baker Academic, 2000.

Hunter, Harold D., and Neil Ormerod. *The Many Faces of Global Pentecostalism.* Cleveland, TN: CPT Press, 2013.

Hunter, James Davison. *To Change the World: The Irony, Tragedy, and Possibility of Christianity in the Late Modern World.* New York: Oxford University Press, 2010.

Hustad, Donald P. "D. L. Moody and Church Music." In *Mr. Moody and the Evangelical Tradition,* edited by Timothy George. New York: T&T Clark International, 2004.

Hutchinson, Mark. "Westbrook, George Gordon (Don) (1898–1966)." In *Australasian Dictionary of Pentecostal and Charismatic Movements.* webjournals.ac.edu.au/ojs/index.php/ADPCM/article/view/230/227.

Hutchinson, Mark, and John Wolffe. *A Short History of Global Evangelicalism.* Cambridge: Cambridge University Press, 2012.

Jacobsen, Douglas G. *Global Gospel: An Introduction to Christianity on Five Continents.* Grand Rapids: Baker Academic, 2015.

Jenkins, Philip. *Jesus Wars: How Four Patriarchs, Three Queens, and Two Emperors Decided What Christians Would Believe for the Next 1,500 Years.* New York: HarperCollins, 2010.

———. *The Lost History of Christianity: The Thousand-Year Golden Age of the Church in the Mid East, Africa and Asia—and How It Died.* New York: HarperCollins, 2008.

———. *The New Faces of Christianity: Believing the Bible in the Global South.* New York: Oxford University Press, 2006.

Johnson, Todd M., and Kenneth R. Ross, eds. *Atlas of Global Christianity.* Edinburgh: Edinburgh University Press, 2009.

Johnson, Todd M., Rodney L. Petersen, Gina A. Bellofatto, and Travis L. Myers, eds. *2010 Boston: The Changing Contours of World Missions and Christianity.* Eugene, OR: Pickwick Publications, 2012.

Johnson, Todd M., and Cindy M. Wu. *Our Global Families: Christians Embracing Common Identity in a Changing World.* Grand Rapids: Baker Academic, 2015.

Johnson, Todd M., and Gina A. Zurlo. "The Changing Demographics of Global Anglicanism, 1970–2010." In *Growth and Decline in the Anglican Communion: 1980 to the Present,* edited by David Goodhew, 37-53. New York: Routledge, 2017.

Kanaga, Lynn D. "The Ministry of the Holy Spirit in Church History, 1550 to 1900 A.D. (Part 2)." *Enrichment Journal Online,* Summer 2011. http://enrichmentjournal.ag.org/201103/201103_000_Holy_Sp.cfm.

Keller, Timothy, and Max Anderson. "A Conversation with Tim Keller on Gospel Movements." *Timothy Keller Sermons Podcast by Gospel in Life,* podcast audio. July 25, 2016. https://itunes.apple.com/us/podcast /timothy-keller-sermons-podcast-by-gospel-in-life/id35266 0924?mt=2.

Kemp, Hugh P. *Steppe By Step.* London: Monarch Books, 2000.

Kerr, John. *Hidden Riches Among the Poor.* Belleville, ON: Essence Publishing, 2003.

Kim, Kirsteen. *The Holy Spirit in the World: A Global Conversation.* Maryknoll, NY: Orbis Books, 2007.

Kling, Fritz. *The Meeting of the Waters.* Colorado Springs, CO: David C. Cook, 2010.

Krapohl, Robert H. *The Evangelicals: A Historical, Thematic, and Biographical Guide.* Westport, CT: Greenwood Press, 1999.

Kuyper, Abraham. "Inaugural Address at the Dedication of the Free University." In *Abraham Kuyper: A Centennial Reader*, edited by James D. Bratt. Grand Rapids: Eerdmans, 1998.

Kyaw Dwe, Clifford. "Tha Byu, Ko." In *A Dictionary of Asian Christianity*, edited by Scott W. Sunquist, 829-30. Grand Rapids: Eerdmans, 2001.

Lahouel, Badra. "Ethiopianism and African Nationalism in South Africa Before 1937." *Cahiers d'études africaines* 26, no. 104 (1986): 681-88.

Lee, Young-hoon. *The Holy Spirit Movement in Korea.* Oxford: Regnum Books International, 2009.

Lim, David S. "Consolidating Democracy: Filipino Evangelicals Between People Power Events, 1986–2001." In *Evangelical Christianity and Democracy in Asia,* edited by David H. Lumsdaine, 235-84. Oxford: Oxford University Press, 2009.

Livingstone, D. N., and R. A. Wells. *Ulster-American Religion: Episodes in the History of a Cultural Connection.* Notre Dame, IN: University of Notre Dame Press, 1999.

Lumsdaine, David Halloran, ed. *Evangelical Christianity and Democracy in Africa.* New York: Oxford University Press, 2009.

Majonis, Joel. "William Wilberforce and Thomas Chalmers: Development of Evangelical Christian Thought and Practices into Methodical Charities." *Journal of Religion and Spirituality in Social Work: Social Thought* 26, no. 2 (June 2007): 63-89.

Mandryk, Jason. *Operation World.* Downers Grove, IL: InterVarsity Press, 2010.

Mantenga, Jay, and Malcolm Gold. *Mission in Motion: Speaking Frankly of Mobilization.* Pasadena, CA: William Carey Library, 2016.

Martin, David. *Pentecostalism: The World Their Parish.* Malden, MA: Blackwell Publishers, 2002.

———. *Sociology of Religion: A David Martin Reader.* Waco, TX: Baylor University Press, 2015.

Matthews, Arthur H. *Standing Up, Standing Together: The Emergence of the National Association of Evangelicals.* Carol Stream, IL: National Association of Evangelicals, 1992.

McNeal, Reggie. *Kingdom Come.* Carol Stream, IL: Tyndale, 2015.

McVicar, Michael J. *Christian Reconstruction: R.J. Rushdoony and American Religious Conservatism.* Chapel Hill: The University of North Carolina Press, 2015.

Melchior, Jillian K. "Leading China's Christian Awakening." *Wall Street Journal*, February 21, 2012. www.wsj.com/articles/SB10001424052970 2033587045772348133382139048.

Mensah, David. *Kwabena: An African Boy's Journey of Faith.* Belleville, ON: Essence Publishing, 1998.

Micklethwait, John, and Adrian Wooldridge. *God Is Back: How the Global Revival of Faith Is Changing the World.* New York: Penguin Books, 2010.

Miller, Donald E., Kimon H. Sargent, and Richard Flory, eds. *Spirit and Power: The Growth and Global Impact of Pentecostalism.* New York: Oxford University Press, 2013.

Miller, Donald E., and Tetsunao Yamamori. *Global Pentecostalism: The New Face of Christian Social Engagement.* Berkeley: University of California Press, 2007.

Mischke, Werner. *The Global Gospel: Achieving Missional Impact in Our Multicultural World.* Scottsdale, AZ: Mission ONE, 2015.

Moeller, Carl, David W. Hegg, with Craig Hodgkins. *The Privilege of Persecution.* Chicago: Moody Publishers, 2011.

Moody, William R. *The Life of D. L. Moody.* New York: Fleming H. Revell, 1900.

Moorhead, James H. *Princeton Seminary in American Religion and Culture.* Grand Rapids: Eerdmans, 2012.

Moreau, A. Scott. *Contextualization in World Missions: Mapping and Assessing Evangelical Models.* Grand Rapids: Kregel Publications, 2012.

Munyenyembe, Rhodian G. *Christianity and Socio-Cultural Issues: The Charismatic Movement and Contextualization of the Gospel in Malawi.* Luwinga, Malawi: Mzuni Press, 2011.

Myers, Bryant L. "Progressive Pentecostalism, Development, and Christian Development NGOs: A Challenge and an Opportunity."

International Bulletin of Missionary Research 39, no. 3 (July 2015): 115-20.

———. *Walking with the Poor: Principles and Practices of Transformational Development*. Maryknoll, NY: Orbis Books, 2011.

Neely, Lois. *From Deep Waters to Higher Ground: The Life Journey of Jonathan and Rosalind Goforth*. Toronto: North York Printing, 2014.

Neuhaus, R. J. *The Naked Public Square*. Grand Rapids: Eerdmans, 1984.

Newbigin, Leslie. *Faith in a Changing World*. London: Alpha International, 2003.

———. *Foolishness to the Greeks*. Grand Rapids: Eerdmans, 1986.

———. *Honest Religion for Secular Man*. Philadelphia: The Westminster Press, 1966.

———. *The Open Secret: An Introduction to the Theology of Mission*. Grand Rapids: Eerdmans, 1978.

———. *To Tell the Truth*. Grand Rapids: Eerdmans, 1991.

———. *A Walk Through the Bible*. Louisville, KY: Westminster John Knox Press, 1999.

Noll, Mark. *Turning Points: Decisive Moments in the History of Christianity*. Grand Rapids: Baker Academic, 2012.

———. *In the Beginning Was the Word: The Bible in American Public Life, 1492–1783*. New York: Oxford University Press, 2015.

Nyman, James. *How to Launch a Church-Planting Kingdom Movement Through Discovery Bible Studies*. Mount Vernon, WA: Mission Network, 2016.

Offutt, Stephen. *New Centers of Global Evangelicalism in Latin America and Africa*. New York: Cambridge University Press, 2015.

Olson, C. Gordon, and Don Fanning. *What in the World Is God Doing?* Lynchburg, VA: Global Gospel Publishing, 2013.

Olson, Roger E. *The Story of Christian Theology: Twenty Centuries of Tradition and Reform*. Downers Grove, IL: InterVarsity Press, 1999.

Onoja, Adoyi. "The Pentecostal Churches: Spiritual Deregulation Since the 1980s." In *Religion in Politics: Secularism and National Integration in Modern Nigeria*, edited by Julius O. Adekunle. Trenton, NJ: Africa World Press, 2009.

Orange, Claudia. *The Treaty of Waitangi*. Auckland, NZ: Bridget Williams Books, 2015.

Orr, J. Edwin. "The Role of Prayer in Spiritual Awakening." 1976. www .kneillfoster.com/articles/RevivalTruths/roleofprayer.html.

Oyugi, Edward, Alloys Opiyo, Mwalimu Mati, Oduor Ongwen, Alice Mudiri, Daniel Somoire, Lumumba Odenda, and Adhu Awiti. "A Tale of Unfulfilled Promises: Kenya, National Report." Social Watch. 1999. www.socialwatch.org/node/10657.

Pabel, Hilmar M., and Mark Vessey, eds. *Holy Scripture Speaks: The Production and Reception of Erasmus' Paraphrases on the New Testament*. Toronto: University of Toronto Press, 2002.

Pecknold, C. C. *Christianity and Politics: A Brief Guide to the History*. Eugene, OR: Cascade Books, 2010.

Pecora, V. P. *Secularization and Cultural Criticism: Religion, Nation, and Modernity*. Chicago: University of Chicago Press, 2006.

Penner, Glenn M. *In the Shadow of the Cross: A Biblical Theology of Persecution and Discipleship*. Bartlesville, OK: Living Sacrifice Books, 2004.

Peterson, Eugene. *The Message*. Colorado Springs, CO: NavPress Publishing Group, 2011.

Pew Research Center. "America's Changing Religious Landscape." Pew Forum. May 12, 2015. www.pewforum.org/2015/05/12/americas -changing-religious-landscape/.

Phillips, Dom, and Nick Miroff. "In Brazil's Political Crisis, a Powerful New Force: Evangelical Christians." *The Washington Post*, May 26, 2016.

Piggin, Stuart. *Making Evangelical Missionaries, 1789–1858: The Social Background, Motives, and Training of British Protestant Missionaries to India*. London: Abingdon, 1984.

Pocock, Michael, Gailyn Van Rheenen, and Douglas McConnell. *The Changing Face of World Missions: Engaging Contemporary Issues and Trends*. Grand Rapids: Baker Academic, 2005.

Pollock, John C., and Ian Randall. *The Keswick Story: The Authorized History of the Keswick Convention*. Fort Washington, PA: CLC Publications, 2006.

Poon, Michael, and Malcolm Tan, eds. *The Clock Tower Story: The Beginnings of the Charismatic Renewals in Singapore*. Singapore: Trinity Theological College, 2012.

Porter, Andrew, ed. *The Imperial Horizons of British Protestant Missions, 1880–1914.* Grand Rapids: Eerdmans, 2003.

Posterski, Don. *Jesus on Justice: Living Lives of Compassion and Conviction.* Mississauga, ON: World Vision Canada, 2013.

Preston, Andrew. *Sword of the Spirit, Shield of Faith: Religion in American War and Diplomacy.* Toronto: Vintage Canada Edition, 2013.

Price, Frederick K. C. *Prosperity on God's Terms.* Los Angeles: Harrison House, Inc., 1990.

Qureshi, Nabeel. *Answering Jihad.* Grand Rapids: Zondervan, 2016.

Rah, Soong-Chan. *The Next Evangelicalism: Freeing the Church from Western Cultural Captivity.* Downers Grove, IL: InterVarsity Press, 2009.

Ranger, Terence O. *Evangelical Christianity and Democracy in Africa.* Oxford: Oxford University Press, 2008.

Raushenbush, Paul B. *Christianity and the Social Crisis in the 21st Century.* New York: HarperCollins, 2007.

Reimer, Reg. *Vietnam's Christians: A Century of Growth in Adversity.* Pasadena, CA: William Carey Library, 2011.

Reimer, Sam. *A Culture of Faith: Evangelical Congregations in Canada.* Montreal: McGill-Queen's University Press, 2015.

Riedl, Rachel Beatty. "Transforming Politics, Dynamic Religion: Religion's Political Impact in Contemporary Africa." *Africa Conflict and Peacebuilding Review* 2, no. 2 (2012).

Riss, Richard M. *Latter Rain: The Latter Rain Movement of 1948 and the Mid-twentieth Century Evangelical Awakening.* Etobicoke, ON: Kingdom Flagships Foundation, 1987.

Rodriguez, Alejandro. *Towards an Institutional or Apostolic Vision.* Ituzaingo, Argentina: Youth With a Mission Argentina, 2009.

Rooy, Sidney H. "Penzotti, Francisco G. (1851–1925)," in *Biographical Dictionary of Christian Missions*, ed. G. H. Anderson. New York: Macmillan Reference USA, 1998.

Ruotsila, Markku. *The Origins of Christian Anti-Internationalism: Conservative Evangelicals and the League of Nations.* Washington, DC: Georgetown University Press, 2008.

Ruthven, Jon. *On the Cessation of the Charismata: The Protestant Polemic on Postbiblical Miracles.* Sheffield, UK: Sheffield Academic Press, 1993.

Rutt, Steven. "An Analysis of Roland Allen's Missionary Ecclesiology." *Transformation: An International Journal of Holistic Mission Studies* 29, no. 3 (2012): 200-213.

Samuel, Vinay, and Chris Sugden. *Mission as Transformation: A Theology of the Whole Gospel.* Oxford: Regnum Books International, 1999.

Sanneh, Lamin. *Disciples of All Nations.* Oxford: Oxford University Press, 2008.

———. *Whose Religion Is Christianity? The Gospel Beyond the West.* Grand Rapids: Eerdmans, 2003.

Sartorio, Enrico. *The Social Religious Life of Italians in America.* Boston: Christopher Publishing House, 1918.

Satta, Ronald F. *The Sacred Text: Biblical Authority in Nineteenth-Century America.* Eugene, OR: Wipf and Stock, 2007.

Sauer, Christof, and Richard Howell, eds. *Suffering, Persecution and Martyrdom.* New York: World Evangelical Alliance, 2010.

Scheidel, Walter. "The Roman Slave Supply." In *The Cambridge World History of Slavery.* Vol. 1, *The Ancient Mediterranean World*, edited by Keith Bradley and Paul Cartledge, 287-310. Cambridge: Cambridge University Press, 2011.

Scheuermann, Rochelle Cathcart, and Edward L. Smither, eds. *Controversies in Mission: Theology, People, and Practice of Missions.* Pasadena, CA: William Carey Library, 2016.

Schirrmacher, Thomas. *Fundamentalism: When Religion Becomes Dangerous.* New York: World Evangelical Alliance, 2013.

———. *The Persecution of Christians Concerns Us All.* New York: World Evangelical Alliance, 2013.

Schraeder, Peter J. "Rendering unto Caesar? State Regulation of Religion and the Role of Catholicism in Democratic Transitions and Consolidation in Predominantly Catholic Countries." In *Democracy, Culture, Catholicism: Voices from Four Continents*, edited by Michael J. Schuck and John Crowley-Buck, 297-309. New York: Fordham University Press, 2016.

Second Vatican Council. *Dogmatic Constitution on Divine Revelation* Dei Verbum *Solemnly Promulgated by His Holiness Pope Paul VI on November 18, 1965.* English translation. www.vatican.va/archive/hist_councils

/ii_vatican_council/documents/vat-ii_const_19651118_dei-verbum _en.html.

Shires, Preston. *Hippies of the Religious Right.* Waco, TX: Baylor University Press, 2007.

Sider, Ronald. *Good News and Good Works: A Theology for the Whole Gospel.* Grand Rapids: Baker, 1999.

———. *Just Politics: A Guide for Christian Engagement.* Grand Rapids: Brazos, 2012.

Sieple, Chris, and Dennis H. Hoover, eds. *The Routledge Handbook of Religion and Security.* New York: Routledge, 2013.

Simas, Marcos, and Carlos Fernandes. "Brazil's Presidential Drama Reflects Political, Denominational Divides." *Christianity Today.* July 15, 2016.

Smail, Tom, Andrew Walker, and Nigel Wright. *Charismatic Renewal: The Search for a Theology.* London: SPCK, 1993.

Smalley, William A. "Cultural Implications of an Indigenous Church." *Practical Anthropology* 5 (1958): 51-65.

Smith, James K. A. *Desiring the Kingdom: Worship, Worldview, and Cultural Formation.* Grand Rapids: Baker Academic, 2009.

———. *How (Not) to Be Secular: Reading Charles Taylor.* Grand Rapids: Eerdmans, 2014.

Snoderly, Beth, and A. Scott Moreau, eds. *Evangelical and Frontier Mission: Perspectives on the Global Progress of the Gospel.* Eugene, OR: Wipf and Stock Publishers, 2011.

Southern, Neil. "Evangelical Journeys: Choice and Change in a Northern Irish Religious Subculture." *Journal of Contemporary Religion* 28, no. 3 (October 2013).

Stark, Rodney. *God's Battalions: The Case for the Crusades.* New York: HarperCollins, 2009.

———. *The Real Story of How Christianity Became an Urban Movement and Conquered Rome.* New York: HarperCollins, 2006.

———. *The Rise of Christianity: A Sociologist Reconsiders History.* Princeton, NJ: Princeton University Press, 1996.

———. *The Triumph of Faith.* Wilmington, DE: ISI Books, 2015.

————. *The Victory of Reason: How Christianity Led to Freedom, Capitalism, and Western Success*. New York: Random House, 2006.

Stark, Rodney, and Xiuhua Wang. *A Star in the East: The Rise of Christianity in China*. West Conshohocken, PA: Templeton Press, 2015.

Stegall, Carrol, Jr., and Carl C. Harwood. *The Modern Tongues and Healing Movement*. Denver: Western Bible Institute, 1950.

Stephanous, Andrew Zaki. *Political Islam, Citizenship and Minorities: The Future of Arab Christians in the Islamic Middle East*. Lanham, MD: University Press of America Inc., 2010.

Stetzer, Ed. "Survey Fail—Christianity Isn't Dying." *USA Today*. May 13, 2015.

Stewart, Adam, ed. *Handbook of Pentecostal Christianity*. DeKalb: Northern Illinois University Press, 2012.

Stiller, Brian C., Todd M. Johnson, Karen Stiller, and Mark Hutchinson, eds. *Evangelicals Around the World: A Global Handbook for the 21st Century*. Nashville: Thomas Nelson, 2015.

————. *An Insider's Guide to Praying for the World*. Minneapolis: Bethany Publishers, 2016.

Strachan, Owen. *Awakening the Evangelical Mind*. Grand Rapids: Zondervan, 2015.

Strelan, Rick. *Strange Acts: Studies in the Cultural World of the Acts of the Apostles*. Berlin: Walter de Gruyter, 2004.

Sunquist, Scott W. *The Unexpected Christian Century: The Reversal and Transformation of Global Christianity*. Grand Rapids: Baker Publishing Group, 2015.

Sweetnam, Mark, and Crawford Gribben. "J. N. Darby and the Irish Origins of Dispensationalism." *Journal of the Evangelical Theological Society* 52, no. 3 (September 2009).

Synan, Vinson, Amos Yong, and Miguel Alvarez. *Global Renewal Christianity: Spirit-Empowered Movements Past, Present, and Future*. Lake Mary, FL: Charisma House Book Group, 2014.

Tarango, Angela. *Choosing the Jesus Way: American Indian Pentecostals and the Fight for the Indigenous Principle*. Chapel Hill: University of North Carolina Press, 2014.

Taylor, William, ed. *Global Missiology for the 21st Century: The Iguassu Dialogue*. Grand Rapids: Baker Academic, 2000.

Taylor, William, Antonia van der Meer, and Reg Reimer, eds. *Sorrow and Blood: Christian Mission in Contexts of Suffering, Persecution, and Martyrdom*. Pasadena, CA: William Carey Library, 2012.

Tennent, Timothy C. *Theology in the Context of World Christianity: How the Global Church Is Influencing the Way We Think and Discuss Theology*. Grand Rapids: Zondervan, 2007.

————. *World Missions: A Trinitarian Missiology for the Twenty-First Century*. Grand Rapids: Kregel Publications, 2010.

Thomas, Scott. *The Global Resurgence of Religion and the Transformation of International Relations*. New York: Palgrave Macmillan, 2005.

Throup, David W., and Charles Hornsby, eds. *Multi-party Politics in Kenya: The Kenyatta and Moi States and the Triumph of the System in the 1992 Election*. Oxford: James Currey, 1998.

Tickle, Phyllis. *The Great Emergence*. Grand Rapids: Baker Books, 2008.

Tiplady, Richard. *One World or Many? The Impact of Globalization on Mission*. Pasadena, CA: William Carey Library, 2003.

Toft, Monica, Daniel Philpott, and Timothy Shah. *God's Century: Resurgent Religion and Global Politics*. New York: W. W. Norton & Company, 2011.

Toryough, Godwin N. "The Biblical Ethics of Work: A Model for African Nations." *Verbum et Ecclesia* 31, no. 1 (November 23, 2010). www.ve.org.za/index.php/VE/article/view/363/479.

Treloar, Geoffrey R. *Lightfoot the Historian: The Nature and Role of History in the Life and Thought of J.B. Lightfoot (1828–1889) as Churchman and Scholar*. Tübingen: Mohr Siebeck, 1998.

Trousdale, Jerry. *Miraculous Movements: How Hundreds of Thousands of Muslims Are Falling in Love with Jesus*. Nashville: Thomas Nelson, 2012.

Vanhoozer, Kevin J. *Is There a Meaning in This Text? The Bible, the Reader, and the Morality of Literary Knowledge*. Grand Rapids: Zondervan, 2009.

Volf, Miroslav. *Exclusion and Embrace: A Theological Exploration of Identity, Otherness and Reconciliation*. Nashville: Abingdon Press, 1996.

Vorster, J. M. "Managing Corruption in South Africa: The Ethical Responsibility of Churches." *Scriptura* 109 (2012).

Wacker, Grant. *Heaven Below: Early Pentecostals and American Culture.* Cambridge, MA: Harvard University Press, 2003.

Weston, Paul, ed. *Lesslie Newbigin: Missionary Theologian; A Reader.* Grand Rapids: Eerdmans, 2006.

Walls, Andrew F. *The Cross-Cultural Process in Christian History: Studies in the Transmission and Appropriation of Faith.* Maryknoll, NY: Orbis Books, 2002.

———. *The Missionary Movement in Christian History.* Maryknoll, NY: Orbis Books, 1996.

Wilberforce, William. *A Practical View of the Prevailing Religious System of Professed Christians, in the Higher and Middle Classes, Contrasted with Real Christianity.* New York: American Tract Society, 1830.

Wilkinson, Michael, ed. *Global Pentecostal Movements: Migration, Mission, and Public Religion.* Boston: Brill, 2012.

Wright, Christopher J. H. *The Mission of God's People: A Biblical Theology of the Church's Mission.* Grand Rapids: Zondervan, 2010.

Wuthnow, Robert. *Christianity in the 21st Century: Reflections on the Challenges Ahead.* New York: Oxford University Press, 1993.

Yang, Fenggang. "When Will China Become the Largest Christian Country?" *Slate*, December 2014. www.slate.com/bigideas/what-is-the-future-of-religion/essays-and-opinions/fenggang-yang-opinion.

Yong, Amos. *In the Days of Caesar: Pentecostalism and Political Theology.* Grand Rapids: Eerdmans, 2010.

———. *Discerning the Spirit(s): A Pentecostal-Charismatic Contribution to Christian Theology of Religions.* Sheffield, UK: Sheffield Academic Press, 2000.

———. *The Future of Evangelical Theology: Soundings from the Asian American Diaspora.* Downers Grove, IL: InterVarsity Press, 2014.

Young-gi Hong, Joshua. "Evangelicals and the Democratization of South Korea." In *Evangelical Christianity and Democracy in Asia*, edited by David H. Lumsdaine, 185-234. Oxford: Oxford University Press, 2009.

AUTHOR INDEX

SUBJECT INDEX

SCRIPTURE INDEX

ABOUT THE AUTHOR

Brian Stiller, a Canadian, was in 2011 appointed global ambassador of the World Evangelical Alliance (WEA), a world community serving some six hundred million Christians (worldea.org). He visits a number of countries each year, learning of issues and opportunities and meeting with churches, pastors, and civil society leadership.

Stiller began his public ministry with Youth for Christ/Canada (YFC) and was its president until 1983. He served as president of the Evangelical Fellowship of Canada for fourteen years, and then as president of Tyndale University College & Seminary, Toronto. He is the author of numerous books, including *An Insider's Guide to Praying for the World* and *Jesus and Caesar: Christians in the Public Square*, and is general editor of *Evangelicals Around the World: A Global Handbook for the 21st Century*.

He can be found at brianstiller.com, and he blogs from the many countries he visits at dispatchesfrombrian.com.